EDUCATION FOR MINISTRY

Reading and Reflection Guide
Volume B, 2018–2019

Living Faithfully in a Multicultural World

EDUCATION FOR MINISTRY

Reading and Reflection Guide
Volume B, 2018–2019

Living Faithfully in a Multicultural World

CHURCH
PUBLISHING
INCORPORATED

Church Publishing
19 East 34th Street
New York, NY 10016
www.churchpublishing.org

Cover design by Laurie Klein Westhafer
Typeset by Beth Oberholtzer

A record of this book is available from the Library of Congress.

ISBN-13: 978-1-64065-109-8 (pbk.)
ISBN-13: 978-1-64065-110-4 (ebook)

Printed in the United States of America

Contents

ix   Acknowledgments

x   About the Authors

xi   Overview of the Year: Reading Assignments for Volume B

xv   About Online Resources

PART I: THE GUIDE

3   Week One: Orientation and Organization

Unit One: Spiritual Autobiography and Listening

18   Week Two: Living in a Multicultural World

33   Week Three

40   Week Four

43   Week Five

46   Week Six

50   Week Seven

Unit Two: Theological Reflection as a Life Skill

54   Week Eight: Last Words

66   Week Nine

69   Week Ten

73   Week Eleven

76   Week Twelve

81   Week Thirteen

First Interlude Unit: Dismantling Racism in America

86   Week Fourteen

88   Week Fifteen

Unit Three: Developing a Sustaining Spirituality

94   Week Sixteen: OMG: Spirituality in the Digital Age

108   Week Seventeen

113   Week Eighteen

117   Week Nineteen

121   Week Twenty

124   Week Twenty-one

Unit Four: Integrating Belief, Behavior, and Doctrine in a Multicultural World

130   Week Twenty-two: Believing
156   Week Twenty-three
160   Week Twenty-four
165   Week Twenty-five
168   Week Twenty-six
172   Week Twenty-seven

Second Interlude: Christian-Muslim Vision and Practice

176   Week Twenty-eight
177   Week Twenty-nine

Unit Five: Vocation

180   Week Thirty: The Mission of the Church
187   Week Thirty-one
191   Week Thirty-two
196   Week Thirty-three
199   Week Thirty-four
203   Week Thirty-five
205   Week Thirty-six: Closing the Year

PART II—RESOURCES

Supplemental Readings in the Christian Tradition

214   Week Three, Reading Assignment for Year Four
      On Being Theologically Literate
223   Week Five, Reading Assignment for Year One
      The Priestly Creation Story
241   Week Thirteen, Reading Assignment for Year Four
      God as Trinity
253   Week Twenty, Reading Assignment for Year One
      Micah

Resources for Listening and Spiritual Autobiography

258   Spiritual Autobiographies: Some Guidelines
260   Listening Skills
264   The Art of Framing Questions

Resources for Reflecting Theologically

268 Primary Aspects of Theological Reflection

269 The EfM Four-Source Model

270 Theological Reflection in EfM

271 The Basic Structure of EfM Theological Reflection in Four Movements

272 Theological Reflection Process Chart

273 Four Phases of Movement in Theological Reflection

274 Framework for Theological Reflections

278 Theological Reflection in a Group

281 Theological Reflection in Motion

Examples of Theological Reflection

The Action Source

286 Theological Reflection Beginning with a Personal Experience (1)

287 Theological Reflection Beginning with a Personal Experience (2)

288 Theological Reflection Beginning with a Personal Experience (3)

290 Theological Reflection Beginning with a Personal Experience (4)

292 Theological Reflection Beginning with a Personal Experience (5)

294 Theological Reflection Beginning with a Dilemma (Action Source) (1)

296 Theological Reflection Beginning with a Dilemma (Action Source) (2)

299 Theological Reflection Beginning with a Wide-angle Lens (Action Source)

The Tradition Source

302 Theological Reflection Beginning with Christian Tradition (Scripture) (1)

305 Theological Reflection Beginning with the Christian Tradition (Scripture) (2)

307 Theological Reflection Beginning with the Christian Tradition (3)

308 Theological Reflection Beginning with a Wide-angle Lens (Tradition Source)

311 Theological Reflection Beginning with a Mind Map (Tradition Source)

313 Theological Reflection Beginning with a Provocative Word (Tradition Source)

The Culture Source

314   Theological Reflection Beginning with a Social Concern (Culture Source) (1)

316   Theological Reflection Beginning with a Social Concern (Culture Source) (2)

319   Theological Reflection Beginning with the Culture Source

320   Theological Reflection Beginning with a Wide-angle Lens (Culture Source)

323   Theological Reflection Beginning with a Provocative Word (Culture Source)

324   Theological Reflection Beginning with a Movie, Video, or Television Episode (Culture Source)

The Position Source

326   Theological Reflection Beginning with a Personal Position (1)

328   Theological Reflection Beginning with a Personal Position (2)

330   Theological Reflection Beginning with Multiple Personal Positions

Resources for Community Life

334   Group Life: The Seminar

337   Issues in the Life of a Seminar Group

341   Activities that Nurture Group Life

       Tools from the Kaleidoscope Institute

       342   The Cycle of Gospel Living

       344   Mutual Invitation

       345   Respectful Communications Guidelines

Acknowledgments

A revision by definition is not *sui generis*. Although this series of *Reading and Reflection Guides* may look different from previous editions of EfM materials, although it may be organized differently, it is nonetheless built on a framework that has evolved over more than forty years of Education for Ministry. Those who have some years of acquaintance with the program will recognize what the new format owes to components developed for its predecessors, among them parallel guides, common lessons, and the many variations of EfM's central discipline of theological reflection.

The developers of those foundational components are by now nearly legion and include not only founder Charles Winters and succeeding leaders like John de Beer and Edward de Bary but also the many EfM coordinators and trainers whose work with mentors all over the globe and over time has shaped the program.

Education for Ministry has been from its inception an experiential and collaborative project. The principal author in this series is Richard E. Brewer, who has a long history of writing and curriculum design in EfM. Significant contributions also were made by Angela Hock Brewer and Karen M. Meridith, the managing editor for the series. In addition, several of the essays and resources, some adapted, others left as originally published in the previous edition, have long been a part of the EfM program, designed, written, and refined by a number of contributors over the years. We are grateful for their work and know that we can look to the future of EfM only because we stand on the shoulders of giants.

Karen M. Meridith, series editor
Executive Director of Education for Ministry
Sewanee, Tennessee
March, 2018

About the Authors

Richard E. Brewer (Rick) is a retired Episcopal priest who served in parochial ministry and in adult Christian formation for forty years. A graduate of the University of the South and The General Theological Seminary, he has lived in Oklahoma most of his life and served as priest and educator in Tulsa and Stillwater Episcopal churches. Additionally, he developed and directed the Deacon Formation Program for the Episcopal Diocese of Oklahoma.

Rick first learned about EfM in 1975 from Dr. Charles Winters, the originator and first director of the program. He has been an EfM trainer since 1978, and a diocesan coordinator, a mentor, and interim assistant director for the EfM program. He conceived and edited the Common Lesson series for the first revision of the EfM materials. He coauthored the Parallel Guides and numerous common lessons with the Reverend John de Beer.

Angela Hock Brewer considers herself a lifelong Episcopalian, although she spent her first twelve years in the Roman Catholic Church. A graduate of the University of Oklahoma, she has served as the Oklahoma Diocesan Chair for Lay Ministry and on the Diocese of Northwest Texas Commission on Ministry for Lay Ministry. Angela is a graduate of Education for Ministry and has served the program for many years as an EfM mentor and trainer.

In addition to their work together on the EfM Reading and Reflection Guides, Rick and Angela co-wrote *Practically Christian: A Guide to Practical Christian Prayer, Action, and Reflection*. They co-directed *Opportunities for Adult Christian Education and Spirituality* (OACES), Inc., which developed a variety of adult Christian formation learning guides and a comprehensive ministry formation program for the Episcopal Diocese of Nebraska.

Karen M. Meridith is the Executive Director of Education for Ministry and Associate Director of the Beecken Center at the School of Theology of the University of the South in Sewanee, Tennessee. She was called to her position in 2010 with the charge to re-envision and redesign the Education for Ministry curriculum. Karen is the managing editor for the four-volume EfM Reading and Reflection Guide series, a contributing writer, and responsible for selecting the textbooks used in the curriculum. A graduate of the University of South Carolina and Episcopal Divinity School, she is also a graduate of Education for Ministry and served as a mentor in the Diocese of Southern Virginia. Karen is an experienced educator and administrator, and has developed curricula and programming for Christian formation at local, diocesan, and national levels of the Episcopal Church.

Overview of the Year:
Reading Assignments for Volume B

Notes

1. Common readings at the beginning of each unit are read by all years.

2. Assignments for years one and two marked with an asterisk are readings in the Bible. Chapters in the survey texts are numbered. When both are assigned, it is suggested that the Bible be read before the survey text chapters. Supplemental essays for individual years are in Part II of the Reading and Reflection Guide.

3. Readings in the interludes and in each of the texts for Year Four are indicated by name of the author(s).

WEEK	UNIT	YEAR ONE	YEAR TWO	YEAR THREE	YEAR FOUR
1	**Introductory Meeting**	Orientation and Organization	Orientation and Organization	Orientation and Organization	Orientation and Organization
2	**Unit One** Spiritual Autobiography and Listening	Common Reading: Living in a Multicultural World	Common Reading: Living in a Multicultural World	Common Reading: Living in a Multicultural World	Common Reading: Living in a Multicultural World
3		Collins: Preface Introduction 1 The Near Eastern Context 2 The Nature of Pentateuchal Narrative	Preface 1 The NT Background: The Roman World 2 The NT Background: The Jewish World	Acknowledgements, Introduction 1 Greece and Rome	Ballard essay: On Being Theologically Literate, RRG Pt II, 214–222 Ford: 1 Introduction
4		Yee: Preface, Introduction	3 The New Testament Writings	2 Israel	Ford: 2 Theology and religious studies
5		* Genesis 1–11 Collins: 3 The Primeval History The Priestly Creation Story RRG Pt II 223–240	4 Jesus 5 The Gospels	3 A Crucified Messiah	Ford: 3 Thinking of God
6		* Genesis 12–50 Collins: 4 The Patriarchs	* Matthew 6 Matthew	4 Boundaries Defined	4 Living before God

Handwritten dates in margin: 9/6, 9/13, 9/20, 9/27, 10/5, 10/12

WEEK	UNIT	YEAR ONE	YEAR TWO	YEAR THREE	YEAR FOUR
7 10/19/18		* Exodus 1–5 Collins: 5 The Exodus from Egypt	* Mark 7 Mark	5 The Prince: Ally or Enemy?	Ford: 5 Facing evil
8	**Unit Two** Theological Reflection as a Life Skill	Common Reading: Last Words	Common Reading: Last Words	Common Reading: Last Words	Common Reading: Last Words
9		* Exodus 16–40 Collins: 6 Revelation at Sinai	* Luke	6 The Imperial Church	Ford: 6 Jesus Christ
10		* Leviticus	8 Luke	7 Defying Chalcedon: Asia and Africa	Ford: 7 Salvation
11		* Deuteronomy Collins: 8 Deuteronomy	* John	8 Islam: The Great Realignment	Ford: 8 Through the past to the present
12		Yee: 1 Character, Conflict, and Covenant in Israel's Origin Traditions	9 John	9 The Making of Latin Christianity	Ford: 9 Experience, knowledge, wisdom 10 Theology for the third millennium
13		* Joshua * Judges Collins: 9 Joshua 10 Judges	* The Acts of the Apostles 10 Acts	10 Latin Christendom: New Frontiers	Coakley essay: God as Trinity, RRG Pt II, 241–252
14	**First Interlude** Dismantling Racism in America	Common Reading: Meeks v–60	Common Reading: Meeks v–60	Common Reading: Meeks v–60	Common Reading: Meeks v–60
15	**First Interlude** Dismantling Racism in Americaa	Common Reading: Meeks 61–136	Common Reading: Meeks 61–136	Common Reading: Meeks 61–136	Common Reading: Meeks 61–136
16	**Unit Three** Developing a Sustaining Spirituality	Common Reading: OMG: Spirituality in the Digital Age	Common Reading: OMG: Spirituality in the Digital Age	Common Reading: OMG: Spirituality in the Digital Age	Common Reading: OMG: Spirituality in the Digital Age
17		* 1 Samuel * 2 Samuel Collins: 11 I Samuel 12 2 Samuel	11 New Testament Letters 12 Paul	11 The West: Universal Emperor or Universal Pope?	McIntosh: 1 Mysteires of Faith 2 The New Encounter with God
18		* 1 Kings * 2 Kings Collins: 13 First Kings 1–16 14 First Kings 17–2 Kings 25	* Romans	12 A Church for All People?	McIntosh: 3 The Splendor of God 4 The Voice of God
19		Yee: 2 Intersections of Ethnicity, Gender, Sexuality, and Nation	13 Romans	13 Faith in a New Rome	McIntosh 5 the Humanity of God

WEEK	UNIT	YEAR ONE	YEAR TWO	YEAR THREE	YEAR FOUR
20		* Amos * Hosea Collins: 15 Amos and Hosea	* 1 Corinthians * 2 Corinthians 14 1 Corinthians 15 2 Corinthians	14 Orthodoxy: More Than an Empire	McIntosh: 6 The Glory of Humanity
21		* Micah * Isaiah 1–39 Micah, RRG Pt II 253–256 Collins: 16 Isaiah	* Galatians 16 Galatians	15 Russia: The Third Rome	McIntosh: 7 The Drama of the Cosmos
22	**Unit Four** Integrating Belief, Behavior, and Doctrine	Common Reading: Believing	Common Reading: Believing	Common Reading: Believing	Common Reading: Believing
23		* Jeremiah * Lamentations * Ezekiel Collins: 17 The Babylonian Era 18 Ezekiel	* Ephesians 17 Ephesians	16 Perspectives on the True Church	Sedgwick: Preface, Introduction, 1 Describing the Christian Life
24		* Isaiah 40–66 * Jonah, et. al Collins: 19 Additions to the Book of Isaiah 20 Postexilic Prophecy	* Philippians * Colossians 18 Philippians 19 Colossians	17 A House Divided	Sedgwick: 2 An Anglican Perspective
25		Yee: 3 The Challenge of Violence and Gender Under Colonization	* 1 Thessalonians * 2 Thessalonians 20 1 Thessalonians 21 2 Thessalonians	18 Rome's Renewal	Sedgwick: 3 Incarnate Love
26		* Ezra * Nehemiah * 1 Chronicles * 2 Chronicles 21 Ezra and Nehemiah 22 The Book of Chronicles	* 1 Timothy * 2 Timothy * Titus * Philemon 22 The Pastoral Letters 23 Philemon	19 A Worldwide Faith	Sedgwick: 4 Love and Justice
27		*Psalms * Song of Songs 23 Psalms and Song of Songs	* Hebrews 24 Hebrews	20 Protestant Awakenings	Sedgwick: 5 The Practices of Faith 6 The Call of God Appendix
28	**Second Interlude** Christian-Muslim Vision and Practice	Common Reading: Heaney, Sayilgan, Haymes vii–85	Common Reading: Heaney, Sayilgan, Haymes vii–85	Common Reading: Heaney, Sayilgan, Haymes vii–85	Common Reading: Heaney, Sayilgan, Haymes vii–85
29	**Second Interlude** Christian-Muslim Vision and Practice	Common Reading: Heaney, Sayilgan, Haymes 86–165	Common Reading: Heaney, Sayilgan, Haymes 86–165	Common Reading: Heaney, Sayilgan, Haymes 86–165	Common Reading: Heaney, Sayilgan, Haymes 86–165

WEEK	UNIT	YEAR ONE	YEAR TWO	YEAR THREE	YEAR FOUR
30	**Unit Five** Vocation	Common Reading: The Mission of the Church	Common Reading: The Mission of the Church	Common Reading: The Mission of the Church	Common Reading: The Mission of the Church
31		*Proverbs * Job * Ecclesiastes (Qoheleth) 24 Proverbs 25 Job and Qoheleth	* James 25 James	21 Enlightenment: Ally or Enemy?	Peace, Rose, Mobley: Foreword Introduction 1 Encountering The Neighbor
32		*Ruth * Esther 26 The Hebrew Short Story	* 1 Peter * 2 Peter 26 1 Peter 27 2 Peter	22 Europe Re-enchanted or Disenchanted?	Peace, Rose, Mobley: 2 Viewing Home Anew 3 Redrawing Our Maps
33		*Daniel * 1 Maccabees * 2 Maccabees 27 Daniel, 1–2 Maccabees	* 1 John * 2 John * 3 John 28 Johannine Letters	23 To Make the World Protestant	Peace, Rose, Mobley: World Protestant 4 Unpacking Our Belongs 5 Stepping Across the Line
34		*Ben Sira (Ecclesiasticus) * Wisdom of Solomon 28 The Deuterocanonical Wisdom Books	* Jude 29 Jude	24 Not Peace but a Sword	Peace, Rose, Mobley: 6 Finding Fellow Travelers
35		Yee: 4 Affirming and Contradicting Gender Stereotypes Collins: 29 From Tradition to Canon	* The Revelation to John 30 Revelation	25 Culture Wars	Peace, Rose, Mobley: 7 Repairing Our Shared World
36	**Final Meeting**	Closing the Year	Closing the Year	Closing the Year	Closing the Year

About Online Resources

All EfM participants have subscriber's access to the Oxford Biblical Studies Internet site, which has articles, maps, timelines, a variety of biblical translations, articles on biblical interpretation, illustrations, and numerous other items. The *New Oxford Annotated Bible (NRSV)* can be accessed on the site.

oxfordbiblicalstudies.com
The login ID is **efm-sewanee** and the password is **ministry**.

There also are resources online that correspond to the Collins and Powell texts, as well as an EfM study guide for the MacCulloch text.[1]

Collins:
http://fortresspress.com/product/short-introduction-hebrew-bible-third-edition
(Links to Research Guide and Study Guide)

Powell:
http://bakerpublishinggroup.com/books/introducing-the-new-testament-2nd-edition/264695
(Link to student study aids)

MacCulloch:
http://efm.sewanee.edu/assets/uploads/MacCulloch_Study_Guide-Babb.pdf

Links to additional resources will be posted on the EfM website **Resources** page on occasion:
efm.sewanee.edu/resources/resources

---

1. These and other hyperlinks in this volume were operational at the time of printing. If you find the link does not work, try searching for the author or title to find an updated link.

PART I

The Guide

Week One: Orientation and Organization

ALL YEARS

Suggested Opening Worship
GOD OF MANY NAMES

Leader	God of a thousand names,
	You come to us in many forms—manna to the hungry
Responders	**water to the parched**
Leader	embrace to the grieving
Responders	**rainbow to the despairing**
Leader	champion of the oppressed
Responders	**defender of the exploited**
Leader	friend to the lonely
Responders	**rescuer to the lost**
Leader	rest for the weary
Responders	**shock to the comfortable**
Leader	peace to the restless
Responders	**gift to the joyful**
Leader	mystery to the knowing
Responders	**revelation to the seeking**
Leader	manna, water, embrace, rainbow, champion, defender, friend, rescuer, rest, shock, peace, gift, mystery, revelation . . . In silence, let us reflect on what God's name is for us at this moment . . .

(Silent reflection)

Let us give thanks to God.

ALL	**God of many names and still the one, true God,**
	You reveal Your name to us in our need,
	yet remain beyond our control or understanding.
	You are God and we are Your people.

> **In trust and love, we commit ourselves to exploring
> and discovering
> who You are and whose we are. Amen.**[2]

Read

Welcome

Welcome to the Education for Ministry (EfM) program, begun in 1975 at the School of Theology of The University of the South in Sewanee, Tennessee, and continuing through you. Education for Ministry is a four-year program in group reflection and study to support formation for Christian ministry in daily life. Assigned texts and essays provide the primary knowledge content in the study of the Christian tradition. The disciplines of individual and group theological reflection facilitate the connection of life experience with this study. The sharing of worship, spiritual autobiographies, and personal stories across the year help to form the relationships that are foundational to ministry.

In this first seminar meeting of the EfM year, the mentor(s) will distribute materials and lead the group in organizing the year and getting to know one another. Between this meeting and the next, participants will prepare the assignments and exercises described in Week Two. Assignments are provided in a Read-Focus-Respond-Practice format that continues through the thirty-six meetings for the year. Notice that this first meeting also follows the Read-Focus-Respond-Practice format.

It is customary to begin each session with worship. Your group may have used the suggested opening above, your mentor may have had another opening worship planned for this session, or your mentor may have asked someone in the group to lead worship. It is likely that responsibility for worship will be shared across the year. Your group will decide how to schedule this.

Take some time in this session to introduce yourselves to one another. The mentor will provide an "ice-breaker" or some other format for these initial introductions. Your group's spiritual autobiographies will contribute to the relationships built in the course of the year together.

The group will be setting community norms during this meeting. A suggested format is given below in the Practice section.

Core Practices in Education for Ministry

The terms "education" and "ministry" in Education for Ministry frequently need unpacking to better understand both the content and the purpose of the program. Some expect EfM to be a course in religion or theology, like

---

2. Revs. Norma and John Brown, "God of Many Names," from *Mission Prayer Handbook (1991–2003)*, Uniting Church National Assembly (Australia), 2. http://pilgrimwr .unitingchurch.org.au/wp-content/uploads/2012/06/mph.pdf

one that might be taught at their local college or university. Some expect it to be geared toward preparation for becoming an ordained minister or pastor, for such is the limited understanding of ministers in contemporary culture.

EfM actually is neither of these, although it does provide an education in the content of the Christian tradition through reading the Bible alongside some basic biblical commentary, church history, and practical introductions to Christian theology and ethics, as well as through encouraging an appreciation for ways in which Christians respond to encounters with those of other faiths. EfM also explores a wider concept of ministry, based as it is in an understanding that baptism, the fundamental rite of entry into Christianity, marks our call to minister to one another in Christ's name in the course of our daily lives.

At its heart EfM is a program in practical theology, that is, a program based in a set of five core practices that form and support us in the various ministries to which we are called.

Living in Community

All ministry begins in relationship, and at its best is reciprocal. As we each share our own stories and listen attentively to another's stories, we come to know each other and the relationship deepens. Empathy deepens, and out of that empathy I minister to you even as you minister to me.

In EfM we begin the year by sharing a focused portion of our spiritual autobiographies. As we listen to one another we may find points of common experience and points at which our empathy is awakened. Sharing spiritual autobiographies forms a foundation on which we build relationships for working together in community through the year. As we continue to share stories of personal experience, name concerns and positions, offer varied expressions of worship, and acknowledge deep spiritual truths and longings, we deepen our connections to one another and actively look for ways to bridge differences that might otherwise separate us. EfM uses the Respectful Communication Guidelines and the Mutual Invitation process from the Kaleidoscope Institute as tools for learning to acknowledge and respect those differences.

Regular Prayer and Worship

EfM expects that weekly worship in the meeting, usually with members taking in turn responsibility for leadership, is a component of the seminar group's work together. Spiritual practices are addressed in the EfM curriculum, particularly in Unit Three each year, but also across the year through the introduction of practices from the Christian tradition like *Lectio divina*, the Ignatian examen, contemplative prayer, and walking a labyrinth. Participants are invited to explore entering into these traditional practices and encouraged to write a Rule of Life.

The different expressions and practices of worship shared weekly by members of the group offer ways to enrich individual spiritual practice, as do trial explorations of different practices from the tradition. In addition, participants are encouraged to be regular in attendance at worship and active participants in congregational life. The goal is to develop a spiritual connection with God and neighbor that grounds and sustains us in the work of ministry.

Theological Reflection

Examining life through a theological lens is the central spiritual discipline in Education for Ministry. The seminar groups practice theological reflection (TR) employing EfM's model that brings four sources of wisdom into conversation, using a method in four movements that lead to new understandings with implications for action in practicing ministry in daily life.

The four sources in the EfM model include three that form our context in daily living: life experience ("Action"), the culture/society around us ("Culture"), and our cherished beliefs and values ("Position"). The fourth source is the Christian tradition handed down over the centuries ("Tradition"). EfM's method for bringing these sources into conversation with one another follows four movements: 1) *identify* a focus from one of the sources for reflection; 2) *examine* the focus; 3) *connect* it to the other three sources; and 4) *apply* new learning to shape action in ministry. In movements two and three, questions are framed using an intentional theological focus.

Using EfM's process for theological reflection often feels awkward at first, yet few expect to be able to play a musical instrument proficiently or master an athletic pursuit without practice. The same is true for spiritual disciplines. With sufficient practice in TR comes the ability to slip seamlessly into bringing the lens of faith to bear on any aspect of life, essential to aligning our behavior with what we say we believe. When faced with making an ethical choice, regular reflective practice can enable one to answer the question: "How do I know this is a faithful way?"

The process for theological reflection is addressed in Unit Two every year with the expectation that theological reflection is practiced weekly (or nearly every week) thereafter in the seminar groups. The curriculum also instructs participants in practicing theological reflection as individuals outside the seminar meeting, with the goal of becoming reflective practitioners of their faith in daily life. Simply put, any seminar group that neglects the practice of theological reflection is not participating authentically in EfM as the program is designed.

Study of the Christian Tradition

A series of four Reading and Reflection Guides provide weekly assignments for reading, reflection, and response that encourage groups to develop a lifelong practice of engagement with the Christian tradition in study. Participants in the first two years read the Hebrew Bible and the New Testament along with commentary that helps them understand the texts in their ancient and modern contexts. In the third year, they study the history of the church. In their final year participants study Christian theology while examining their own personal theologies, consider ethics through the lens of the Anglican tradition, and read first-person stories of interreligious encounter.

In addition, the Reading and Reflection Guides offer contextual themes that shape ministerial formation over four years, viewing the study of the Christian tradition through lenses of personal and global contexts for our ministry in daily life as we grow in spiritual maturity and live into the journey with God. The regular study of the Christian tradition in EfM forms a foundation for theological reflection in the service of faithful living.

Vocational Discernment

Listening for and responding to God's call to ministry in daily life, the focus of Unit Five each year, is a practice that undergirds the whole EfM curriculum. It is assumed that all Christians are so called.

In the group we begin with attentive listening to one another as we share spiritual autobiographies and continue that listening through shared prayer and worship, shared stories of our daily lives, shared theological reflection across the year. Through such listening we often find we can help one another identify specific gifts and the deep moments of longing or joy that may signal a call to a ministry in which the person can offer those gifts. As individuals the practice of regular prayer opens us to listening for God's call, a call that we can take to the community for reflection and support.

Responding to God's call is shaped by the regular practice of attention to personal and community contexts. What are the needs of the community around me? What gift can I offer? Attention to the fruits of theological reflection will shape response as well. What implications for my own or others' action in ministry can be taken from this TR? What are the next steps? What or who will be needed to support me in this response? How can I support you in your call? The seminar group becomes a community of affirmation, support, and accountability when regular attention is paid to vocational discernment with and for its members.

Expectations

The Participants

You, the participants in an EfM seminar group, are all adults. You set your own learning goals and need the latitude to learn as each individual does best. This requires a certain commitment to the program, but every participant does not need to work in the same way or with the same intensity. EfM has the flexibility for each of you to work in his or her own way.

There are some basic expectations of each participant:

• Attend the seminar sessions or at least maintain the community by letting others know when you will be absent.

• Read the materials and complete the work assigned to the best of your ability.

• Participate in the discussions, reflections, and worship of your seminar group.

The Mentor

The role of the mentor is crucial to the life of the group. The term "mentor" originates in Greek mythology. Mentor was a friend of Odysseus who remained in charge of his household while he was away. "Wisdom" in the form of Athena took shape in Mentor to be the guide and teacher of Telemachus. A teacher who guides is a description of an EfM mentor.

The EfM mentor brings skills in working effectively with small groups of people. The responsibility for the life of the group belongs to everyone, but the mentor is the initial convener. The mentor works to allow everyone an opportunity to learn, to share, to discover. At the same time, the mentor is also a member of the group. The mentor is also there to learn, to share, and to discover. The mentor has a second role, that of administrator for the group. The mentor handles registrations, receives and distributes materials, files reports, and is accountable to the administrative staff in Sewanee.

The mentor serves the group neither as a teacher whose most important task is to provide information nor as a therapist. The mentor is a guide in a journey of discovery. Some groups have co-mentors who work together as a team. This can be very helpful to the process since it can be very difficult to lead and participate simultaneously.

Mentor training and accreditation by an EfM trainer is required. It is an important component of the EfM program. Mentors must renew their accreditation every eighteen months.

The Seminar Group

The EfM seminar group is the crucible for learning in the EfM program. A seminar group usually contains no fewer than six and no more than twelve participants and a mentor (or two co-mentors). The group provides an environment that supports the exploration and expression of ideas so that discovery and learning occur. It is a place of trust and confidentiality as participants in the seminar reflect upon ways to pursue a life of faith on a daily basis.

Seminars usually meet for two-and-a-half to three hours once a week over a period of thirty-six weeks during the academic cycle. For many of us this cycle begins in September and ends in June, but the group may decide to meet more frequently for shorter periods of time or less frequently for longer periods of time. Less frequent meetings can be very helpful when participants are scattered or they live in a region where bad weather can make travel difficult for extended periods. Some seminar groups meet online.

EfM seminars regularly engage in three different aspects of learning. These may not all be done in any one session, but attention needs to be given to all three aspects.

- There is time for social and spiritual needs to be addressed. This is a way to build trust, friendship, and community. It is an opportunity to support each other and maintain the freedom we all need to express our thoughts and feelings.

- There is time to discuss the materials which participants read in the texts. It is not a time for classroom presentations, rather an occasion to raise questions, wrestle with the materials, obtain clarifications, and generally share impressions about what has been read.

- There is an opportunity to engage in reflective activity. This may come in the form of a spiritual autobiography, one of many forms of theological reflections, studying and following a spiritual discipline, or exploring the meaning of the ministries we have.

The Program

The EfM Program expects participants, mentors, and trainers to remain faithful to the program. EfM is a program for adults and one expectation of the program is that adults take responsibility for their lives, set their own goals, and seek the support necessary to move forward. The program asks participants and mentors to provide an arena in which learning can take place on a mature adult level.

The relationship of EfM and the University of the South to the local church and to the judicatory/diocese is one of collaboration. Together we join to provide a program of theological education for the laity that carries a number of benefits.

- Portability—Participants can begin in one location and continue their work in another one.

- Accreditation—EfM grants Continuing Education Units to indicate completion of the work.

- Access to an international network

- A training opportunity for the laity

- Connection with the University of the South and its School of Theology

- Basic theological education to support the laity in responding to the call to ministry in daily life. For some the theological groundwork in EfM may be supplemented with additional opportunities to prepare for ecclesial roles such as that of lay reader, vocational deacon, or educator.

Providing the program is something in which various agencies participate. The local church provides a setting and may offer some financial assistance to participants. The diocese may contract with EfM, which lowers the tuition for participants. When there is a contract with the local jurisdiction, a function of that contract is the appointment of a coordinator who maintains a liaison with the EfM program in Sewanee, arranges for mentor training locally, acts as a communicator for EfM, and promotes the program.

What EfM Is NOT

- *EfM is not only Bible study.*
    EfM participants study what the Bible says, but they also learn how to understand the Bible within its historical context and literary setting. Biblical studies form the primary work of the first two years. EfM is more

than a Bible study in which one reads the Bible, seeks to understand it, and then applies it to daily life. EfM takes seriously God's revelation through all of Christian tradition, from the earliest biblical messages, through the development of liturgy and theology, and even in the context of the challenges we face in our own times.

- *EfM is not a program in personal therapy or problem solving.*

    While EfM groups develop a close community in order to delve deeply into matters of faith and theology, the group does not exist as a problem-solving agency or as a setting for analyzing or addressing personal and social problems. In an EfM group, members may wish to share various aspects of their lives, but EfM is not a place to probe or press individuals to talk about those things they would prefer to leave unexamined.

- *EfM is not a closed community.*

    The content of EfM materials and the processes we use for reflection are not secrets. A group may invite a guest such as someone who brings some special information or someone who would like to participate for a session in order to decide if he or she might like to join. On the other hand, we do respect one another's privacy. This means that we expect the group to maintain confidentiality about personal matters. The rule of thumb is: secrets—no; privacy—yes. Participants may share with others what they have learned and how that was learned, but they are expected to retain in confidence specific personal aspects of their colleagues' lives which may have been shared during the course of the program.

- *EfM is not an academic program leading to a degree or an ordination program.*

    Local arrangements may permit EfM to become part of the work leading to a degree or to ordination, but the School of Theology of the University of the South makes no recommendations about ordination nor does it grant course credit for completing the Education for Ministry program.

The EfM Curriculum

The EfM curriculum is presented in a cycle of four Reading and Reflection Guides. A theme for each volume in the cycle provides a lens for focusing the work throughout the year. Weekly assignments guide participants' responses to the readings. Weekly preparation includes practice in the disciplines of listening and theological reflection.

Volume A: "Living Faithfully in Your World"

Volume B: "Living Faithfully in a Multicultural World"

Volume C: "Living as Spiritually Mature Christians"

Volume D: "Living into the Journey with God"

Each volume contains five units that explore and nurture the core practices for developing foundational skills for ministry in daily life:

Unit One: *Spiritual Autobiography and Listening* uses creating a spiritual autobiography and developing effective listening habits to focus on sharing stories to develop relationships.

Unit Two: *Theological Reflection as a Life Skill* introduces the EfM theological reflection model to integrate life experience and faith.

Unit Three: *Developing a Sustaining Spirituality* encourages, through prayer and worship combined with study and theological reflection, a four-fold spiritual discipline that can help sustain us in the practice of ministry.

Unit Four: *Integrating Belief, Behavior, and Doctrine* offers opportunities to examine and build a personal theology.

Unit Five: *Vocation* focuses on discerning and responding to God's call to ministry in daily life.

Terms in the EfM Curriculum

Common Reading: A common reading is assigned to all year levels. Each unit begins with an introductory essay read by all participants. Interlude texts are also assigned for common reading.

Identify, Explore, Connect, Apply: Theological reflection is described in four movements: *Identify, Explore, Connect, Apply.* This pattern also underlies the *Read, Focus, Respond, Practice* pattern of the Reading and Reflection Guide.

Interlude: An interlude is a two-week session in which all participants in a group read and respond to a common text chosen in relation to the theme of the Reading and Reflection Guide. There are two interludes in each program year.

Interlude Text: The text assigned to an interlude session is called an interlude text or interlude book. Two interlude books are read each year. The books address special topics that reinforce the theme of the Reading and Reflection Guide for that program year.

Participants: Those enrolled in a seminar group are generally referred to as participants or group members.

Program Year: The approximately nine-month period (thirty-six sessions) during which the group seminar meets is its program year. An EfM group can begin its program year in any month *except June, July, or August.*

Read, Focus, Respond, Practice: The guide for each session follows the sequence of *Read* (assigned reading), *Focus* (questions or terms specific to the assigned reading), *Respond* (connects the reading to the unit theme), and *Practice* (suggested application for individual and/or group work). This sequence provides a four-fold discipline for the practice of ministry.

Reading and Reflection Guides: These guides outline what is needed for participants to prepare for each of the thirty-six seminar meetings in a program year, including individual reading assignments and suggested ways to focus, respond, and practice what is being learned. There are four volumes, A–D, used in a cycle. All groups use the same Reading and Reflection Guide volume in a program year.

Readings in the Christian Tradition: Textbooks provide participants with their weekly readings in the Christian tradition: the Hebrew Bible in Year One; the New Testament in Year Two; church history in Year Three; and theology, ethics, and interfaith encounters in Year Four.

Theme: Each volume of the Reading and Reflection Guide has a central theme that is carried through each of the units and interludes. Volume A's theme is ministry in your own particular context. Themes for the subsequent volumes are (B) ministry in an intercultural and interfaith context, (C) growth into spiritual maturity, and (D) the journey into a deepening relationship with God.

The Seminar Schedule

There are thirty-six seminar weeks, weekly meetings of about two to three hours each. Groups meeting online may have shorter sessions, with some work shared online asynchronously. Each seminar meeting will include components of worship, community life, theological reflection, and reflective discussion of the participants' work prepared for that week. In the first few weeks, all participants prepare a spiritual autobiography and share a selected part of that with the group. Holiday breaks will be set as agreed in the group.

Focus

You will receive the assigned texts appropriate to your year in the program as provided by the Education for Ministry program. Examine them briefly as they are distributed.

- **The Reading and Reflection Guide, Volume B, 2018–2019–"Living Faithfully in a Multicultural World."**
  The Guide supports EfM participants in preparing for their weekly seminar sessions. While it may not be possible to do everything assigned each week, giving priority to regularly completing as much of the work in the Guide as possible will enhance your formation for ministry through study and theological reflection.

- **Interlude books** bring additional voices into the study and support the theme of the year.

Living into God's Dream: Dismantling Racism in America, edited by Catherine Meeks.

Faithful Neighbors: Christian-Muslim Vision and Practice, edited by Robert S. Heaney, Zeyneb Sayilgan, and Claire Haymes.

- **Texts for the assigned readings in the Christian tradition** provide a foundation in the study of the Bible and church history, and in the practice of viewing life experience and choices through a theological lens.

  Years One and Two will a need a Bible for reading assignments, and all participants will benefit from bringing a Bible to the seminar for use during theological reflection. The most recent Oxford Annotated edition of the New Revised Standard Version of the Bible is recommended, but any translation may be used as long as it includes the Apocrypha. A Bible with study notes is helpful. Paraphrased Bibles are not recommended for study.

  - **Year One:** *A Short Introduction to the Hebrew Bible*, 3rd ed. by John J. Collins; *The Hebrew Bible: Feminist and Intersectional Perspectives*, edited by Gale Yee.

  - **Year Two:** *Introducing the New Testament*, 2nd ed. by Mark Allan Powell.

  - **Year Three:** *Christianity: The First Three Thousand Years* by Diarmaid MacCulloch.

  - **Year Four:** Four texts

    Theology: A Very Short Introduction by David Ford.

    Mysteries of Faith by Mark McIntosh.

    The Christian Moral Life: Practices of Piety by Timothy F. Sedgwick.

    My Neighbor's Faith: Stories of Interreligious Encounter, Growth, and Transformation edited by Jennifer Howe Peace, Or N. Rose, and Gregory Mobley.

Respond

Spend a few minutes as a group exploring the Reading and Reflection Guide. Note that there are two parts to the guide, the assignments for the weekly seminar meetings and a collection of supplemental resources. Note also that on pages xi–xiv in the front of the guide you will find an overview chart of all the reading assignments for the year and a list of hyperlinks for online resources.

Part I of the EfM Reading and Reflection Guide supports participants in learning at home *between* the weekly seminars, providing reading assignments as well as ways to focus and reflect on the week's study and prepare for the seminar. Mentors support participants *in* the weekly seminars by facilitating the group's conversation and reflection to draw on the participants' work from the Guide in a variety of ways. The work of the seminar group as a learning community is significantly enhanced when individual participants are faithful in doing the work assigned in the Guide.

Note that each of the six units in Part I begins with an essay that all year levels read together in place of a reading in the assigned textbooks. The Interlude sessions also are for the group together with all years reading the same text. In the remaining sessions each year level will have its own individual assignment for Read and Focus. The Respond and Practice assignments are for all year levels together.

- The **Read** section lists the reading assigned for the week. Most of the time each year level will have its own separate reading assigned. Other times, at the beginning of a unit and during the Interludes, the reading assigned will be for all years together.

- The **Focus** section is specific to each year level's reading assignment and may include terms to define, topics or names to note, or a question regarding that week's study in light of the themes of the year and the particular unit.

- The **Respond** section poses an idea that all participants can relate to from the perspective of their own individual study for the week. Respond may provide a vehicle for seminar discussion, encouraging the connecting of personal responses to those of others in the group in relation to the theme of the year or unit.

- The **Practice** section provides participants a suggested practical application in connecting learning to daily life, including practicing skills for ministry such as listening or theological reflection between group meetings. Mentors may choose to use an individual theological reflection model from the week's Practice as a starting point for group theological reflection, giving participants opportunity to experience how group reflection and personal reflection on the same topic may both differ and compliment each other. Personal theological reflection can help us to go deeper in our theological understanding as it draws on the four sources from our individual perspectives. Theological reflection in a group also offers depth through insights from varied perspectives as participants share from their own life experiences and differing cultural and social contexts. Each way of reflecting is important in shaping a whole life attuned to listening for and responding to God's call to us.

Part II of the Guide contains resources to support the work of the year. Supplemental reading assignments are collected at the beginning of Part II. Also in Part II are sections that provide additional information about spiritual autobiographies, listening, theological reflection (including the basic structure of the four movements in the EfM method and examples of reflections beginning in each of the four sources), and resources to enhance an understanding of community life. The Respectful Communication Guidelines from the Kaleidoscope Institute are on the last page of Part II to make it easy to find them for regular use and review.

Practice

If you have not already made introductions, you may want to do so now. What would you like to share briefly to help other group members begin to get to know you? A suggested format for introductions and beginning the work of reflecting on our multicultural world is below.

Our Stories: A Way to Deepen Personal Connections

The spiritual autobiography encouraged for this seminar year helps participants to notice the pattern of diversity that has shaped and continues to shape each person. Beginning in the preparation for Week Two, each will have the opportunity to explore those life dimensions and decide what to share openly with the group at the agreed upon time.

Read the following excerpt from Unit One, Week Two (page 21):

> [This year's *Reading and Reflection Guide* volume] invites participants to notice the different cultures present in their lives. These cultures have distinctive qualities and features that differentiate one from another. A people's mores, assumptions, values, sciences, artifacts, and philosophies work together to form their culture. Culture refers to the patterns that order the social interactions ranging from the economic and political interests to educational and family concerns. In short, a group's ways of being in relationship to other people and groups. Culture includes the physical environments and the ways of relating to the geographic conditions.
>
> Language, dress, food, celebrations, rituals, music, stories, myths, and religious practices distinguish a person's ethnic background—a background that is lived out within a cultural ethos. People from very diverse ethnic backgrounds come together creating the diverse features of a common society.

Take a few moments to recall stories you have heard about your family's history, or perhaps information you have discovered through some kind of ancestry research. If, for a variety of reasons, little is known of your family history, recall the environments in which you have grown up and what cultural contributions may have come from those arenas. Note multicultural threads that have contributed to your identity.

Using Mutual Invitation share one or two of the threads you identified as part of your introduction to the group.

The Kaleidoscope Institute's Mutual Invitation is recommended as a helpful process to use to make sure each person in the group is invited to share during these initial introductions as well as during check-in and times for group discussion through the year. A description of Mutual Invitation is on page 344 in Part II. The process is designed to facilitate conversation across cultural differences and may feel awkward at first but will become easier as you practice. The extension of a gracious invitation can do much to encourage each person in the group to share with greater ease.

Begin to set community norms by reading aloud the Kaleidoscope Institute's Respectful Communication Guidelines on page 345 in Part II. Your mentor will facilitate the group in considering how these will form the foundation for your norms, as well as what you might need to add in order to help the group do its work as a learning community this year. You may want to review the norms you compose over several weeks before agreeing on a final set. Your group also may find it helpful to read the Respectful Communication Guidelines aloud at the beginning of each meeting, at least for the first several weeks of the year. Some groups do this every week to mark a safe space for sharing. You are encouraged to review your community norms periodically through the year to see if additions or changes need to be made. Everyone in the group should be willing to agree to abide by the norms you set together.

Finally, in the upcoming week prepare for your next meeting using the work assigned for Week Two. This will be the pattern for the year: Complete the assigned work in the week prior to the seminar meeting. Looking ahead will help you allow adequate time to complete the reflective work as well as sometimes long reading assignments, a practice that will enhance your learning and your experience in EfM this year.

A Closing Prayer

All: God, Creator of variety and difference,
Creator of hearts, minds, and bodies,
you have called us into relationship with each other
so we can know you more fully.
Help us see you in our neighbours,
in those who are familiar
and in those who are not yet familiar.
Creator of wholeness,
help us learn to do more than celebrate difference.
Help us be transformed by the gifts of diversity
to become the blessed community.
Amen.[3]

---

3. from "Who Are We? Resources for Canadian Multiculturalism Day" © 2013 The United Church of Canada/L'Église Unie du Canada. Licensed under Creative Commons Attribution Non-commercial Share Alike Licence. To view a copy of this licence, visit http://creativecommons. org/licenses/by-nc-sa/2.5/ca. Any copy must include this notice.

UNIT ONE

Spiritual Autobiography and Listening

Week Two

ALL YEARS

Read

Living in a Multicultural World

Sometime in the latter half of the twentieth century in Manhattan, New York, Carolyn A. Rose composed a collect that expressed a vision for humanity. Anyone living in New York City as she did in the 1950s and '60s experienced refugees and immigrants flooding into the city and knew firsthand the tensions and pressures present whenever people from diverse cultures interact. The prayer likely emerged from the pressures of plurality she felt.

> *O God, who created all peoples in your image, we thank you for the wonderful diversity of races and cultures in this world. Enrich our lives by ever-widening circles of fellowship, and show us your presence in those who differ most from us, until our knowledge of your love is made perfect in our love for all your children; through Jesus Christ our Lord. Amen.*[4]

The primary petition of the collect envisions a dynamic world in which "ever-widening circles of fellowship" reveal God's love. Decades later, in South Africa, a vision of God fueled the passions of a people who were emboldened to abolish an oppressive apartheid system. Archbishop Desmond Tutu promoted the vision that guided people into a new world. He extended his ongoing commitment to the vision in his book *God Has a Dream*:

> Dear Child of God, before we can become God's partners, we must know what God wants for us. "I have a dream," God says, "Please help Me to realize it. It is a dream of a world whose ugliness and squalor and poverty, its war and hostility, its greed and harsh competitiveness, its alienation and disharmony are changed into their glorious counterparts, when there will be more laughter, joy, and peace, where there will be justice and goodness and compassion and love and caring and sharing. I have a dream that swords will be beaten into plowshares and spears into pruning hooks, that My children will know that they are members of one family, the human family, God's family. My family."[5]

---

4. Collect "For the Diversity of Races and Cultures," *The Book of Common Prayer* (New York: Church Hymnal Corporation, 1979), 840.

5. Desmond Tutu, *God Has a Dream: A Vision of Hope for Our Time* (New York: Image Books Doubleday, 2005), 19–20.

Bishop Tutu continues,

> In God's family there are no outsiders. All are insiders. Black and white, rich and poor, gay and straight, Jew and Arab, Palestinian and Israeli, Roman Catholic and Protestant, Serb and Albanian, Hutu and Tutsi, Muslim and Christian, Buddhist and Hindu, Pakistani and Indian—all belong.

A gap occurs between vision and reality; between what is desired and what currently exists. The gap creates a tension that seeks resolution. Either the vision atrophies and dissolves into merely a notion or the current situation moves toward realizing the vision. A vision that is loved can provide motivation and energy to transform current realities into the vision.[6] Ministry occurs in the gap between vision and reality. Carolyn Rose's heartfelt prayer for "ever-widening circles of fellowship" and Desmond Tutu's dream of an inclusive world create lenses through which learners can recognize the knowledge, skills, actions, and attitudes needed to realize the vision. Once people fall in love with God's dream, they enter into a partnership with God.

One way to understand ministry is to see it as the participation with God realizing God's dream. Ministry happens among and within the complexities of the world. Clearly, contemporary life is complex and fast-paced, filled with multiple encounters with ethnic diversity. *Education for Ministry* brings people together by forming a reflecting community of colleagues committed to helping one another to know better what it means to live as an adult Christian in an increasingly pluralistic world.

The Reading and Reflection Guide: Volume B is built on the theme "Living Faithfully in a Multicultural World." Advancements in travel have brought races and cultures together geographically in unprecedented ways. Technology, especially in the advancement and use of communication satellites, has shrunk our world into what Marshall McLuhan aptly described in the 1970s as a "global village." All of humanity has been brought into an awareness of the "wonderful diversity of races and cultures." While all may not celebrate the diversity, the fact of great cultural and racial diversity is undeniable. The following excerpt from Diana Eck's *A New Religious America* sets the stage for the work ahead as she describes the current reality of the contemporary religious scene.

> The huge white dome of a mosque with its minarets rises from the cornfields just outside Toledo, Ohio. You can see it as you drive by on the interstate highway. A great Hindu temple with elephants carved in relief at the doorway stands on a hillside in the western suburbs of Nashville, Tennessee. A Cambodian Buddhist temple and monastery with a hint of a Southeast Asian roofline is set in the farmlands south of Minneapolis, Minnesota. In suburban

---

6. Robert Fritz has worked extensively on structural tensions and has written several books on how the tension, once established, brings visions into life. http://robertfritz .com

Fremont, California, flags fly from the golden domes of a new Sikh gurdwara on Hillside Terrace, now renamed Gurdwara Road. The religious landscape of America has changed radically in the past thirty years, but most of us have not yet begun to see the dimensions and scope of that change, so gradual has it been and yet so colossal. It began with the "new immigration," spurred by the Immigration and Nationality Act of 1965, as people from all over the world came to America and have become citizens. With them have come the religious traditions of the world—Islamic, Hindu, Buddhist, Jain, Sikh, Zoro-astrian, African, and Afro-Caribbean. The people of these living traditions of faith have moved into American neighborhoods, tentatively at first, their altars and prayer rooms in storefronts and office buildings, basements and garages, recreation rooms and coat closets, nearly invisible to the rest of us. But in the past decade, we have begun to see their visible presence. Not all of us have seen the Toledo mosque or the Nashville temple, but we will see places like them, if we keep our eyes open, even in our own communities. They are the architectural signs of a new religious America. . . .

We are surprised to find that there are more Muslim Americans than Episcopalians, more Muslims than members of the Presbyterian Church USA, and as many Muslims as there are Jews—that is, about six million. We are astonished to learn that Los Angeles is the most complex Buddhist city in the world, with a Buddhist population spanning the whole range of the Asian Buddhist world from Sri Lanka to Korea, along with a multitude of native-born American Buddhists. Nationwide, this whole spectrum of Buddhists may number about four million. We know that many of our internists, surgeons, and nurses are of Indian origin, but we have not stopped to consider that they too have a religious life, that they might pause in the morning for few minutes' prayer at an altar in the family room of their home, that they might bring fruits and flowers to the local Shiva-Vishnu temple on the weekend and be part of a diverse Hindu population of more than a million. We are well aware of Latino immigration from Mexico and Central America and of the large Spanish-speaking population of our cities, and yet we may not recognize what a profound impact this is having on American Christianity, both Catholic and Protestant, from hymnody to festivals. . . .

In the past thirty years massive movements of people both as migrants and refugees have reshaped the demography of our world. Immigrants around the world number over 130 million, with about 30 million in the United States, a million arriving each year. The dynamic global image of our times is not the so-called clash of civilizations but the marbling of civilizations and peoples. Just as the end of the Cold War brought about a new geopolitical situation, the global movements of people have brought about a new georeligious reality. Hindus, Sikhs, and Muslims are now part of the religious landscape of Britain, mosques appear in Paris and Lyons, Buddhist temples in Toronto, and Sikh gurdwaras in Vancouver. But nowhere, even in today's world of mass migrations, is the sheer range of religious faith as wide as it is today in the United States. Add to India's wide range of religions those of China, Latin America, and Africa. Take the diversity of Britain or Canada, and add to it the crescendo of Latino immigration along with the Vietnamese, Cambodians, and Filipinos. This is an astonishing new reality. We have never been here before.[7]

Reading and Reflection Guide Volume B: Living Faithfully in a Multicultural World invites participants to notice the different cultures present in their lives. These cultures have distinctive qualities and features that differentiate one from another. A people's mores, assumptions, values, sciences, artifacts, and philosophies work together to form their culture. Culture refers to the patterns that order the social interactions ranging from the economic and political interests to educational and family concerns: in short, a group's ways of being in relationship to other people and groups. Culture includes the physical environments and the ways of relating to the geographic conditions.

Language, dress, food, celebrations, rituals, music, stories, myths, and religious practices distinguish a person's ethnic background—a background that is lived out within a cultural ethos. People from very diverse ethnic backgrounds come together, creating diverse features of a common society. Increasingly, ethnic identity has become marbled as different cultures interact.

Spiritual Autobiography

At the beginning of every program year EfM participants reflect on and prepare spiritual autobiographies, then share a portion with their seminar groups. This is a foundational part of the work for the year and is not optional. Everyone, participant and mentor alike, participates in this exercise. Since reflecting on and sharing your own story and listening deeply to the stories of others are fundamental skills for the practice of ministry in daily life because ministry begins in relationship, the sharing of spiritual autobiographies provides the seminar group an opportunity to begin forming the learning community in which we will work and reflect together through the year.

The suggested format for framing an autobiography changes yearly, giving participants over the four years in EfM multiple spiritual lenses through which to consider their own lives. Why go through this each year? One reason that seems consistently true is that after completing my own account and hearing the autobiographical accounts of others, I become aware of additional pieces of my own story that I may not have recalled earlier. As life continues to unfold, year by year, day by day, my own story unfolds. My story this month is different from my story even six weeks or six months ago. Another reason is that choosing the slice of my larger story to offer as spiritual autobiography each year provides an avenue for reflecting on where my own experience encounters that shared by others in my seminar group,

---

7. Diana Eck, *A New Religious America* (San Francisco: HarperSanFrancisco, 2002), 1–4.

while simultaneously engaging with the greater story of the people of God encountered through EfM study and reflection.

A spiritual autobiography may contain both religious material—significant people or times within the religious community—and everyday material—people and times in your life that have influenced who you are now and how you understand God's presence or absence in your life.

The work you do on your spiritual autobiography is private, "for your eyes only." This allows you to be free, without concern about how others will interpret either the context or expression. Preparing a spiritual autobiography each year provides a way to deepen your understanding of Christian life and ministry. By virtue of your baptism you were called to ministry, guided and pushed by personal gifts, passions, skills, experiences, and interests.

Once you prepare your spiritual autobiography, you need to decide what you want to share with your seminar group. Martin Buber, twentieth-century philosopher and Jewish theologian, is reputed to have said that he could never hold a significant conversation with another person until he had heard the other's life story. The purpose of sharing autobiographies is to build trust and understanding within the group and to begin to make connections within your own story. We need the experience of hearing other life stories to know that we are not alone in God's world. By sharing appropriate stories of our lives we form learning communities that can challenge and support us throughout our lives.

Your mentor will relate her or his own story and help the group structure the time for sharing of autobiographies. Most groups give each member around ten minutes to tell his or her story. Spiritual autobiographies are the focus of most of the seminar time for the first few meetings of the year. This is a special time for your group. This component of your group's life will carry you to the next phase of your year together. This may be the first time to tell your story in this way. It may seem a bit daunting at first. Remember that you should offer what you feel comfortable sharing in the group. This is not an opportunity for "group therapy" or psychologizing, so the group should not engage in raising questions about motives or probe for information beyond what you share. Feel free to say "no" or to say that you do not wish to explore questions that others may raise out of curiosity or concern.

Sharing your spiritual autobiography is a way to say, "Here I am," and to join your EfM group as a full participant. Over the years in EfM you will probably find that your spiritual autobiography changes. You may find yourself free to talk about things that were previously guarded. You also may find that your freedom to be yourself will grow as you discover ways in which your personal story, the life of the group, and the story of God's people relate to each other.

The format for this year's spiritual autobiography is given in the **Practice** section below.

Listening as an Act of Ministry

An ellipse is a figure with two foci that create the elliptical shape. The work in *Unit One: Spiritual Autobiography and Listening* has two points of focus. One centers the work of constructing a narrative of one's life, especially from the viewpoint of living among several cultures. The other focus works with listening as an act of receiving the story of another. Attending to another's life requires deep, compassionate listening. A primary skill for ministry is listening. The following is taken from *9 Skills for Listening to Life* by Geoffrey Caine,[8] providing a profile of the features of listening and the various attitudes and skills necessary for effective listening.

Why Listen?

Life is messy. Life is noisy. Life is rushed. That means that while life is rich with possibility, it is also full of missed opportunities, problems big and small, miscommunication, and mistakes. So the more tools we have for dealing with the demanding aspects of life, the better.

One set of tools, lying right under our noses, is the underutilized and surprising power of listening.

I gained a fresh understanding of listening when I left Australia and came to live in the United States many years ago. You might say that I'm an accidental immigrant. I came to visit someone. Seven days later we were married. Four days after that I discovered that I was going to immigrate. Life can be like that. And this was quite a shock for someone who used to pride himself on taking the time to think things through. I'm thrilled that I immigrated, but it was difficult. I landed in California. Others may think that California is laid back, but the people here do things fast! They speak more quickly than I do, jump from this to that, and have a whole set of references that meant nothing to me when I first arrived. So finding the right way to jump into an everyday conversation, let alone getting a feel for what people were talking about, was tough for me. All that, and I also needed to find a way to earn a living! I had no choice but to adapt and learn to live here. That forced me to listen in an entirely new way.

In this constantly changing world, most of us are immigrants in some way, and we can all benefit from deeper and more powerful listening. People move from state to state, relationship to relationship, job to job, project to project. Then there's the online world. Writer Marc Prensky talks about the online world in terms of digital natives and digital immigrants—people at home with the world of information technology and others who are just dipping their toes in the digital water. If ever you want to see a failure to communicate, you can see it between many of the citizens of those two worlds. One of the most basic tools available to all of these immigrants is the power of listening.

---

8. Geoffrey Caine, *9 Skills for Listening to Life* (Livingston, NJ: Funderstanding, 2013), 10–32.

It's not that most people have suddenly stopped listening. It's just that as everything about the world speeds up, and as the tsunami of online opinions heats up, and as the urgency to make instant decisions flares up, listening tends to get trampled underfoot.

This is unfortunate because listening and thinking are soul mates. If we don't–or can't–listen, then the odds are that we are not doing enough thinking. That's a disaster-in-waiting for everything from marital peace, to making good business decisions, to getting a genuinely great education. . . .

As educators, managers, parents and others, we have to realize that the people with whom we live and work passionately love and want to feel heard. And so do we. Being heard in and of itself enhances motivation, builds relationship, encourages cooperation, and contributes to better results.

Listening and being listened to are great gifts, and they can be freely available everywhere. We do have to work for them, however.

5 Pillars of Great Listening

Listening, like any other skill, needs to be built on firm foundations. Some may be obvious, some are surprising. The interesting thing about the foundations of listening is that we have access to all of them because they are literally second nature to us. And yet they are often so much a part of us that they have become invisible.

For instance . . . good listening often calls for thoughtful attention. But paying attention involves more than just intellect and thought. In order to listen with full attention, many elements of the body, brain, and mind need to work together. There needs to be a blend and a balance of thought, feeling, physical posture, and relationship. So it pays to be aware of, and to strengthen, the foundations upon which good listening are built. It's a little like preparing the soil before planting a garden or strengthening the immune system as the basis for good health. Let's look at five pillars that together form a solid foundation for good listening.

1. We listen with our bodies as well as with our minds
Reflect for a moment about what your body does when you listen to someone tell a story, or when you're at a fantastically interesting conference, or even caught up in a dispute at work. It's not a matter of being right or wrong, but just of noticing what you do.

- When listening to that story with interest, do you find yourself leaning forward, focusing hard, and breathing more heavily? Or do you lean back out of boredom, wish that you could close your eyes, and find yourself adopting a pattern of breathing that resembles falling asleep? (Did you know that when people are bored their brains release a chemical that is just like an anesthetic?)

- When listening to music, are you jazzed up and excited as your head keeps time, or do you sit back with eyes closed as the gentle sounds waft over you?
- When engaged in a dispute, do your fists clench, your shoulder muscles tighten, while your stomach churns? Or, as one alternative, are you firmly centered, well balanced, and alert for whatever might come next?

Musician Steven Halpern calls the body a "human instrument." We can improve listening by taking charge of our breathing, posture, and how relaxed we are. (Research shows that when we are extremely stressed, parts of the brain associated with planning and effective decision making are bypassed and we revert to automatic and very primitive responses such as fight or flight. That state doesn't make for very good listening!)

Listening is also coupled with our other senses. The behaviors, movements, reactions, and context that we notice with our eyes always color the meanings that we discern with our ears.

2. We listen to both thoughts and feelings (even if we are unaware of it)

My wife and I regularly talk, sometimes vigorously, about our finances. Now I used to be a lawyer (I left the profession many years ago but some aspects of lawyering have become part of my DNA). When the issue gets intense, I act like a lawyer again. I get formal. I want specifics. I formulate my words and arguments with rigorous clarity and precision. I look for that formal clarity in others. And it drives my wife nuts. She, apart from having been a professor of education, has a background in therapy, and is very sensitive to the tone that people use. When I get overly formal, she feels that relationship is being lost, and has no desire to listen to my words.

We may want to be in the same conversation, but we're not. I am focusing on the facts; she is focusing on the relationship. And until the twain meet, we don't go anywhere.

All communication operates at these two levels: the content of the message and the emotional pull and tug underneath. Almost all people respond to the emotional tug first. Marketers, politicians, and radio and TV shock-jocks all rely on this fact. So does every media outlet where new items are framed in terms of stories, with a setting and characters and drama. As Krishnamurti said,

> . . . when you are listening to somebody completely, attentively, then you are listening not only to the words, but also to the feeling of what is being conveyed, to the whole of it, not part of it.

Some people are very good at communicating at both levels. It is equally important to be good at hearing at both levels.

Perhaps the most important aspect of the social, emotional and physical nature of listening is the sheer joy and satisfaction of feeling heard. We all love and need to feel heard. This applies to children feeling heard by their parents (and vice versa), spouses feeling heard by each other, employer and employees, students and teachers, colleagues at work, customers, clients, and more.

3. Listening is interactive

Every one of us, even the loners among us, is a social being. Our worlds, and the ways in which we make sense of things, are shaped by interacting with others. Current research in social neuroscience, for instance, shows that there are neuro-cognitive (brain-mind) systems that link what one person feels while doing something to what another feels while observing the action.

From the perspective of listening, this means that our words and actions contribute to what others perceive and how they speak and behave. Have you ever been to a gathering and found yourself talking to someone whose eyes were constantly surveying the room in a search for someone more interesting (or influential or useful) to talk to? Or found yourself talking to someone who appears to be totally unresponsive? Did you feel listened to? Did you feel like continuing the conversation? Compare that with how it feels to be the focus of someone's attention, to have that person authentically and enthusiastically respond to you, and fully share a moment in time with you.

Listening is almost always a dynamic interplay between people. Someone chooses the topic. Some people are more enthusiastic than others. Some responses seem approving and others disapproving. These differing reactions can send a conversation along very different paths. The bottom line is that what we do and say, and how we respond in a conversation, has an enormous impact on what other people say and how they say it. To a very great extent, listeners shape what they hear.

Even no response at all is a response. Imagine that someone is holding forth and has taken over a conversation. The silence of the listeners contributes to the space that the speaker fills with his or her words. And we may or may not want to be there listening. That's why author and consultant Harrison Owen coined the phrase "the law of two feet" as one of the attributes of what he calls "open space technology." People can stay. Or they can leave.

4. Listening is selective

At any point in time, there is always more going on than we can possibly absorb. Sometimes we are attuned to what a particular person is saying, and we automatically listen more fully to that which interests us. Our attention can be grabbed by people who seem to share our beliefs, but also by people who seem to be criticizing what we believe. Every one of us has a nonsense index, and we usually dismiss or ignore things that don't seem to make immediate sense to us.

These are just some of the ways in which each and every one of us filters input and selectively makes sense of the mass of words and sounds and activities that surround us. We can't help but be selective, because we all have biases, preferences, expectations, and ways of seeing and making sense of the world. So to a large extent people do not hear where others are coming from; they hear where *they themselves are coming from.*

We can, however, become more aware of our own tendencies. We can make a point of listening to things with which we do not immediately agree or that do not immediately make sense. Good listeners work to get on the same page and enter into the same stories. We cannot avoid being selective, but we do have a choice about what we actually select.

5. We are always listening to life

Hearing and listening are key components of everything that we do and everything that interests us. We listen in varying ways to the news, to our friends (and, sometimes, our enemies), to teachers, to bosses, to lovers, to passers-by. We listen to and contribute to gossip about neighbors, celebrities and others. We hear the cheers and jeers of fans at a football match or any other sporting event. We listen to the wind and the rain and the sounds of birds, planes and traffic of all kinds.

Indeed, sometimes it can seem as though we are afraid of silence. Nowadays the sounds of TVs, radios, and canned music fill the air in restaurants, airports, malls—almost everywhere people congregate. And every movie has a soundtrack intended to stimulate emotional responses to the movie. Life expresses itself through sound. And so hearing and listening matter everywhere.

How do we become better listeners?

The goal is to be willing and able to listen deeply, effectively and naturally in many different circumstances. The process is developmental. It is a matter of building a scaffold of skills and practices. Ultimately, as these skills become integrated, the scaffold begins to fall away and deeper listening follows naturally.

Focus

List the four or five greatest challenges you have experienced in the face of the information provided above. What image, picture, or metaphor expresses life in a multicultural world?

Respond

How have your inherited culture and your experience with interacting with other cultures influenced your view of God, faith, religion, worship, and your deep desires and loves?

How might the process of developing skills in listening as expressed above in Caine's image of building a scaffold of skills and practices apply in general to developing all skills?

How have you experienced the five pillars of listening? When have you felt listened to? When have you been the listener? Which of the five pillars do you do well? Which remain for you to develop further?

In the seminar meeting, responding to and reflecting on reading assignments must be done on a limited basis so that all participants have time to contribute. For this reason giving a "book report" is discouraged. A more helpful way to summarize learning from your study across the weeks each year is to use this ABCD schema:[9]

A	B	C	D
What amazed you or gave you an "aha!" moment in this week's study?	What bothered you in this week's study?	What confused you?	What delighted you?

Although each group can decide whether this or another frame for text reflections is most helpful to them, the Response sections through the year will include a reminder to use ABCD as you prepare what you will share in the seminar.

Practice

Begin to prepare your spiritual autobiography.

Your Spiritual Autobiography

The old Navaho woman sits silently in front of her loom weaving as generations before her have done. Outside her hogan, she works with the upright loom swiftly forming the natural yarn into a sacred rug pattern. Her rug seemingly forms by itself. She has done this for so many years that routine, not thought, guides her hands. The familiar actions quiet her mind thereby allowing images to form within her. The images carry her thoughts into a daydream: "Our lives are like this rug. We are formed by the Cosmic Woman who makes this world on her loom. Each of us becomes as she weaves us into her Earth Rug. The various colors and textures interrelate to form the world. Each different thread has a place. Each contributes to the whole. Nothing is unintended. All have purpose. Everything belongs."

The Earth Rug image reflects your work within this program. You are striving to know the traditions of God's people so that you can find your place within the intercultural worlds.

---

9. Offered by an Oklahoma mentor, Lauri Wakkins, during mentor training in 2013 and refined by other mentors in a conversation in *Reflections*, an online forum for mentors hosted by the EfM administration.

The following exercises may guide you in reflecting on your personal history. Such reflection is for your private consideration. Later, you will be asked to decide what you are willing and ready to share with members of your seminar. The story you share within the seminar might be part of what you discover as you do the exercise. However, your seminar preparation is separated from this exercise to encourage you to reflect privately first.

As you reflect on your experiences, you may encounter thoughts and feelings that you are not ready to share. Often, events in our lives need to be protected from outside judgments. Paul Tournier tells of the importance of having privacy. "A creative work is a very fragile thing while it is being produced. It needs secrecy. It can die away, lose its impetus and its conviction by being divulged prematurely. . . . A criticism, a comment, even praise, can disrupt the creative impetus."[10] Your life is a creative work. The experiences and events that form you need the same initial protection that any creative activity needs. Without allowing you to have the protection of secrecy, the new life emerging within may "lose its impetus and its conviction by being divulged prematurely." He continues, "Yes, a certain secrecy, to just the right extent, ought to enclose every precious thing, every precious experience, so that it can mature and bear fruit." You may wish to maintain a diary or journal to provide a private place where you can write your reflections, memories, and discoveries.

Over the course of the four years of EfM, you will be asked to consider your personal history from several perspectives, as if you are constructing several autobiographies of your life, each from a different standpoint. This year's exercise is designed to enrich your self-awareness and assist you in knowing yourself more fully with reference to living in a multicultural world, using concepts and categories to assist in understanding the multicultural dimensions and dynamics within a person's life and among those with whom that person lives and works.

Each of us begins life in the midst of "givens." Identify the givens present in the beginning of your life and trace your journey through time: family structure, where you were born and lived, rituals of the family, religious world, political events of the time you were born and since, and so forth. Consider how you presently understand where you come from, who your people are, and who you are. The work of constructing an autobiography includes identifying the inherited self that has been shaped, described, and defined by a given culture. Identifying one's cultural identity and how that identity shapes knowing the holy, God, and meaning is a beginning point for the autobiographical work this year. Each person is embedded in a nexus—a web of interconnections and relationships with other people and social institutions. Institutions, while being products of human creativity, become entities that transcend the individuals who cre-

---

10. Paul Tournier, *Secrets: Revealing Insights Into the Instruments of Mature Emancipation* (Atlanta: John Knox Press, 1977), 20–21.

ated them. Institutions embody cultural values and transmit those values to subsequent generations.

1. Write a brief paragraph that describes your inherited self. For example:

I am a white Anglo-Saxon heterosexual male whose family of origin were Episcopalians for several generations. I only speak English although I have studied Spanish and German. My family of origin consists of pioneers who settled the United States from Scotland, England, and Ireland. My paternal roots came out of the hills of Tennessee, while my mother's heritage stems from Pennsylvania and Iowa.

Another example:

I am second generation Asian-American. I am a lesbian woman whose family came to the United States in the nineteenth century as construction workers on the railroad. My first language is Mandarin Chinese. I grew up in a Buddhist household. In my adulthood I became a Christian through encounters with the Roman Catholic Church in Los Angeles.

2. Construct a description of your personal experience of interacting with other cultures and how they have influenced your understanding of the world, society, humanity, religion, and God. Additionally, in contemporary society there is an intracultural diversity within each person. The intrapersonal diversity creates an eclectic identity that impacts how God, humanity, nature, and the self is experienced and understood.

Primary question: How has your experience with different cultures shaped your identity and your spirituality?

3. Begin with recalling the various experiences, events, and interactions you may have had with people from cultures different from your own. Awareness of their difference may have come in hearing a different language, seeing people dressed in different clothing, tasting different food, experiencing different religious ceremonies, or listening to music markedly different from your own. You may have heard someone speaking about different groups of people using the third-person plural pronoun "they." As you recall conversations or comments notice what feelings were associated with them. Was the "other" spoken about in fear, fascination, or affection?

Interaction with people from different cultures often occurs whenever a person moves into a different geographic area. Or perhaps refugees from war or persecutions brought people from different ethnic backgrounds and cultures into your neighborhood. Other contact may have occurred when traveling on vacation or business.

Record twenty or twenty-five different experiences or impressions of different cultures.

4. Select five or six memories, then write a short paragraph consisting of no more than three or four sentences. For example:

As I child, I remember being hurriedly ushered into our house because "a band of gypsies" had come into our yard. They were scavenging anything that was not anchored. I recall peeking out of the window and seeing a woman in a long, dark dress hold a pot that I had been playing with in the dirt. The adults around me were excited and fearful.

I recall when our school was racially integrated and for the first time, blacks and whites were in school together. The Dunbar School was closed and we all attended classes and played sports together.

While attending school in New York City, I encountered Hasidic Jews on the subway. It was my first time seeing the way they dressed. Their suits and full beards, their locks of hair wrapped around their ears, barely visible under that black hat, distinguished them from the other passengers on the subway. Before that, my only knowledge of the existence of a Hasidic Jew was from a passing reference to Martin Buber as a member of the ethnic and religious group.

5. Consider different decades of your life in light of your awareness of different cultures. Express how your experiences have shaped who you are and contributed to your spiritual formation. You might create a narrative or story from these various experiences or treat your encounters as if they were small pieces of material from which you could create a collage or mosaic that communicates something about you and your spirituality.

6. Prepare a ten-minute presentation that tells of your experience of living in a multicultural world. Include in it how your sense of self, God, truth, belonging, compassion, and/or justice has been shaped by your multicultural experiences.

At the seminar each person will be scheduled a time, ideally in the next three or four weeks, to offer what was prepared from his or her spiritual autobiography.

Scheduling Spiritual Autobiographies

The seminar group sets the schedule for sharing spiritual autobiographies. It is most important to share them as early in the program year as possible and to share them in a way so that all of the group can hear each spiritual autobiography shared. Many groups schedule a time to hear one to three spiritual autobiographies each week over several weeks, depending on the number in your group. Others have found, given the busy schedules of adults, that it is difficult to have all members present for every spiritual autobiography every week and have developed alternate ways for making sure all spiritual autobiographies are heard. Some gather for a retreat-like meeting where all the spiritual autobiographies are shared in a single day, often on a weekend. Some break the spiritual autobiography format into a series so that each week every person in the group responds briefly to the same prompt or question. An explanation of this series format for sharing spiritual autobiographies is given in Part II of this Guide on page 258–259. Your mentor may have learned about other ways to schedule.

Alternate Format for Sharing Spiritual Autobiographies

Everyone in the group does the work assigned in "Your Spiritual Autobiography" above. The difference is in how the spiritual autobiographies are shared in the seminar meetings.

Use Mutual Invitation (see page 344 in Part II of the *Guide*) and allow a brief silence before inviting the next person to share. Each participant answers the framing question or prompt in two to three minutes. There is no cross talk. After everyone has had a turn, the mentor leads the whole group in a closing prayer of thanksgiving for the gifts shared.

The following is an example of how framing questions or prompts drawn from the assignment can guide the sharing over five meetings. Your group may want to compose their own questions or prompts.

Week One: SELF
Share experience(s) with other cultures that have contributed to your sense of self.

Week Two: GOD
Share a story that illustrates how living in a multicultural world has contributed to your understanding or vision of God.

Week Three: TRUTH
Share one or more ways in which living in a multicultural word has shaped your definition of and understanding of truth.

Week Four: BELONGING
Share an experience where your sense of belonging was challenged by an encounter with a culture other than your own.

Week Five: COMPASSION OR JUSTICE
Share a story about how your feeling of compassion (or justice) was awakened (or challenged) by an encounter with a person or group you experience as "other."

Week Three

A Reminder about Online Resources

As you begin the readings in the Christian tradition, remember that all EfM participants have subscriber's access to the Oxford Biblical Studies Internet site. This resource has articles, maps, timelines, a variety of biblical translations, articles on biblical interpretation, illustrations, and numerous other items. The *New Oxford Annotated Bible (NRSV)* can be accessed on the site.

oxfordbiblicalstudies.com
The login ID is **efm-sewanee** and the password is **ministry**.

There also are resources online that correspond to the Collins and Powell texts, as well as an EfM study guide for the MacCulloch text.[11]

Collins:
http://fortresspress.com/product/short-introduction-hebrew-bible-third-edition

Powell:
http://bakerpublishinggroup.com/books/introducing-the-new-testament-2nd-edition/264695

MacCulloch:
http://efm.sewanee.edu/assets/uploads/MacCulloch_Study_Guide-Babb.pdf

Links to additional resources will be posted on the EfM website Resources page on occasion:
efm.sewanee.edu/resources/resources

About Electronic Books

All of the books used in EfM are available for purchase in e-book formats, most from Amazon and some directly from the publisher. Fortress Press offers the e-book versions of the Year One texts at no charge to all enrolled participants, mentors, trainers, and diocesan coordinators. In addition, EfM provides free e-book files for the Reading and Reflection Guide each year. Instructions for accessing and downloading these texts will be provided in *EfM News* (the electronic newsletter) as the program year begins in September.

---

11. These and other hyperlinks in this volume were operational at the time of printing. If you find the link does not work, try searching for the author or title to find an updated link.

About Reading Theological Works

Reading theological books may be a new experience for some participants. Most of us are accustomed to reading in our daily lives specifically for information and in small pieces, and more and more many of us read only from sources—especially in social media—that are curated for a narrow viewpoint. A theological text is meant to be part of a conversation. There is no need to accept the author's every assertion as gospel, nor to throw the book at the wall simply because it challenges your viewpoint. Engage with the author. Be open to what you might learn and how you might be stretched by a different perspective. Write in your book (gasp!), make notes, come back over and over to see if you are able to find another way into what the author is sharing. And, finally, reflect, reflect, reflect. How can you put these words into conversation with your life and your theology?

You may find this blog post from Kwok Pui Lan helpful:

http://kwokpuilan.blogspot.com/2011/02/
how-to-read-theological-book.html

And as Kwok frequently reminds her students: A hermeneutic of suspicion is needed, but should be balanced by a hermeneutic of compassion. An ancient author, and even one from more recent centuries, is writing to a particular audience, one that may not share your worldview or use your vocabulary. Nonetheless, an author from the long tradition of Christian witness can speak to us across the centuries with insights for faithful living today.

About the Reading Assignments

In various weeks throughout the year there may be long reading assignments in the Reading and Reflection Guide as well as in your textbooks. The practice of looking ahead can help you plan time to comfortably complete each assignment.

In particular for Year One, in order to provide opportunity to read a substantial portion of the Hebrew Scriptures, reading assignments will sometimes be long, although it is not always necessary to read closely. Please think about what you need to do in order to provide enough time for your preparation. For example, if you have a long commute each day or if you are someone who enjoys audiobooks, you might consider listening to an audio version of the biblical passages assigned.

Year Three readers might consider purchasing *Christianity* in audiobook format, available through Audible.com. Also, a six-part video miniseries from the BBC features MacCulloch speaking on key themes from the book (although it does not track exactly with the chapters). Your local or diocesan library may have the set on DVD. Many Year Three participants have found the series helpful to their understanding of the sweep of church history.

YEAR ONE

Read

Collins, Preface, Introduction, Chapter 1, "The Near Eastern Context," and Chapter 2, "The Nature of the Pentateuchal Narrative."

Some EfM participants have observed at the end of their first year that they wished they had read Collins's Chapter 29 at the beginning of the year. It is very brief. If you wish to read it now, do so. Note how this chapter provides a context for reading the ancient writings of the Hebrew Bible today.

Focus

Terms and names to note: anthropomorphic; Torah; Pentateuch; Julius Wellhausen; Hermann Gunkel; Rolf Rendtorff; Gerhard von Rad; Erhard Blum; sources in the Hebrew Scripture; e.g., documentary hypothesis; J, E, P, and D sources.

"Critical" does not mean debunking scripture, and it does not mean proving its truth. Religious people should and will find truth in their scriptures, but they may also be interested to learn something about where their scripture came from, who wrote it, and how editors collected it for them to read.[12]

Through this year you will be reading nearly the whole of the Hebrew Bible as well as two texts that will offer important interpretive perspectives to your understanding of the Hebrew Bible. John Collins's *A Short Introduction to the Hebrew Bible (Third Edition)* is a widely used, acclaimed textbook that provides an overview of current biblical scholarship through an historical-critical lens. If you have been accustomed primarily to devotional Bible study, Collins's approach may feel strange to you, but foundational to the EfM curriculum is that learning about the origins of the Bible as a text provides a needed context for deeper engagement with its contents in reflection and future study. Gale Yee's *The Hebrew Bible: Feminist and Intersectional Perspectives* is intended to supplement standard introductions to the Hebrew Bible by offering commentary from contemporary female biblical scholars. In addition to a brief historical look at feminist and intersectional biblical scholarship in general, the book offers essays, corresponding to each of the standard divisions used in Collins's survey, that explore feminist and intersectional concerns raised by the biblical narrative. You may find yourself challenged by the essays in this collection. If you are new to reading scholarly work, the Kwok essay noted above may help you find your place in the conversation.

Note: Next week, the Introduction to the Yee text is long, setting the background for a better understanding of the development of feminist biblical scholarship and defining important terms. Plan ahead to allow time for this important foundational information.

---

12. http://www.wfu.edu/~horton/r102/hc-method.html. "What is the Historical-Critical Method?"

YEAR TWO

Read

Powell, Preface, Chapter 1, "The New Testament Background: The Roman World," and Chapter 2, "The New Testament Background: The Jewish World"

Focus

Terms and names to note: schools of philosophy; mystery religions; animism; Gnosticism; Nag Hammadi; honor and shame; Pax Romana; Sadducees; Pharisees; Essenes; Zealots; Herodians; Samaritans; Gentiles; Hellenism; Septuagint; "Chrestus"; Herod the Great; Herod Antipas; Pontius Pilate; Herod Agrippa I; Josephus

Powell notes three worlds that comprise the world of the New Testament. What are they? Identify some of the many cultures of the New Testament world.

YEAR THREE

Read

MacCulloch, Acknowledgements, Introduction, Chapter 1, "Greece and Rome"

Focus

Terms and names to note: Christians of the Middle East; Latin-speaking Church; Orthodoxy; repentance and conversion; Bible as central text of Christianity; "[b]ooks are the storehouses for human ideas"; historical truth; conventions used throughout MacCulloch's book; Logos; Hellas; polis; *ekklesia*; Plato's influence on Christianity; Hellenistic Greece; *res publica* (republic); Roman Republic; imperial monarchy

The Greek understanding of *polis* provides a way to flesh out a fuller understanding of living within a social and intellectual context [cf. pages 25, 26]. It involves knowing the collective consciousness that greatly influences a person's or a people's identity. The *polis* greatly shapes how one behaves, thinks, and lives. Note as you read how the Greek and Roman cultural contexts shape Christianity.

Until recently, Christian history has traced the movement from Jerusalem, through the Roman Empire, and on to Europe, steadily moving westward to the New World. Such a focus of history is no longer practical.

MacCulloch's book has been chosen for Year Three study precisely because of his taking a more global approach. He presents Christian history by following three paths: the movement west from Jerusalem that became the Western-Latin expression of Christianity; the path into the Middle East and Far East; and the Eastern Orthodoxies of Byzantium empires.

What is gained or lost in such an approach? Note as you read through the year how each of these paths has shaped a particular Christian culture.

YEAR FOUR

Read

Ballard, "On Being Theologically Literate" on pages 214–222 in Part II of this Reading and Reflection Guide; and Ford, Chapter 1, "Introduction: theology and the religions in transformation"

Focus

What role does theological literacy play in your faith life at this time?

How is the work of theology related to a life of "multiple overwhelmings"?

Over the next several weeks, you will be reading two different texts and an essay on the work of doing theology. David Ford's *Theology: A Very Short Introduction,* begun this week, examines the basic questions that arise when thinking about God and centers an understanding of God in worship. Sara Coakley's essay, "God as Trinity: An Approach Through Prayer," proposes that we can best experience the wholeness of the triune God in personal and corporate prayer. Mark McIntosh's *Mysteries of Faith* explores Christian doctrines using a central image of relationship. These works are very different from one another, yet each in its way offers a practical approach, a way of examining and constructing our own theologies centered in practice. As you read, notice how each author handles core theological concepts, such as the nature of God, the divine/human nature of Jesus Christ, the Trinity, the question of evil, the relationship of creation to creator, and other theological questions that may occur in the course of doing your own work in theology. It may help to keep a journal in which you can consider these questions over the weeks spent on these texts.

- What does each author contribute to your work and identity as a theologian?

- What concerns do you have about assertions made by one or more of these theologians?

- What surprises you?

- What new understandings are forming?

- What are points of congruence and divergence between your theology and those presented in these texts?

ALL YEARS

Respond

What purposes, attitudes, and assumptions do you bring to your reading and study of the Christian tradition?

How have your attitudes and assumptions been fashioned by the various cultures identified in your spiritual autobiography work? How have those attitudes and assumptions affected your reading of the Christian tradition?

Use the notes or highlights you made during your assigned reading this week to reflect on the key contexts (concerns, interests, and issues) faced by the men and women of faith. What are some concerns for those who would have their lives reflect their faith?

Use ABCD as you prepare what you will share in the seminar.

Practice

For the next few weeks the seminar will center on reflecting on your reading and reflecting on spiritual autobiographies. When you share your autobiographical reflections, what do you need to do to communicate your thoughts? When you listen to others, what do you need to do to listen well? Which of Caine's "5 Pillars of Great Listening" directly support you in listening to others as they present their spiritual autobiographies?

Carefully defined concepts clarify complex and emotionally volatile situations. The plurality of religious traditions and cultures has come to characterize every part of the world today. Diana Eck's work on the Pluralism Project at Harvard University uses several helpful definitions to sort out the complexities that arise from the interaction of diverse cultures. Chief among the terms is pluralism itself. Consider these four points about pluralism to guide living faithfully in a multicultural world:

- First, pluralism is not diversity alone, but *the energetic engagement with diversity.* Diversity can and has meant the creation of religious ghettoes with little traffic between or among them. Today, religious diversity is a given, but pluralism is not a given; it is an achievement. Mere diversity without real encounter and relationship will yield increasing tensions in our societies.

- Second, pluralism is not just tolerance, but *the active seeking of understanding across lines of difference.* Tolerance is a necessary public virtue, but it does not require Christians and Muslims, Hindus, Jews, and ardent secularists to know anything about one another. Tolerance is too thin a foundation for a world of religious difference and proximity. It does nothing to remove our ignorance of one another, and leaves in place the stereotype, the half-truth, the fears that underlie old patterns of division and violence. In the world in which we live today, our ignorance of one another will be increasingly costly.

- Third, pluralism is not relativism, but *the encounter of commitments.* The new paradigm of pluralism does not require us to leave our identities and our commitments behind, for pluralism is the encounter of commitments. It means holding our deepest differences, even our religious differences, not in isolation, but in relationship to one another.

- Fourth, pluralism is *based on dialogue.* The language of pluralism is that of dialogue and encounter, give and take, criticism and self-criticism. Dialogue means both speaking and listening, and that process reveals both common understandings and real differences. Dialogue does not mean everyone at the "table" will agree with one another. Pluralism involves the commitment to being at the table—with one's commitments.[13]

Over the next several weeks individual dimensions of pluralism will be presented to put into practice. Begin by identifying two or three feelings in response to how Eck shapes pluralism. What picture or image best envisions pluralism as she uses the term?

---

13. http://www.pluralism.org/pages/pluralism/what_is_pluralism

Week Four

YEAR ONE

Read

Yee, Preface and Introduction: Definitions, Explorations, and Intersections

Focus

Terms and names to note: feminism; ideological criticisms; first wave feminists; second wave feminists; sexism; sex/gender system; postmodernism; queer theory; intersectionality; "matrix of domination"; "heterogeneity, hybridity, multiplicity"; postcolonial feminism; *The Woman's Bible*; "depatriarchalizing the Bible"; traditional vs. feminist interpretations of Eve; "texts of terror"; *The Women's Bible Commentary*; deconstructive criticism; gender criticism; womanist criticism; Kimberlé Crenshaw; Mary Wollstonecraft; Betty Friedan; Mary Daly; Judith Butler; Combahee River Collective; Audre Lorde; Elizabeth Cady Stanton; Sojourner Truth; Phyllis Trible; Musa Dube

Note the students' questions on page viii. Are any of these questions that you also wonder about? Which questions surprise or challenge you? What questions of your own would you add?

Yee writes:

> The historical and literary criticisms reveal that the Hebrew Bible is mainly the work of elite men. Although they were only a tiny minority of the population of ancient Israel, their upper-class male sociohistorical and religious imprints are dominant and normative throughout the text. Furthermore, biblical scholars and religious interpreters of the bible, such as clergy, have primarily been male. Thus the composition of the biblical text as well as its interpretation throughout the ages tends to focus on male interests and ideologies.[14]

What has been your own understanding of feminism? What messages about feminism have you encountered in the culture/society around you?

YEAR TWO

Read

Powell, Chapter 3, "The New Testament Writings"

Focus

Terms and names to note: testament; apostolic; catholic; seven categories of New Testament writings; Justin Martyr's account of Christian worship;

---

14. Gale A. Yee, ed., *The Hebrew Bible: Feminist and Intersectional Perspectives* (Minneapolis: Fortress Press, 2018), 17–18.

canon; stages in the transmission of the Gospel Tradition; Marcion; exegesis; hermeneutics

Name three methods of exegesis.

In "Exegesis and Hermeneutics" Powell states, "All the exegetical methods and academic disciplines described above are used by people who operate with different hermeneutical assumptions and interests. The methods themselves are simply tools that are employed for very different purposes by people with different attitudes and goals."[15]

Reflect on how considering the interpreter's assumptions, interests, and purpose can contribute to your reading of biblical commentary.

YEAR THREE

Read

MacCulloch, Chapter 2, "Israel"

Focus

Terms and names to note: Maccabees; Tanakh; Apocrypha; the first and second exiles; Samaritans; the first and second temple; Septuagint; Hellenized Jews; creation out of nothingness; development of the notion of afterlife and individual soul; Hasmonean dynasty; Sadducees; Pharisees; Essenes; Zealots

Chapter 2 concludes Part I, "A Millennium of Beginnings," in which MacCulloch traces the social and intellectual "seeds" of Christianity. The two histories (Greco-Roman and Israel) continually influence Christian life and thought.

MacCulloch writes, "Even through their hardest and most wretched experiences of fighting with those they love most deeply, [Israel is] being given some glimpse of how they relate to God."[16] MacCulloch connects this struggle with Jacob's formational struggle with the angel of the Lord, with God, at the River Jabok. This way of drawing meaning from experience allowed Israel to view history through the eyes of faith. History became the arena in which they could see God at work, bringing them into being as a people bound to God. Some might consider this a rewriting of history, merely a means of self-justification. There is plenty of room for that view. However, this is also a way of interpreting history, of seeing God at work in the life and experience of an individual and a group; this is salvation history—history that tells the story of God's work of redemption.

---

15. Mark Powell, *Introducing the New Testament* (Grand Rapids: Baker Academic, 2009), 60.

16. Diarmaid MacCulloch, *Christianity: The First Three Thousand Years* (New York: Penguin, 2009), 50.

YEAR FOUR

Read

Ford, Chapter 2, "Theology and religious studies: how is the field shaped?"

Focus

Terms and names to note: four elements of wise and creative theology; *ressourcement*; *aggiornamento*; "confessional" theology; "neutral" religious studies; Frei's five types of theology; Vatican II; Hans Frei; Rudolf Bultmann; Paul Tillich; Karl Rahner

Where do you place your own theology in relation to Frei's types?

ALL YEARS

Respond

In learning to live faithfully in an increasingly multicultural and multi-faith world, we often hear calls for tolerance. On one hand, tolerance can be understood along a spectrum from simply "putting up with someone" to actively showing respect to the other. What from your reading assignment illustrates humanity moving along this tolerance spectrum? On the other hand, tolerance does not always equal inclusion. Consider the difference between saying, "I tolerate you here" and "I welcome you here." Think of some examples from your reading or from the culture around you where tolerance does not equal respect or inclusion.

Use ABCD as you prepare what you will share in the seminar.

Practice

Return to Geoffrey Caine's "5 Pillars of Listening." He identified them as:

1. We listen with our bodies as well as with our minds

2. We listen to both thoughts and feelings (even if we are unaware of it)

3. Listening is interactive

4. Listening is selective

5. We are always listening to life

Select one or two pillars from the list. Identify behaviors, barriers, and/or attitudes that block listening. For example, describe a behavior that impedes or even prevents the exercise of listening with both thoughts and feelings. Or consider how different kinds of stress prevent listening with one's body.

Become aware of how you or others you know impede listening. Especially attend to how the barrier to listening may be present when people of different cultures converse.

Week Five

YEAR ONE

Read

Genesis 1–11
Collins, Chapter 3, "The Primeval History"
"The Priestly Creation Story" essay provided in Part II of this Guide, pages 223–240.

Focus

Terms and names to note: primeval; two creation stories; 'adam; Atrahasis myth; Epic of Gilgamesh; Sons of God (Genesis 6); Enuma Elish; covenant; Baals; cult; Sabbath; ex nihilo; Zoroastrianism; Manichaeism; dualism; Plato; Neo-Platonic; via negativa

Stories delight and entertain. They come in various forms and styles. Myths, epics, legends, novellas, and fables each tell some tale that entertains as they instill values, guidance, and meaning. Often the values live implicitly within the hearers of the stories only to surface in moments of crisis that call for decisive action. Some myths come into being to explain why things are as they are; others prescribe "right" behavior; while others venture into offering explanations along with establishing meaning.

All people, to some degree or another, seek answers to fundamental questions. What is truth and can I know it? What endures? What is real? Is there purpose to my life? Where did we come from and where are we going? Stories in all their forms, one way or another, offer answers to basic concerns. Begin noticing how such questions play out in different cultures

"The Priestly Creation Story," an excerpt from an earlier version of the Education for Ministry curriculum reprinted in Part II of this Guide, is a theological reading. Consisting of only ten verses in Genesis, this passage poetically presents a full doctrine of creation. It also offers a doctrine of God. The story shows God as wholly Other yet present to creation. God transcends all that is, thereby providing a corrective to all forms of dualism. Many theological difficulties get untangled by the implications in the story.

The Priestly creation story is a mature statement of Israel's belief about God and the relationship of all that exists to God. Describe the development of your personal view of the relationship between God and creation, that is, between God and all that is not God.

Explore creation stories from other cultures such as Native American or Australian Aborigine lore. What do you learn as you compare them with the Hebrew Bible's creation story?

YEAR TWO

Read

Powell, Chapter 4, "Jesus," and Chapter 5, "The Gospels"

Focus

Terms and names to note: gospel as a literary genre; parables; miracle stories; pronouncement stories; passion and resurrection narratives; sayings of Jesus; the synoptic puzzle (aka problem); the Q source; Griesbach hypothesis; Diatessaron; two doctrines of Jesus; kingdom of God; themes in Jesus' teaching; the historical Jesus

The historical Jesus emphasizes Jesus as a Palestinian man of a particular time, yet some artwork depicts Jesus with different ethnic features. What does such artwork say about Jesus as Savior?

YEAR THREE

Read

MacCulloch, Chapter 3, "A Crucified Messiah"

Focus

Terms and names to note: cluster of words (*evagelion*, *evangelium*, Gospel); Julius Africanus; *epiousios*; parables; *abba*; *Kyrios*–"Jesus is Lord, the word for God"; Paul of Tarsus; *epistole*; Paul's use of the word "church"; Johannine Christ; Jewish revolt and fall of Jerusalem

Change in the eastern region of the Roman Empire eventually upset the Roman Empire's social order. The history of Christianity began with seemingly insignificant events. How did the importance of those events become clear through the lenses of experience and hindsight? What does this suggest for our own view of history?

Notice how the clash of cultures shaped Christian beginnings.

YEAR FOUR

Read

Ford, Chapter 3, "Thinking of God"

Focus

Terms and names to note: "real"; omnipresence; omniscience; the "divine"; Trinity; the God worshipped by Christians; being "multilingual" in faith

In your experience, how is God known?

Ford defines the divine as "what is worshipped." How is this a helpful (or not helpful) definition for you?

The Trinity is a core doctrine in Christianity. How do you understand the Triune God? What are your questions about and/or challenges with this doctrine?

ALL YEARS

Respond

Diana Eck advocates developing the attitude and skill of dialogue to live creatively in a multicultural world. "Pluralism requires the nurturing of constructive dialogue to reveal both common understandings and real differences. Not everyone at the "table" will agree with one another; the process of public dialogue will inevitably reveal areas of disagreement as well. . . ."[17]

When, where, and how have you experienced constructive dialogue? How can you encourage constructive public dialogue?

Use ABCD as you prepare what you will share in the seminar.

Practice

Geographic regions within a country develop patterns of local culture, just as different parts of the world exhibit the distinctive patterns of their overall cultures. Invite one person this week into a conversation about the local culture out of which that person came and your own. Make some notes about the experience. What similarities and differences do you find? What distinctive details amaze, bother, confuse, or delight you?

If you didn't have enough time before the seminar to accomplish the above practice, try to recall a conversation you may have had that brought to light differences in your culture and another's. Or recall what differences and similarities there were between the cultural upbringing you had and that of another person, such as a college roommate, a life-partner, or a coworker.

---

17. Diana Eck, "From Diversity to Pluralism," http://pluralism.org/encounter/challenges

Week Six

YEAR ONE

Read

Genesis 12–50
Collins, Chapter 4, "The Patriarchs"

Focus

Terms and names to note: the Patriarchs; Abraham; Sarah; Isaac; Rebecca; Jacob; Rachel; Leah; Benjamin; Joseph; Miriam; pharaoh at time of Joseph; Jethro; Horeb; Legends–etiological, ethnological, etymological, and ceremonial; Hermon Gunkel; *Sitz im Leben*; *bris*; Abraham Cycle; Jacob Cycle; Joseph Story

Why do we recommend you read the Bible assignment before reading the Collins text? Collins's *Shorter Introduction* is a secondary text commenting on the primary text, the Bible itself. Reading the Bible first allows you to encounter the text uninfluenced by others and provides a base for then understanding what scholars and others say about it. Robert Denton, professor at the General Theological Seminary, with a smile often reminded his students that they would be amazed by how much the primary text could illuminate the commentary. Each person has unique experiences that shape how scripture is interpreted. While the work of biblical scholars is enormously valuable, only you can bring your distinctive experience to the learning process. Your experience with the text then can be brought into dialogue with what scholars have written. It is in that dialogue that deeper learning occurs.

What light does Collins shed on your own reading of the Genesis assignment?

What sources do the "authors" of the stories of the patriarchs use to explain meaning?

Notice what sources Collins uses in this chapter. Examples of such sources include academic disciplines, biblical references, personal experience, or beliefs or conclusions that he asserts.

YEAR TWO

Read

The Gospel according to Matthew (Try to set aside enough time to read the whole gospel in one or two sittings.)
Powell, Chapter 6, "Matthew"
Note: EfM suggests reading the assignments in the Bible before reading Powell's commentary, as your own experience of reading the text can then be brought into conversation with what the scholar has to offer in interpreting the text.

Focus

Terms and names to note: five speeches of Jesus; Beatitudes; binding and loosing of the law; *oligopistoi;* Eusebius; Ecclesiastical History

The Gospel writers tell the story of the Good News of God in Christ. The Gospel in its entirety communicates the story. However, seldom do people hear the entire story, rather they experience the scripture verse by verse or in short pieces they hear within worship. Such reading is like watching a trailer of a film and believing you have seen the movie. Individual scenes make little or no sense without the context of the whole story. So too it is important to know the entire Gospel, allowing you to experience its drama. Once you have a sense of Matthew's story, you are positioned better to interpret individual scenes, teachings, and events. Notice any new insights emerging about stories from this Gospel that you may have heard many times before.

What are some of the cultural hallmarks of the audience for whom the Gospel according to Matthew seems to have been written?

YEAR THREE

Read

MacCulloch, Chapter 4, "Boundaries Defined"

Focus

Terms and names to note: *Hermas (The Shepherd)* and the *Didache* online or in Bettenson (if you have access to that book) or elsewhere and read what you can or want; Letter to Philemon; *Didache*; gnosis, Gnosticism, Nag Hammadi; Docetism; key points of difference between gnostic and Jewish attitudes; Marcion; Diatessaron; *presbyteroi*; *diakonos*; *episkopoi*; the importance of Antioch and Jerusalem in the early church; Clement; Ignatius; Victor; Stephen of Rome

References to primary sources are sprinkled throughout the chapter. Try to find two or three primary sources to read, even if only a portion of the work. Henry Bettenson's *Documents of the Christian Church* includes many primary sources from the early Christian tradition.[18] Used and new copies of this book in several editions are available to purchase and through some libraries. Online, the Christian Classics Ethereal Library at www.ccel.org includes numerous documents of the early church in its collection. For example, *The Teaching of the Twelve Apostles, Commonly Called the Didache.*[19]

---

18. Henry Bettenson's *Documents of the Christian Church* has been published in four editions by Oxford University Press. Any edition will give you a taste of these early documents.

19. http://www.ccel.org/ccel/richardson/fathers.viii.i.html Note: This and all links provided in the Reading and Reflection Guides were active and working at the time of printing. Sometimes links are changed for various reasons. If this one does not work, try searching for "Didache" in your browser search engine or on the Christian Classics Ethereal Library main page: http://www.ccel.org

YEAR FOUR

Read

Ford, Chapter 4, "Living before God: worship and ethics"

Focus

Terms and names to note: religious and non-religious forms of worship; five basic forms of prayer; idolatry; ethics; the shaping of desire; theological anthropology; Dietrich Bonhoeffer

How do you define God? In what ways are your ethics shaped by your concept of the Trinity? In what ways are your ethics shaped by the culture in which you grew up?

ALL YEARS

Respond

"From the historical perspective, the terms 'exclusion,' 'assimilation,' and 'pluralism' suggest three different ways in which Americans have approached this widening cultural and religious diversity."[20] Exclusion isolates the different groups, thereby reducing if not eliminating the difficulties of difference, for segregation creates neighborhoods of separation. Assimilation seeks to eliminate separating differences by bringing all into a common "melting pot" where distinctions melt away into one another. The option of pluralism means honoring each other's differences through the demanding practice of dialogue. "Pluralism involves the commitment to being at the table—with one's beliefs." [21]

Constructive dialogue requires knowing what one's core values and commitments are. As you have reviewed your life through the exercise of constructing your autobiography, what core values and commitments were uncovered? What can you draw on to remain authentically who you are as a Christian while being welcoming to other religious traditions and open to learning from them?

Use ABCD as you prepare what you will share in the seminar.

Practice

Continue to utilize the ABCD means of summarizing your study for the week.

If you have enough time in your preparation, find some information about another ethnic culture with which you are unfamiliar and about

---

20. Eck, http://pluralism.org/encounter/challenges
21. Eck, http://pluralism.org/encounter/challenges

which you are curious. Do you have any opportunity for talking with someone who comes from that culture?

Find out what religious gathering places of other cultures are near you. Plan a time to visit one, if possible. Note any indication that ethnic and religious cultures are sometimes intertwined. Where do you find evidence of your own culture expressed in your Christian tradition?

Week Seven

YEAR ONE

Read

Exodus 1–15
Collins, Chapter 5, "The Exodus from Egypt"

Focus

Terms and names to note: Manetho; Hyksos; Hecataeus; Ramesses II; Habiru; *Yam Sup*; Passover; "charter myth"; history; legend; folklore; founding myth; YHWH; Adonai (Lord); *HaShem*; *'ehyeh 'aser* (I AM WHO I AM); *'ehyeh*; *eimi ho on* (I am the one who is); absolute Being; YHWH is on the side of the weak; "salvation history"

Name the images/metaphors for God that the writer of Exodus uses to tell the story of God's action of liberation for the children of Israel. Select two or three of the images for God and explore the qualities of God the image reveals.

YEAR TWO

Read

The Gospel according to Mark
Powell, Chapter 7, "Mark"

Focus

Terms and names to note: John Mark; intercalation; major themes in Mark; messianic secret; *inclusio*

Every discussion, written or spoken, draws on material to form the presentation. The content (images, story, ideas) comes from different sources, which may be other writings, personal experiences, or beliefs held. Notice the different sources that Powell uses throughout his chapter on Mark.

YEAR THREE

Read

MacCulloch, Chapter 5, "The Prince: Ally or Enemy?"

Focus

Terms and names to note and become familiar with pronunciation: parousia; Apostolic Tradition; Celsus; *in catacumbas*; Origen; Plotinus; Mani; Manichee/Manichaean; Diocletian; Syriac Church; Osrhoene; Dura Europos; Armenia; Ephren; Odes of Solomon; Trdat (Tiridates)

Christianity not only survived but grew under the wave of persecutions from 100 to 300 CE. People willing to suffer and die for what they believe wield powerful inspiration. When religious conviction is stronger than the fear of pain and death, it is as if the persecutor's sword sharpens one's beliefs into passionate convictions. Clarity comes as a person discovers relationships that matter more than death. The witness born from martyrdom has transformative power for both believers and non-believers.

What might stories of martyrs contribute to the cultural identity of a people?

YEAR FOUR

Read

Ford, Chapter 5, "Facing Evil"

Focus

Terms and names to note: personal, structural, and natural evil; theodicy; the double mystery of evil and goodness; metanarrative; Anselm of Canterbury; Bonaventure; Augustine

What experience have you had or heard about that supports a belief that God can bring good out of evil? In what way can evil be seen as a form of idolatry?

ALL YEARS

Respond

Diaspora, syncretism, xenophobia, and separatism emerge as refugees, conquerors, and immigrants enter new lands. What part have any of these social interactions played in your readings? What experience have you had with such interactions?

Summarize your learning from the unit's study. What have you learned to do or do better during these weeks? What have you learned about listening? What stands out for you as a key learning in these first weeks of EfM?

Use ABCD as you prepare what you will share in the seminar.

Practice

Return to Week Three to review Caine's ideas about listening. Pick one of the areas he names to practice deeply this week. What does that activity contribute to Christian ministry? *#5 always listening*

— keeps you supple and open to new things

UNIT TWO

Theological Reflection as a Life Skill

Week Eight

ALL YEARS

Read

In this essay former Archbishop Rowan Williams reflects theologically on his experience in New York City on September 11, 2001. He was staying only a few blocks from the World Trade Center, preparing for a conference hosted by Trinity Church, Wall Street.

Read the essay from two standpoints. First, read it as a presentation intended to guide others in making sense of the horrific event. Second, read it as something that Williams writes to support his coming to terms personally with the experience in light of his theological convictions as a twenty-first-century person and a well-educated theologian.

Last Words[22]

Last words. We have had the chance to read the messages sent by passengers on the planes to their spouses and families in the desperate last minutes; and we have seen the spiritual advice apparently given to the terrorists by one of their number, the thoughts that should be in their minds as they approach the death they have chosen (for themselves and for others). Something of the chill of September 11 lies in the contrast. The religious words are, in the cold light of day, the words that murderers are saying to themselves to make a martyr's drama out of a crime. The nonreligious words are testimony to what religious language is supposed to be about—the triumph of pointless, gratuitous love, the affirming of faithfulness even when there is nothing to be done or salvaged.

It should give us pause, especially if we think we are religious. You don't have to be Richard Dawkins to notice that there is a problem.

On the morning of September 11, I was getting ready to spend a day talking religious language with a group of clergy and spiritual directors. I am still thinking about what it meant to be interrupted like that; and to be presented with the record of a solemn and rich exhortation cast in evocative spiritual terms designed to make it easier for some people to kill others.

It isn't (say it now and get it over with) a problem about Muslims, about some kind of religiousness that is "naturally" prone to violence. It's true that Islam seems to think differently about its language for God from the way

---

22. Rowan Williams, *Writing in the Dust: After September 11* (Grand Rapids, MI: Wm. B. Eerdmans, 2002), 3–12.

Christians and Jews do: Muslims will regard what we say as too ambiguous, too larded with irony or paradox, self-indulgent in comparison with the sober directness of the Qur'an. But Christians at least have used their irony and paradox often enough to slip out from under the demands of justice or compassion. They have found plenty of ways to be absent from what they say, to play with commitment. The Jewish-Christian Bible is not a very straightforward set of texts, after all. No wonder postmodernism blossoms on post-Christian soil.

We'd better acknowledge the sheer danger of religiousness. Yes, it *can* be a tool to reinforce diseased perceptions of reality. Muslim or not, it can be a way of teaching ourselves not to see the particular human agony in front of us; or worse, of teaching ourselves not to see ourselves, our violence, our actual guilt as opposed to our abstract "religious" sinfulness. Our religious talking, seeing, knowing, needs a kind of cleansing.

Someone who is about to die in terrible anguish makes room in their mind for someone else; for the grief and terror of someone they love. They do what they can to take some atom of that pain away from the other by the inarticulate message on the mobile. That moment of "making room" is what I as a religious person have to notice. It isn't "pious," it isn't language about God; it's simply language that brings into the world something other than self-defensiveness. It's a breathing space in the asthmatic climate of self-concern and competition; a breathing space that religious language doesn't often manage to create by or for itself.

God always has to be rediscovered. Which means God always has to be heard or seen where there aren't yet words for him. Saying something for the sake of another in the presence of death must be one place of rediscovery. Mustn't it?

Careful. You can do this too quickly. It can sound as though you're gratefully borrowing someone else's terrible experience to make another pious point. And after all, not everyone dies with words of love. There will have been cursing and hysteria and frantic, deluded efforts to be safe at all costs when people knew what was going on in those planes. And would anyone want their private words of love butchered to make a sermon?

It proves nothing. But all I can say is that for someone who does believe, or tries to, the "breathing space" is something that allows the words of religious faith for a moment not to be as formal or flat or self-serving as they usually are.

The morning after, very early, I was stopped in the street in New York by a youngish man who turned out to be an airline pilot and a Catholic. He wanted to know what the hell God was doing when the planes hit the towers. What do you say? The usual fumbling about how God doesn't intervene, which sounds like a lame apology for some kind of "policy" on God's part, a policy exposed as heartless in the face of such suffering? Something about how God is there in the sacrificial work of the rescuers, in the risks they take? I tried saying bits of this, but there was no clearer answer than there ever is.

Any really outrageous human action tests to the limit our careful theological principles about God's refusal to interfere with created freedom. That God has made a world into which he doesn't casually step in to solve problems is fairly central to a lot of Christian faith. He has made the world so that evil choices can't just be frustrated or aborted (where would he stop, for goodness sake? he'd have to be intervening every instant of human history) but have to be confronted, suffered, taken forward, healed in the complex process of human history, always in collaboration with what we do and say and pray.

I do believe that; but I don't think you can *say* it with much conviction outside the context of people actually doing the action and the prayer. In the street that morning, all I had was words. I wasn't surprised that they didn't help. He was a lifelong Christian believer, but for the first time it came home to him that he might be committed to a God who could seem useless in a crisis.

Perhaps it's when we try to make God useful in crises, though, that we take the first steps towards the great lie of religion: the god who fits our agenda. There is a breathing space: then just breathe for a moment. Perhaps the words of faith will rise again slowly in that space (perhaps not). But don't try to tie it up quickly.

Breathing. A bit paradoxical to talk about that. When we finally escaped from our building, it was quite hard to breathe normally in the street: dense fumes, thick, thick dust, a sort of sandstorm or snowstorm of dust and debris, large flakes of soft grey burned stuff falling steadily. In the empty street, cars with windows blown in, a few dazed people, everything covered in this grey snow. It can't have been silent, there must have been (I know there were) shouts, sirens; a few minutes later, there was the indescribable long roar of the second tower collapsing. But I remember it as quiet; the very few words spoken to each other, the ghostliness of it all; surreal associations for Frost's lovely poem, "Stopping by Woods on a Snowy Evening" ("The only other sound's the sweep / Of easy wind and downy flake"). Or a "heart of the storm" feeling.

In that time, there is no possibility of thinking, of explanations, resolutions. I can't remember much sense of panic, much feeling about the agony going on a couple of hundred yards away, let alone much desire for justice or vengeance. It was an empty space. I don't want to forget that, as feeling returns in various ways. We don't know fully what goes on when, in the middle of terror or pain, this emptiness and anaesthesia set in (it happens in plenty of contexts). But somehow the emptiness "resources" us. Not to run too fast to explore the feelings and recover the words seems important.

Simone Weil said that the danger of imagination was that it filled up the void when what we need is to learn how to live in the presence of the void. The more closely we bind God to our own purposes, use God to help ourselves avoid our own destructiveness, the more we fill up the void. It becomes very important to know how to use the language of belief; which is why the terrible simplicity of those last messages matters so intensely.

And why also we have to tread so carefully in not making some sort of religious capital out of them. Ultimately, the importance of these "secular" words has to stand as a challenge to anything comfortingly religious we might be tempted to say. This is what human beings *can* find to say in the face of death, religion or no religion. This is what truly makes breathing space for others.

Words like "transcendent" hang around uneasily in the background of my mind. Careful again. But that moment of pointless loving communication is the best glimpse many of us will have of what the rather solemn and pompous word means. I have to *begin* with this. I know I shall be feeling my way towards making some verbal shape out of it all in terms of my Christian faith, but there is nowhere else to start except with that frightening contrast: the murderously spiritual and compassionately secular.

The EfM Four-source Model of Theological Reflection

The mix of cultures evidences a complex array of values, perspectives, practices, and social patterns that challenge, confuse, excite, and at times even frighten Christians formed within the western, English-speaking world. The challenge of living as a Christian within and among an ever increasing diversity of cultures and faiths calls for the development of a strong identity that is fortified by an awareness and knowledge of the richness of the Christian heritage. A person can thrive within this environment by developing skill in the discipline of theological reflection.

The practice of theological reflection draws on an array of skills. Essentially, theological reflection is a way of thinking that joins personal experience and cultural realities in conversation with the knowledge and values of the Christian tradition. People "do theology" whenever they reflect on questions that lead to searching for ultimate meaning and significance. Theology, as practiced in EfM, is about increasing knowledge of God so that people grow more fully in knowing God.

The theme for our work this year, *Living Faithfully in a Multicultural World*, invites us to reflect theologically on the common good of contemporary humanity in relationship to the vision of God revealed and interpreted within the Christian tradition.

Terms for Talking about Theological Reflection

Movement: primary steps of theological reflection—*identify* something that matters, *explore* the topic, *connect* to other areas of life and meaning (Sources, Voices), and *apply* learning to ministry.

Source/Category/Voice: interior and exterior areas of life from which a person draws when making sense out of something that has happened: *personal experience/action, faith tradition, culture/society (contemporary and/or traditional),* and *personal beliefs/positions.* For instance, a person's belief forms in relationship to something that happened, something that was read, something that was learned. Each of those areas speaks with some kind of voice, contributing to how a person makes sense out of what has occurred. A belief about the sanctity of life can be explored to discover what formed that belief in a search for deeper awareness of God and of meaning.

Theological Perspective: questions asked in applying a theological lens to the reflection commonly use traditional terms developed in systematic theology (*creation, sin, judgment, repentance, redemption*); reframing or rephrasing them can bring out subtle differences in understanding. For example, in this volume you will be asked to consider the perspective questions in terms of *wholeness, brokenness, recognition, reorientation, and restoration.*

Every person uses images, ideas (concepts), feelings (intuitions), values, and behavior (action) as the substantive content for reflecting. Whenever one's thought process engages the heritage of the faith tradition in which one was raised, the reflection becomes theological in tone. While thoughts cannot be separated into discrete isolated units for consciousness, clarifying distinctions can be useful. The EfM program draws on or listens to four primary categories or sources/voices in theological reflection: **Faith Tradition; Culture/Society; Personal Experience/Action;** and **Personal Belief/ Position.** Each of these categories emerged from conversations in small groups over the past several decades. The following statements summarize the categories.

"She has the Midas touch"–a voice of Culture via Greek mythology

"Don't we have Good Samaritan laws?–a voice of Christian Tradition in scripture

"This is a strange place. I have a feeling we are not in Kansas anymore, Toto."–a voice of Culture via the movies to interpret experience

"I believe that all people are good to begin with."–a voice of Position or Personal Belief

"That's how I felt when I fell out of a tree and broke my arm."–a voice of Personal Experience

Each of these statements makes an assertion that states a belief, opinion, or position. Yet, while the person making the statement expresses a belief, the way to communicate a fuller meaning is to use images or words that pull from other sources. Each statement "borrows" from some other story or experience to flesh out meaning centered on something that mattered. **Faith Tradition, Culture/Society, Personal Experience/Action, and Personal Belief/Position** provide a common language for individuals and groups to use as they engage in theological reflection. The vocabulary might feel a bit like jargon; however, the words provide some definition that can guide and clarify the theological discussion, whether it is within a group conversation or an individual's internal conversation.

Faith Tradition: Whenever the language, concepts, terms, or images in a conversation come from the Bible or some other document or story that is part of the Christian lore, then one is drawing from the Christian Tradition source. Words like "creation" or "sin"; images like "Good Shepherd" or "walking on water" come from the Christian scriptural tradition. Concepts such as providence, eschatology, or incarnation make use of the terms used by theologians. In EfM's theological reflection model, the umbrella term "Tradition" more accurately refers to the Christian heritage and is the source that marks the reflective conversation as theological. However, someone *formed* in (not simply having a passing interest in) another faith tradition would hear the voices from *their* sacred writings or stories, their wisdom figures, or their leaders, and the contributions from such connections would enrich the reflection.

Culture/Society: This source of the four-source model refers to a very large body of material. Literature, music, paintings and other artifacts are part of the Culture source. References from a movie or from a novel would be examples of something from the contemporary Culture source. The Culture source also includes traditional social or ethnic norms that might be referenced by "My grandmother used to say. . . ." The Culture source contains both written and oral content, and may have been handed down from one generation to another.

Notice that the Tradition and Culture sources have a common characteristic. They have an objective quality independent from an individual; that is, they are sources "from outside" a person. The material from these two sources resides in the "other." It may be contained in printed material or recorded in a way that can be referenced in much the same way as a footnote in a research paper. The oral content of the Culture source has a less impartial quality. What one's grandmother transmitted (Culture) often gets incorporated in the psyche of the person. Nevertheless, the content of the aphorism distinctly comes from outside the grandchild. Cultural and ethnic messages transmitted within a society are placed within the Culture source of the EfM model. These too have a quality of being embedded from the outside into the individual.

The other two sources in the theological reflection model have a more subjective nature. They can be modified with the pronoun "my" and refer to personal experience; drawing a distinction between them becomes somewhat awkward.

Personal Experience/Action: Behavior and activity define this source; what actually happened that can be communicated using neutral words. For example, a person draws from the Action source when she describes what happened such as, "One Halloween our family attended a city-wide celebration. I went as a pink bunny rabbit with a carrot in hand. I got separated from my siblings and followed the crowd as it left the stadium. My family found me walking along the side of the road. I was crying and felt alone. When they got me into the car, I was told that my rabbit ears had been tied together by someone." This is something that happened within a person's experience and which fostered some learning and viewpoints and attitudes that would continue long after the incident. The experience was formational to some extent and became a source/voice in that person's life.

Personal Belief/Position: Behavior centers on what is seen and heard. Any experience also contains the feelings and thoughts that shape the meaning attributed to the experience. Opinions, beliefs, viewpoints, and convictions held by a person constitute the position pole of the four-source model. A person's position arises out of the mix of behavior, images, feelings, and viewpoints. A person's history and the meaning attributed to the past contribute to the formation of beliefs. Positions rest, however tentatively, on the meaning attributed to behavior, learning, or life events.

The content of theological reflection comes from combining distinctive voices. Human consciousness employs reason, emotion, imagination, and praxis (the practical side of something, rather than its theory) to create meaning and value in life. Theological reflection, individually or with others, is a search for a glimpse of truth and meaning.

Reflection: What and How?

Reflection happens as the mind moves through the four steps of identifying a focus, exploring the focus, connecting to the sources/voices, and applying that focus to ministry. It begins as a topic is identified. Several skills help to arrive at a clear focus for conversation: recognizing that there is something that draws attention such as an experience, a painting, a piece of scripture, and so forth; focusing on the object of attention; discerning where the important consideration needs to center, that is, where the "heart-beat" is of the incident, movie, passage in scripture, painting, and so forth.

Once the topic for reflection is selected, it is possible to begin exploring its dimensions. As the various dynamics are considered, the mind naturally makes connections with other sources, as if each source has a voice that joins in the reflection. As the variety of voices converse, new awareness and insights emerge. Perhaps an individual or group experiences the sensation of being grasped by truth. New understanding leads to considering how insights might be applied. Identifying, exploring, connecting, and applying constitute the movements, phases, or steps of reflection. [23]

---

23. EfM's model of theological reflection follows these four movements as it considers the perspectives of the four sources in conversation with one another. In Part II you will find examples of the reflections used in the Reading and Reflection Guide series on pages 286–332. The only real difference between the examples is where each begins (i.e., from which source).

Focus

Rowan Williams's short essay on his experience of being in New York City on September 11, 2001, describes his theological reflection on his experience. Review the article and identify the various "voices" present in it. For example, he recalls knowing that people in the planes sent messages to their loved ones. Another voice would be his reference to Dawkins as a well-known atheist. Listen especially to the voices of Culture and the Christian Tradition. Notice the voices from Personal Experience and Personal Beliefs.

Respond

Theological reflection is a discipline that contributes to the formation of Christian ministry, with particular emphasis this year on how your own call to ministry is lived out in a multicultural context. Each person has an individual, unique identity. However, each person also has a corporate identity—a self that is "we." Our work in ministry formation this year will attend especially to the communal dimension of human identity—the self that is "we." The various approaches and disciplines, especially the discipline of theological reflection, emphasize the common humanity shared by all.

The communal heritage of a person influences the person's view of reality; the guiding values underlying how the person approaches life (that is, the canon of thought employed); and how truth is experienced, known, and expressed. Humankind is increasingly in need of a renewed sense of common humanity and an enlarged ecological perspective.

Theological reflection throughout this volume will engage the social identities a person experiences and how those identities have been fashioned and continue to be shaped by the interaction of the ethnic richness present in a multicultural environment. Inherited values impact daily decisions, often operating in an unconscious, tacit way. As people grow in their awareness of their inherited selves and listen deeply to other corporate identities, basic assumptions get uncovered. "Doesn't everybody do things this way?" is met with a resounding "No!" How authority and power are understood and trusted impact daily decisions. The confidence a person has is not only a product of individual experience, but is also the result of inherited, communal assumptions that color expectations. Distrust or trust of a particular ethnic group has been woven into the cultural inheritance that formed the person. For example, a person who grew up as a member of the majority race in a prosperous country generally views governmental authorities, such as police, as trusted servants of society. Another person who grew up as a member of a marginal ethnic group that for generations was oppressed by governmental authorities will be hard-pressed to trust any governmental authority, especially the police. Additionally, interaction among different cultures with differing assumptions can generate misunderstandings and miscommunication. Theological reflection provides a way to bring out cultural biases and clarify how miscommunication and conflict emerge in the interaction of cultural differences.

Theological reflection within a growing awareness of multicultural and global realities becomes an effective instrument to help realize the vision of God encountered in scripture and liturgy. The Episcopal Book of Common Prayer uses phrases that call for contributing to the common good as a way to reveal God's Realm. For example, the Prayers of the People, Form IV, in the Book of Common Prayer, prays, "Guide the people of this land, and of all the nations, in the ways of justice and peace; that we may honor one another and serve the common good."[24] Sprinkled throughout the prayer book one can find references to the call to act for the benefit of the entire human community.

As a person reflects theologically on experience and is encouraged to fold communal and ethnic understandings into the reflection, the importance of ethical implications easily arises. Identity moves from individualistic preoccupations into communal concerns—issues that involve all people. Global economic and political interactions encouraged, if not forced, by globalization, and environmental impacts on air and water demand attention.

What relationship do these global issues have to inclusive theological terms such as "heaven" or "the people of God"?

Use ABCD as you prepare what you will share in the seminar.

Practice

Theological reflection is a discipline that is learned best through practice. The goal of theological reflection is to help us more clearly hear God in the midst of our life; in the midst of moments or encounters that can draw us more deeply into awareness of God. Throughout the *Guide*, there are many opportunities to reflect. The four movements of identifying a focus, exploring the focus, connecting to other voices around and in us, and applying the learning are the elements that will be common to all of the reflection outlines. Reflecting so that doors are opened to those who have grown up in and been formed by differing cultures leads men and women into ministry with others. Multicultural experience begins to become intercultural experience, something more than just having a variety of cultures around us, but rather opportunity to awaken to the wonder of God's extravagant diversity in creation and to learn. This unit begins with the practice of reflecting theologically on a personal experience.

---

24. *The Book of Common Prayer* (New York: Church Hymnal Corporation, 1979), 388.

THEOLOGICAL REFLECTION BEGINNING WITH A PERSONAL EXPERIENCE

Identify a focus. Describe a short conversation that you recently had about something that mattered to you. Write it out or make some notes on what was said. Recall the tone, the points made, and the parts of the conversation that have stayed with you. What was it about? What does it mean to you now? Starting from a conversation like this places you in the Action/Experience aspect of your life.

Name the central theme of the conversation (what it was about) and then try to come up with an image that captures that theme. If you could draw a picture of the theme, what would it be? Or, explore by naming the central issue in the conversation. Either image or issue will work as a focus for reflection.

Explore the issue or image focus by asking a question or two, such as:

How does that image or issue express facets that are creative and those that are destructive?

How would God be present in such a matter?

What values are present?

How would grace be represented?"

Connect to other areas of your life. Listen for voices that speak from society or **Culture**, that is, from the world around you; from the Christian **Tradition**; and from your **Personal Beliefs**. Connect freely, without trying to do these in any order.

How and where do any of the questions stimulate response from you?

How do people or groups in your **Culture** deal with the image or issue?

How does the Christian **Tradition** (scripture, hymns, prayers, and so forth) speak to that matter?

What do you **Believe** or wrestle with about the theme upon which you are reflecting?

What other times have you had to deal with this matter (**Personal Experience**)?

What are you becoming aware of as you explore and connect to the issue or image? What do you see in a new way?

Apply

What difference, however great or small, does this reflection have for your daily life? What implications for ministry are there?

Further Practice for Reflecting Theologically

Playing with Images

Use any kind of image. The following are suggestions only.

- A shaker of salt

- A bowl of water

- A lit candle

- An unlit candle

Pick any one or more of the above images and respond as follows:

- Draw the item depicted or find that item and set it before you.

- What are the characteristics and qualities of that item?

- Where do you find that image in the scriptures or hymns or prayers of your faith tradition?

- Where do you find that image represented in the world around you? What cultural issues, if any, are there relative to that image?

- When have you had an experience that was related to that item or image in some way?

- What do you believe about the matters that the image may be surfacing for you?

Match the questions above to the four movements of theological reflection: identifying a focus for reflection, exploring the focus, connecting the focus to other voices, and applying learning.

Match the four "voices" or sources to the last four questions in the exercise: Personal Experience; Position or Belief; Culture; Christian (or other faith) Tradition.

Feelings Have Roots

Use the following sets of thoughts and feelings to create images that capture those dynamics.

Feelings: angry, sad, tired	Thoughts: I can't do this anymore
Feelings: joyful, expectant	Thoughts: Is this real? I want to hold on forever.

Create one or more pictures that represent the sets of thoughts and feelings.

What does the image bring to mind for you?

Identify the source of your recalled connection—a personal experience, a piece of scripture, a piece of music, and so forth.

Where do you turn to make sense of such a connection? Think along these lines: If you recalled a personal experience based on the thoughts and feelings and image, what helps you interpret that experience? If you recalled a piece of scripture, what helps you draw meaning from that?

As your reflection deepens, what do you begin to understand, proclaim, question?

Write a brief prayer that relates to insights and implications that may surface from this reflection.

What ministry does your reflection suggest? Or how will your reflection contribute to ministry in your life and with a variety of cultures you may encounter?

Week Nine

YEAR ONE

Read

Exodus 16–40
Collins, Chapter 6, "Revelation at Sinai"

Focus

Terms and names to note: Mosaic/Sinai covenant; Hittite treaties; Assyrian treaties; vassal treaty; theophany; Baal; Asherah; Festival of Unleavened Bread; Sukkoth; Book of the Covenant; apodictic law; casuistic law; Yahwist Decalogue; ritual Decalogue; unwritten (oral) law

Note how Israel's covenant with God is part of the foundation of Israel's identity.

YEAR TWO

Read

The Gospel according to Luke

Focus

Name three aspects of Luke's account of the Good News that differ from the other two synoptic gospels, Mark and Matthew. What do these aspects contribute to an understanding of the identity of Jesus?

Imagine the writer of Luke making a list of images for Jesus. What would be on that list?

Describe how Luke's images shade and color the gospel he proclaims.

YEAR THREE

Read

MacCulloch, Chapter 6, "The Imperial Church"

Focus

Terms and names to note: Constantine; Chi Rho, Milvian Bridge; Codex Vaticanus; Codex Sinaiticus; *Hagia Eirene*; *Hagia Sophia*; Helena; Athanasius; Basil; Arius; Miaphysites; Nestorius; *sedes, cathedra, basilica*; *catechesis; eremos, monachos, abila, homoousion, homoios, hypostasis, ousia, Theotokos*; monasticism; *The Acts of Thomas*; Councils; Chalcedonian Definition; dates: 312, 325, 481

History presents a narrative that the author creates from primary or other secondary sources. What sources can you identify that MacCulloch uses in this chapter?

YEAR FOUR

Read

Ford, Chapter 6, "Jesus Christ"

Focus

Terms and names to note: resuscitation vs. resurrection; Christology; catholic; the Councils; the divinity and humanity of Jesus Christ; Alexandrine vs. Antiochene Christology; hermeneutical gap; Augustine; Irenaeus; Jaroslav Pelikan

How does Ford's "defensible historical core" (pages 86–89) compare to your own understanding of Jesus? What are some losses and gains in translation of sacred texts? How does this affect your understanding of the biblical text? Why is the Jewishness of Jesus important?

ALL YEARS

Respond

The issues raised in each of the year's readings are real, ongoing, and perhaps difficult. Identify some of the issues faced by those considered in your reading this week. What has your experience taught you about one or more of those issues?

Use ABCD as you prepare what you will share in the seminar.

Practice

THEOLOGICAL REFLECTION BEGINNING WITH THE CHRISTIAN TRADITION

Use your assigned reading this week to:

Identify the focus of what you read and state it briefly;

Explore the focus by identifying theological views of the world, sin, judgment, repentance, and/or redemption that may have been present in your reading;

Connect by identifying how your identified reading focus gets addressed in the Culture in which you live; i.e., are there political implications related to the focus you identified; is there a movie you have seen that dealt with the matter of your reading focus; are there social agencies that deal with the matter you focused on? How is God acting in today's world to respond to that focus?

recalling **Personal Experiences** related to the focus; in other words, when have you had something occur in your life that relates to the reading focus you identified?

recording your own **Beliefs/Positions** about the matter and making note of how those beliefs were formed. How is your belief affected by your theological reflection on the matter?

Apply

Given your reflection on the focus of your reading, what do you want to do or feel called to do? For example, does the reflection increase your interest in helping in a community project or agency? Are there areas you want to study more about? Is there someone in your life that you want to reach out to?

What implications are there for living faithfully in a multicultural world?

Find some way to discover how those in another culture relate and/or respond to the focus you used for your reflection.

If possible, make a commitment to one small action you could take in the near future as a result of your reflection and think about what you need to do or what would support you in order for you to take that action.

Week Ten

YEAR ONE

Read

Leviticus and Numbers
Collins, Chapter 7, "Priestly Theology: Exodus 25–40, Leviticus & Numbers"

Focus

Terms and names to note: the Tabernacle; sacrificial system; Day of Atonement; stories of Nadab and Abihu and of Korah; impurity laws; Holiness Code; relationship of ethics and holiness; Cultic Calendar; Book of Numbers

YEAR TWO

Read

Powell, Chapter 8, "Luke"

Focus

Terms and names to note: Theophilus; "the beloved physician"; Luke's Gospel in relationship to the Acts of the Apostles; the major themes in the Gospel of Luke; passages from Luke widely used in Christian liturgies

Use the ABCD to identify your response to Powell's presentation of Luke's Gospel.

Which of the major themes Powell identifies do you find interesting or even compelling?

Who is Luke's intended audience? How does Luke tailor his gospel to the culture of his audience?

YEAR THREE

Read

MacCulloch, Chapter 7, "Defying Chalcedon: Asia and Africa"

Focus

Terms and names to note: *The Life of Barlaam* and *Joasaph*[25]; Miaphysites; Dyophysite "Nestorianism"; Tome of Leo; *Henotikon*; Jacob Baradeus; Syriac Orthodox Church; Sergius; Peter the Iberian; Armenian Church; *Trisagion*;

---

25. An eBook English translation of "*The Life of Barlaam and Joasaph*" can be found at https://www.gutenberg.org/files/749/749-h/749-h.htm

Theopaschism; Ethiopia; *abun*; Ezana; täwahedo; Kebra Nagast; King Kaleb; Dyophysite Christians; failure of the Marib Dam; School of the Persians in Edessa; Sebokht; "Mar Thoma" Church; Cosmas Indicopleustes; Thomas Christians; Evagrius Ponticus; Alopen; library pagoda of Ta Qin

Identify the central opposition for an individual or a group that defied Chalcedon (Kal-SEE-dun).

YEAR FOUR

Read

Ford, Chapter 7, "Salvation—its scope and intensity"

Focus

Terms and names to note: salvation; predestination; God's salvific will; universal salvation; secondary creation; theological virtues; eschatology; Aquinas; Calvin; Anselm of Canterbury; Martin Luther

Identify some different Christian understandings of salvation. What is your theology of salvation in relation to these? How does salvation have a corporate dimension? How might inter-religious dialogue help you as a Christian better understand a doctrine of salvation?

ALL YEARS

Respond

Consider how dynamics of multicultural interaction were present at the time in your reading this week.

What tensions, if any, arose for those you read about? How were those dealt with?

Use ABCD as you prepare what you will share in the seminar.

Practice

The following passages involve the people of Samaria, a group that fostered strong feelings among the Jews. Carefully read the passages and identify two or three topics common to both.

> When the days drew near for him to be taken up, he set his face to go to Jerusalem. And he sent messengers ahead of him. On their way they entered a village of the Samaritans to make ready for him; but they did not receive him, because his face was set toward Jerusalem. When his disciples James and John saw it, they said, "Lord, do you want us to command fire to come down from heaven and consume them?" But he turned and rebuked them. Then they went on to another village.
>
> Luke 9:51–56

But wanting to justify himself, he asked Jesus, "And who is my neighbor?" Jesus replied, "A man was going down from Jerusalem to Jericho, and fell into the hands of robbers, who stripped him, beat him, and went away, leaving him half dead. Now by chance a priest was going down that road; and when he saw him, he passed by on the other side. So likewise a Levite, when he came to the place and saw him, passed by on the other side. But a Samaritan while traveling came near him; and when he saw him, he was moved with pity. He went to him and bandaged his wounds, having poured oil and wine on them. Then he put him on his own animal, brought him to an inn, and took care of him. The next day he took out two denarii, gave them to the innkeeper, and said, 'Take care of him; and when I come back, I will repay you whatever more you spend.' Which of these three, do you think, was a neighbor to the man who fell into the hands of the robbers?" He said, "The one who showed him mercy." Jesus said to him, "Go and do likewise."

Luke 10:29–37

Note: Though the above scripture passages are quoted from the NRSV translation, reading the passages in a variety of translations can be helpful.

THEOLOGICAL REFLECTION BEGINNING WITH THE CHRISTIAN TRADITION

Identify: The passage above from Christian tradition is the identified starting point. Focus by considering where the key energy/heart of the scripture passage is, what the passage seems to be about. Develop an image in words or a drawing that illustrates the heart of the passage. You might try to think in visual terms, as if you were making a video or a painting that conveys the feeling.

Explore the image using a question from the theological themes of Creation, Sin, Judgment, Repentance, or Redemption; that is,

What kind of community does the image-world suggest? (Creation)

What might get in the way of relationships in that image-world? (Sin)

What could make those in that world realize there's something wrong? (Judgment)

What would represent a change of direction? (Repentance)

What might a new, life-giving creation look like? (Redemption)

Connect with:
Note: Connecting happens best if some freedom is allowed. Listen to each of the "voices" or "sources" underlined below and let your responses emerge in any order. You may not make a connection in one area; that is okay. That may occur at a later time, or not at all. Mainly, allow your inner life to speak, connecting you to these areas of potential meaning and revelation.

Experience—When has something happened in your life that is like the world of the image/metaphor? Compare your experience with the exploration above.

Contemporary Culture/Society—Who or what has taught you something that is helpful when life is like the image? In our world, where is opposition to that image? Where is support for it?

What key issues do the metaphor and personal experience and contemporary culture raise?

State your beliefs and positions relative to those issues.

Apply meaning and purpose to the reflection by identifying learning and clarifying questions.

How do the beliefs and insights of the exploration support you in ministry?

Notice where you might want to make some changes in action or viewpoint about the matter covered in the reflection.

What prayer would you offer in this matter?

Week Eleven

YEAR ONE

Read

Deuteronomy
Collins, Chapter 8, "Deuteronomy"

Focus

As you read Deuteronomy, define the Mosaic covenant and notice how the covenant underwent renewal and reinterpretation.

What can you find out about the history of the baptismal covenant in the Episcopal Book of Common Prayer over time? Compare that history of covenantal renewal and reinterpretation to that of the Mosaic covenant. What inspires the change?

YEAR TWO

Read

The Gospel according to John

Focus

Make note of anything you had to look up and any surprising ideas or images that you found in reading John's Gospel. Especially note how John's Gospel presents the message of Jesus. Compare John's proclamation (*kerygma*) with that in the other gospels. What do you notice? What challenges you?

YEAR THREE

Read

MacCulloch, Chapter 8, "Islam: The Great Realignment"

Focus

Terms and names to note: *Qur'an*; *al-ilah* (Allah); how Christian *divisions* contributed to Muslim conquests; Mosques of Umar (Dome of the Rock); John of Damascus; Timothy I; Ta Qin monastery; Bishop Alopen's writing; Khan of the Keraits's vision of St. Sergius; Kublai Khan and Dyophysite Christianity; Christians of Baghdad; North African Church; Coptic patriarchs; Ethiopian Christianity; *The Miracles of Mary*; Prester John myth

What do you find surprising in this chapter? What information about the history of Christianity in this particular context is new to you?

YEAR FOUR

Read

Ford, Chapter 8, "Through the past to the present: texts and history"

Focus

Terms and names to note: Pentecostal; Charismatic; deification; liberation theologies; the context of the text; genre; the canon of scripture; the "levels" or "senses" of the text; commentary; original languages of the Bible; hermeneutics; critical history; presuppositions; Ernst Käsemann; Friedrich Schleiermacher; Paul Ricoeur

Ford's guidelines for interpreting texts on pages 137–139 is extensive. Do you find any surprises in this list? Which do you already do regularly in your reading of the Bible or theological texts? Which would you like to add to your practice? What would you like to suggest be added to Ford's list? How does the study of history contribute to your reading of the Bible or other theological texts?

ALL YEARS

Respond

What challenges and opportunities for multicultural interaction occurred during the time period you read about and thought about this week?

Identify the cultural diversity you encounter today and compare that to what things were like as you grew up. What have been or are the challenges and opportunities of cultural diversity you have experienced, or currently experience?

Name one culture different from your own that you would like to learn more about.

Use ABCD as you prepare what you will share in the seminar.

Practice

THEOLOGICAL REFLECTION BEGINNING WITH THE CHRISTIAN TRADITION

Use your text reading this week to

Identify the focus of what you read;

Explore by identifying the views of the world, sin, judgment, repentance, and/or redemption that may have been presented in your reading;

Connect by identifying how the author(s) drew on his or her contemporary culture in writing the chapter;

identifying the beliefs that the author seemed to hold and how those interact with your beliefs;

recalling personal experiences related to the chapter's focus;

Apply by making notes of what you want to share with the seminar group as you reflect on your reading.

If your group chooses to use this reflection assignment in the seminar, note how group reflection differs for you from reflecting on your own as an individual.

What are the advantages of individual reflection? What is lost?

What are the advantages of reflection with a group? What is challenging?

Week Twelve

YEAR ONE

Read

Yee, Chapter 1, "Character, Conflict, and Covenant in Israel's Origin Traditions" by Carolyn J. Sharp

Focus

Terms and names to note: cultural norms; cultural performance of power; valorizing of male authority; androcentric; elite; cisgender; the *shalom;* relational fidelity; agent; feminist visions of mutuality; patrilineal; phallocentrism; polygynous; hermeneutics of emancipation; Exodus tradition as liberatory; syncretism; reciprocal obedience; cultural ethos; ritual impurity and cleansing; halakhic discourse; systemic inequities; Phyllis Trible; Hagar; *El-roi;* Dinah; Shiphrah and Puah; Julia Kristeva

What is new for you in this chapter? What is challenging to your understanding of the stories presented in the Pentateuch?

Use ABCD as you prepare what you will share in the seminar.

YEAR TWO

Read

Powell, Chapter 9, "John"

Focus

Terms and names to note: Book of Signs; Book of Glory; Logos; beloved disciple; abundant life; Paraclete; Sacred Heart piety; Raising of Lazarus; Washing the Feet; *Christ of Saint John of the Cross*

Identify the meaning of major themes in John's Gospel: true revelation of God; Jesus as God; Glorification of Jesus in his death; world and Jews; loving one another.

How does John's Gospel support your own understanding of God? Of Jesus? What does Powell's commentary add to your understanding? What about Powell's commentary do you find challenging?

YEAR THREE

Read

MacCulloch, Chapter 9, "The Making of Latin Christianity"

Focus

Terms and names to note: *Papa*; catholic; Latin Rite; St. Lawrence; Basilica of St. Peter; Damasus; Jerome; Vulgate; Faltonia Betitia Proba; Prudentius; Ambrose; Augustine's *Confessions*; Monica; Manichaeism; *tolle lege*; Donatists; *City of God*; Pelagius; 410 CE; Augustine's analogy of Trinity; double processions of Holy Spirit; Martin; Sulpicius Severus; *capellae*; Cassian; Benedict; Rule of St. Benedict

What are you finding challenging in MacCulloch's history of the church? What connections are you making to the church today?

YEAR FOUR

Read

Ford, Chapter 9, "Experience, knowledge, and wisdom," and Chapter 10, "Theology for the third millennium"

Focus

Terms and names to note: epistemology; levels of knowing–experience, understanding, judgment; corrigibility; *docta ignorantia*; wisdom vs. knowing information; Bernard Lonergan

Ford names nine aspects of knowing God. What questions does this list raise for you in your experience as a person trying to live a faithful life?

How does Ford envision theology's role in the third millennium? What role does theology play in your understanding of the call to ministry in everyday life?

ALL YEARS

Respond

One of the ideas offered by the writer of the Gospel according to John is "abundant life." What does that term mean to you personally? Carolyn Sharp, in the Year One assignment on the Pentateuch, speaks of the *shalom* as a vision of God's abundance. How does John's picture of abundant life relate to the vision of *shalom* in the Pentateuch?

What might the term "abundant life" mean in a larger societal context? If you are not in Years One or Two, what connections to "abundant life" can you find in what you are reading? What is the picture of abundant life you find in your own culture?

Use ABCD as you prepare what you will share in the seminar.

Practice

THEOLOGICAL REFLECTION BEGINNING WITH A SOCIAL CONCERN

Philosophical anthropology studies the nature of humankind. Questions of identity, both individual and communal, comprise the field of study. Theological anthropology addresses human nature in relation to God. Both philosophical and theological anthropology address related questions: What is the end (*telos*) of human beings? What does human flourishing involve? What is "the common good"—the actions, values and policies that allow people to flourish? In theological terminology, what is God's vision for all people? Such questions involve thinking about the meaning of terms such as the Kingdom of God, heaven, and the *eschaton* (end-time).

The following theological reflection outline provides a way to consider philosophical and theological anthropological matters.

Identify a focus.
Develop a list of social concerns that are presently being deliberated in your Culture/society. The items on the list might come from politics, news media, documentaries, current cinema, or advertisements.
For example:

• Environmental concerns

• Universal health care

• National security

• Distribution of wealth

• Economic wellbeing

Select one topic from the list you create and reflect theologically on that voice from the Culture source. You will have a chance to make additional connections to the voice of Culture when you add the Connect movement to your reflection.

Explore some dimensions of your selected social concern. For example:

• Notice what is revealed about human nature in the identified concern, both individually and corporately. What human values seem to be operating around the social concern? Describe what the identified social concern seems to assert about "the common good"; that is, if the concern you are working with is "economic wellbeing," how does that concern relate to the common good?

• What characteristics of God are present or absent in that concern? Possibly, a social concern around national security could reflect God's characteristic of protector. What about God's self-emptying?

Identify the deep hopes that are present or implied in the nature of the social concern.

Connect to other sources. Describe various ways the identified social concern gets manifested at the present time. For example, if universal health care is the identified concern under reflection, then identify the ways in which that concern has come to the foreground in the Culture/society where you live, such as:

- U. S. news report on congressional action

- Canadian experience of universal health care

- English experience of universal health care

Where do you hear God's voice in your social structure, or your culture?

Learn something new. Find a way to hear the voice of Cultures/societies other than your own, such as how other countries handle the same or similar concern. How do varying cultural groups handle such a matter, perhaps even within the same country? Please resist the temptation to "talk off the cuff" about another place or people; rather, try to talk to someone from that culture or look up information that you could consider authoritative and reliable.

Personal Experience: Name concrete ways in which the issue has intersected your life. For example:

- Retirement brought change in how medical insurance was obtained

- Got ill and had to receive medical attention over an extended period of time

- Health of a friend's parent deteriorated and he/she required extended health care

- Visit to emergency room of hospital and noticing who was there and why

- Change in a person's life that required addressing the need for medical insurance

When have you had personal experience related to that concern or issue? What emotions have you experienced as that concern has intersected your life: fear, frustration, sorrow mixed with gratitude? Name your thoughts and feelings in relation to the focus you have selected.

Personal Belief/Position: What seems to be at stake in the reflection as you have explored and connected to the identified concern? What statements of conviction are you willing to make? What is alive for you in this matter?

- State what you value and hold important that is touched by the identified social concern.

- State your best vision or hope for the world and for creation.

Tradition: Listen to the voice of Christian tradition, especially the way Christian tradition speaks to the questions of God, common good (reign of God), or human nature.

What specific stories from the Christian tradition speak to the concern? Note what scripture stories, perhaps ones you remember from your childhood, give shape to the concern.

As you access the various voices in Personal Experience, Christian Tradition, Culture(s), and Personal Beliefs, what rings true for you or seems new to you? Express, as best you can, any intuitive sense of what "should" be, "ought" to be, could be, or "must" be done relative to the social concern. In other words, what matters to you about this?

Describe actions that you could take that might contribute to the reign of God, the common good, in the matter of the social concern on which you reflected.

Apply the insight and new awareness from the reflection within the context of the social concern you named above.

How do the dimensions of the social concern point to the common good?

In what way does participation in the social concern/issue contribute to a vision of God's reign?

How does human flourishing revealed through the reflective theological conversation point toward action and behavior and practices?

In other words, what are you going to do (ministry) with what you have considered?

What would support you? Where/how will you reach out for that support?

Week Thirteen

YEAR ONE

Read

Joshua
Judges
Collins, Chapter 9, "Joshua"; Chapter 10, "Judges"

Focus

As you read the book of Joshua, note the concerns of the people. Especially think about the nature of God that the narrative presents and how that understanding of God shaped their understanding of the world and of themselves.

Judges in the Hebrew Bible are more aptly described as warlords than magistrates. Collins writes that the selection criterion for a judge was might. As you step back into the time of Judges, why do you think these stories would be recorded and valued? State how you think the people would have seen God to be present.

YEAR TWO

Read

The Acts of the Apostles
Powell, Chapter 10, "Acts"

Focus

Terms and names to note: the role of the Church in Jerusalem; Stephen; the relationship between Paul and the Roman Empire

Make note of what surprises you in reading Acts; what you have to look up; and the events, images, or ideas that interest you. Note key points in the differences between Paul and Peter, and their goals.

Powell notes that the commonly used title "Acts of the Apostles" is misleading because Luke's focus actually is on the acts of God the Holy Spirit. Do you agree or disagree? What evidence can you show to support your opinion?

YEAR THREE

Read

MacCulloch, Chapter 10, "Latin Christendom: New Frontiers"

Focus

Note how MacCulloch organizes five hundred years of Latin Christian history around several themes: how changing allegiances affect the church; the mission to expand the church; the role of converts in shaping the identity of the church; and the church's relationship with empire.

Identify a few key persons and events related to these themes. What aspects of these themes do you find in the church today?

YEAR FOUR

Read

The Coakley essay: "God as Trinity: An Approach through Prayer" in this EfM Reading and Reflection Guide, Part II, pages 241–252.

Focus

Terms and names to note: hypostases; Karl Rahner; David Hume; doxologies; Schleiermacher; *richesse*; St. John of the Cross; Hippolytus; Origen; Mithras; Basil the Great; Gregory of Nyssa

What is your understanding of the relationship of the three "persons" of the Trinity? Does Coakley's essay raise questions for you?

What is your experience with the question of gendered language in speaking of God? What are the issues for you? How do you address them? Write a position statement on the topic of gendered language in liturgy.

ALL YEARS

Respond

What multicultural issues arose in the lives of people you read about in the material you studied this week? What resources were available for interaction among the people in the variety of cultures?

Use ABCD as you prepare what you will share in the seminar.

Practice

Theological reflection is the central discipline of EfM, and it is expected that individuals and groups will regularly engage in theological reflection, especially in the weekly seminar. As with all spiritual disciplines, practice is the key to becoming proficient, and with proficiency comes greater comfort and ease in the process.

Reflections in a group work best when all contribute; more experienced members can help the process by encouraging participation from those less experienced. Note group reflection does not mean that the group simply is sharing individual refection work you have already prepared at home. Group reflection is a fresh opportunity to incorporate multiple viewpoints and insights that can inform your own perspective.

As your group reflects together in the seminar, notice for yourself how reflecting in community differs from personal reflection. There is a time for each process as we engage deeply with the intersection of faith and life.

For this reflection, in some way, visit another <u>Culture</u> this week. Remember that culture is not always synonymous with ethnicity, but for this practice exercise it will be helpful to choose another culture that is unfamiliar in some significant way.

- Perhaps there are places of worship in your community, town, and city representing faith traditions with which you are unfamiliar. Go there if possible. Talk to people there.

- Are there movies you could watch about another culture?

- Are there family members you could talk to?

- What about books or friends?

THEOLOGICAL REFLECTION BEGINNING WITH THE CULTURE SOURCE

Identify

Once you have explored another culture in some way, identify a focus, then create an image or metaphor of your limited understanding of that culture, if possible.

Explore the focus from some theological perspectives, such as:

- What beliefs about creation are reflected in the image?

- What is considered sin in the world of your image?

- How does one find forgiveness in that image world?

- What constitutes ultimate fulfillment as that culture understands it?

- What do you regard as the meaning of life for that culture? ·

- What is the meaning of death?

Connect by listening to other voices. (Reminder: You can do the following in any order.)

Christian Tradition—What passages in scripture or church history come to mind as you explore the image above? Read the passages or material you recall.
Compare and contrast the world you found in the scripture or church history passage with the world you explored with the theological questions.

Personal Experience—What has occurred in your life that provides answers to some of those theological questions?

Compare and contrast your personal experience with the experiences of those in the culture you explored briefly. What differences and similarities are there? What begins to matter to you as you make the comparisons?

Contemporary Culture/Society—How does your culture/society view that of the one you explored? What are the challenges and possibilities?

Personal Beliefs—What beliefs of yours are challenged by those of the other culture? How could that challenge create road blocks? How could it create opportunity? What would you have to give up in order to change your beliefs? What might someone from the culture you explored have to give up?

Apply the reflection by noting your insights and how those insights might make a difference in ministry in your life.

FIRST INTERLUDE

Dismantling Racism in America

Week Fourteen

ALL YEARS

Read

Meeks, Preface and Chapters 1–4, pages v–60

Focus

Terms and names to note: Racism and prejudice; White privilege; Beloved Community; Thurman's four phase development of hate; reconciliation; racist institutions and systems; socially constructed identity; essentialism of race; Brown's working definition of racism; phenotype; master status; implicit racial bias; "othering"; assigning value to race; colorblindness; projection; self-integration; the necessity of inner work; the necessity of outer work; "postracial"; racial healing; internalized oppression; "playing a race card"; microaggressions; "post traumatic slave syndrome"; The *New Jim Crow*; White supremacy; counterprojection; the shadow; W. E. B. Dubois; Howard Thurman; C. G. Jung

Respond

How do you define racism?

What is your earliest memory of recognizing racial differences? What details can you remember about the incident, including emotions?

Growing up, what were you taught/told about members of races other than your own?

Consider the idea of "master status." What do you focus on first when meeting someone new?

Practice

THEOLOGICAL REFLECTION BEGINNING WITH A PROVOCATIVE WORD[26]

Identify: This theological reflection begins with a word that has impact. For the purpose of this reflection and the practice, we suggest using "**RACISM.**"

What revelations on the meaning of the word do you have? Anything it denotes or connotes?

When you encounter this word what feelings are evoked? Write them down. What feeling carries significant weight for you? Select one (or a combination) to focus the reflection.

---

26. Adapted from a design by Patricia Bleicher, EfM mentor

Explore: Ask the questions

Next, ask the six "journalist's questions" about the feeling the word conveys:

WHO was involved when you were feeling_____?
(Source/Action . . . tell the stories from your life)

WHAT image comes to mind about the feeling(s) _____?
(Image . . . explore the metaphor–its reflection of Wholeness, Brokenness, Recognition, Reorientation, and/or Restoration)

Connect: Go to the other sources we use to help explore meaning

WHERE does this feeling come from and WHERE is it found in society?
(Source/Culture)

WHEN does this feeling come up in the Bible, lives of saints, hymns, and so forth?
(Source/Tradition . . . explore the world of tradition)

WHY is this feeling manifest in our lives? (Source/Position)

HOW might God redeem any negatives in this (Hope in Christ)
Consider insights and implications

What have you learned for the next time you feel_____?

Apply: Write a collect using the outline:

Dear God . . .	**(naming of God's aspects)**
You . . .	**(connect situation of the image to that aspect)**
We pray that . . .	**(petition of our hearts)**
So that . . .	**(result we desire)**
Amen.	

Week Fifteen

ALL YEARS

Read

Meeks, Chapters 5–9, pages 61–146

Focus

Terms and names to note: koinonia; normative; interpersonal, institutional, and systemic or structural racism; colonialism; busing/desegregation in Boston; master narrative; safeguarding the feelings of White people; spiritual director as architect of safe space; "soft Zionist"; "the Tragic Gap"; dueling narratives; Mobius strip; *Tikkun Olam*; Bodhisattvas; James Baldwin; Parker Palmer; Thich Nhat Hanh; contemplative practice; "forgiveness is not . . . "; importance of covenant; "thin" places; intersections among slavery, lynching, mass incarceration, and the death penalty

In what ways is the South America's Holy Land?

What is your experience of anti-racism training?

Respond

Racism is so deeply ingrained in our social policies and practices that we can perpetuate it unknowingly in environments that are race silent. In such a climate we no longer can afford the illusion that this is a problem only for people of color. . . . If racism is an exploitive system set up by White people, maintained by White people, and benefiting White people, who has primary responsibility for dismantling it? Although Euro Americans may stand in solidarity with the Black Lives Matter movement, for example, their primary role is in White spaces where no one is talking about race. . . . It can be uncomfortable to speak up about equity and diversity, advocating in White spaces for a different reality. It can be risky to be known as the person who always raises awkward questions. Yet this is work crucial to the spiritual well-being of all people; it is not work Whites do on behalf of Afro Americans or Latinos or others. It is only by taking ownership of dismantling racist systems and overcoming our own racial assumptions that we can create the just, loving, compassionate world for which we long.[27]

The following questions are meant to inspire personal reflection. You may wish to journal on this through the week between meetings, and even beyond.

If your group decides to use the questions for discussion in the seminar, please remember that for all of us the work is ongoing. Some may find their

---

27. Diane D'Souza, "A White Lens on Dismantling Racism" in *Living into God's Dream*, ed. Catherine Meeks (New York: Morehouse, 2016), 91.

own memories of experiences difficult, painful, or regrettable. Some personal positions may be difficult to share and/or difficult to hear. Be gentle with one another and assume such honest sharing is done with good intent. This is a good time to begin by reviewing the Respectful Communication Guidelines and use Mutual Invitation, honoring the ability to pass or pass for now and building in time for pondering before responding. Listen deeply. It is not necessary to try to form some immediate plan or action.

The questions are framed from a predominantly North American perspective where white persons are in the dominant culture. If you are in another country, please feel free to substitute the dominant culture of your context and reframe the questions as appropriate.

- If you are a white person, what has been your experience of talking about racism, racial injustice, or racial reconciliation with other white persons or in groups in which there are no persons of color? What concerns have you felt or heard expressed? What personal experiences and positions have you shared in these conversations?

- If you are a person of color, what has been your experience of talking about racism, racial injustice, or racial reconciliation in conversations with white persons or groups? In what ways has your experience differed when talking in a group where white persons are not present?

Practice

D'Souza recounts how a preview of the movie *Selma* led to action in Boston. Consider watching and reflecting on *Selma* with your EfM group. As indicated below, the group will need to agree to view it either together or individually, either as "homework" or in the seminar meeting. Please note that if you choose to view it together during the seminar, you will need to decide beforehand whether to extend the meeting time in order to have adequate time for *viewing and reflection* in one meeting, or use two meetings, viewing it together during the first meeting and reflecting during the second meeting.

Selma is widely available. Your local library or school may have a copy to borrow or you may prefer to use an Internet streaming service or connection if you have access. An alternate option is the documentary *Traces of the Trade: A Story from the Deep North*.[28]

THEOLOGICAL REFLECTION BEGINNING WITH A MOVIE, VIDEO, OR TELEVISION EPISODE (CULTURE SOURCE)

This theological reflection has been designed to meet the particular needs of groups who are wanting to engage in theological reflection beginning from a movie, video, or television show (or episode). The design is intended to raise particular questions about the group's engagement with the movie/video/ television episode and draw connections to the larger theological themes.

---

28. http://www.tracesofthetrade.org/buy-use-the-film/

Theological Reflection on a movie can be done as an individual reflection, however this exercise is framed for a group.

Identify

Begin by identifying a movie/video/television episode. The group agrees to view it either together or individually. The movie may be viewed during an EfM seminar meeting time or as "homework" in anticipation of the reflection. (If a full-length feature is to be viewed during the seminar, the group will need to decide beforehand whether to extend the meeting time in order to have adequate time for viewing plus the full reflection or if the movie will be viewed during one week's meeting and the reflection done during the subsequent meeting.)

After viewing:

- Classify the genre (comedy, drama, action, documentary, nature, adult, children, etc.) and the period in which the piece was made.

- What is the film about? Avoid a detailed plot summary, but describe the themes, overarching concerns, or prominent features.

    Where was this evident in the film?

    What scene captured the essence of what the movie was about?

    Identify a focus for reflection (someone may list various suggestions from which to choose).

    A broad focus will look at a particular character or theme

    A narrow focus will look at a single scene

- After the focus is chosen, invite the group to share briefly how each identifies with the focus.

Explore

Use theological perspective questions to explore the focus:

- For a scene

    What happened? What is the world like?

    What went wrong/right? What was broken/mended?

    What was surprising?

    What was cause for celebration?

    Where in this scene did you see joy, pain, surprise, coming together?

- For a character

    What happened?

    What went wrong/right?

    What surprised him/her?

    What was cause for celebration?

- For a theme

  Where in the movie do we find the theme?

  How is it depicted? What makes it bearable?

  What enhances/destroys/builds up the theme? What obstacles are encountered?

  Is there a resolution?

  Is there change?

Connect

The question for connecting to the Christian Tradition depends on whether the group is exploring a character, theme, or scene. Where do we find resonances with characters in scripture or the tradition? OR Where do we find similar themes in scripture or the tradition? OR Where do we find similar scenes in scripture or the tradition? Identify/choose one similarity and explore it using the theological perspective questions used above.

Are there other voices from culture/society that address these themes, ideas, perspectives? Does the scene/theme/character confirm or challenge some aspect of culture/society? What does this scene/theme/character express in or for the culture/society that created it? At the time of its creation? Now? Are there underlying values, attitudes, etc.?

Apply

Consider your own position: What do I believe about what we have discussed? Has my position changed from my initial impression? Were I to view this film again, how might I view it differently?

What insights arise for me from this reflection? Can I make use of them in my life? What would help me? What resources would I need? How does this relate to my ministry? What is God calling me to be, do, or change?

What do we want to bring from this reflection into our current life together? What would our community look like if we could implement the values and perspectives we have discussed? What are we called on to do or change together? (The group may want to form a consensus statement.)

UNIT THREE

Developing a Sustaining Spirituality

Week Sixteen

ALL YEARS

Read

Introduction

Whether as a member of a minority group within a dominant culture or as a member of the cultural majority in a changing society, a person may experience the inner disturbances that transition brings. Christians seeking to live faithfully in a multicultural world need a spiritual life that sustains them through many kinds of transition. It must be capable of helping us respond not only to the refugees and immigrants created by regional wars, economic deprivation, natural disasters, and climate change but also to a rapidly changing world that transcends traditional cultural and religious boundaries.

She frequently sits with her morning coffee in a local shop whose surroundings are familiar and comfortable. Often she meets a friend for conversation and catching up. This particular morning she is alone and notices around her a number of others, some also alone, some sitting in small groups. They seem oblivious not only to her but also to each other, with eyes focused on screens of various sizes. Still she is aware that somehow conversation is occurring. She cannot understand a single word, yet she sees smiles and animated facial expressions as fingers fly over keys. She feels disoriented, left out, somehow less real to them than the person(s) with whom they are energetically connecting. It is a feeling not unlike the culture shock when visiting in a foreign country where one does not speak the language. She finds she is both drawn to and fearful of exploring the possibilities of encounters and relationships in this new digital world.

How does spirituality—in particular its traditional components of prayer, worship, and study—fit into the culture of the digital world? What does a spiritual community look like in the digital world? What might church become as we navigate this brave new world?

The Rt. Rev. Steven Charleston is a citizen of the Choctaw Nation of Oklahoma. He comes from a family with a long history of service in the Native American community and the church. His great-grandfather and grandfather were both ordained pastors who preached in their native language in rural communities throughout the state. Following in their footsteps, Bishop Charleston was ordained at Wakpala, South Dakota, on the Standing Rock Sioux Reservation.

Bishop Charleston has been the national director for Native American ministries in the Episcopal Church, a tenured professor of systematic theology at Luther Seminary, the bishop of the Episcopal Diocese of Alaska, and the president and dean of the Episcopal Divinity School in Cambridge,

Massachusetts. He is the founder of Red Moon Publications. Currently he is the Visiting Professor of Native American Theology at the Saint Paul School of Theology at Oklahoma City University. He is no stranger to navigating between and among cultures, whether in society or in the church.

Bishop Charleston's online meditations have been collected into six volumes available from Red Moon Publications. He is also the author of *The Martian Trilogy* he calls "spiritual science fiction novels." [29] The following is his Kay Gill Butler Lecture presented in April 2014 at the General Theological Seminary (GTS) in New York.

OMG: Spirituality in the Digital Age[30]

Good evening and thank you for being here. I am very honored to be invited to share this year's Kay Butler Gill Lecture. I want to express my gratitude to those who made this possible, to the Trustees, faculty and to the Dean, to the seminary staff who have welcomed me so warmly, and to the whole GTS seminary community. It is a privilege to be with you. And I hope it will be some fun as well.

Before I begin let me offer a brief aside to any of you who may have heard me speak before. If you have, you may be expecting an extemporaneous sermon that would sound more like a Baptist camp meeting than a sedate lecture in a venerable Episcopal school. Please, don't be disappointed. I assure you that my evangelical corpuscles are still active, even if in this instance I try to channel them into a more sedate form. I am offering my lecture in this more traditional style for a couple of reasons:

First, in this talk I want to think about what *is* evangelical . . . not be evangelical, if you see what I mean.

The reason is because our subject this evening is about a form of evangelism. It is about how we share spiritual and religious beliefs, how those "sharings" are received and transmitted, about how we communicate with one another. My purpose in this lecture is not to demonstrate one form of that process, even the traditional form of a sermon-like exposition, but rather to invite you into a reflection on how information and communication technology has impacted the process, how it has re-defined things like evangelism, sermons, meditations and spirituality. So to do that more deliberately, I have chosen to present my ideas to you in as clear and objective a manner as I can. I will save my altar call till later.

A second reason to go a little slower in this talk is that the concepts I want to ask you to consider are not always self-evident. I believe that in our pride, we may believe that we are shaping technology, when, in fact, technology is shaping us. As a Science-Fiction writer, I appreciate the dif-

---

29. http://www.redmoonpublications.com/red-moon-publications-author-charleston.html
30. http://news.gts.edu/wp-content/uploads/2014/04/Charleston-Lecture.pdf.

ference. And I want you to join me in pondering some of these nuances, taking old assumptions out and re-considering them, putting some of our post-modern "truisms" to the test to see what new things we can discover.

Finally, I am delivering my lecture in this way because I don't really know what I am talking about. (But that never stopped any bishop before so I will forge ahead!) I say that "I don't know" and I believe that is the strength of my presentation. I am not an expert in the field of electronic delivery systems. As you will see in a moment, I did not have some cunning master plan of how to create a communications network to rule the world. In fact, I am of that generation that looks to twelve year olds to explain how things work. But it is precisely in my own naiveté that I think I have begun to see the contours of what religion will be in the years to come. Not the religion of technical experts or trained scholars, but the religion, the spiritual life, of everyday people like me.

So please sit back, open the windows of your imagination, and let's see what we can find together through the lenses of my simple experience.

To begin, let's go back to the point of origin, to the place where my journey into spirituality and social media first began.

It was in 2011. I was serving as the interim Dean of a cathedral. As part of that job I was encouraging the congregation to improve its website. I was appealing to the technically-minded members of the community to engage some web designers to re-do the site as one of the most important aspects of outreach for the community. In doing this, I was successful in getting the website overhauled, but I also opened a Pandora's Box for myself because four of these church members started gently harassing me to join them on Facebook.

I did not want to be on Facebook. I did not think I liked Facebook. My wife had been enjoying it as a way to stay in touch with her family and friends, so I had a vague idea of what it was: a kind of endless electronic bulletin board to post messages and images that could be seen and responded to by anyone, or by a smaller self-selected community of what has come to be called "Facebook friends."

My problem was, I didn't want to be a Facebook friend. By nature, I am an extreme introvert; I was afraid that I would not have anything interesting to say or show on Facebook. But my four cathedral colleagues were persistent. "How could you encourage people to use technology when you won't use it yourself?" That was the gist of their ongoing pestering of me. So finally, I relented. I signed up and became an official Facebook participant in the very beginning of 2011.

I remember this time-line very well because I remember the first time I sat down to stare at a blank Facebook wall. It was the electronic version of the blank piece of paper in the old typewriter, waiting for me to begin The Great American Novel.

I stared at it with absolutely no idea of what to say. I was stepping into a global forum of something like 700 million people, and I was speechless. Even though, at that moment, I only had an audience of four people, the original four who were my first and only Facebook "friends," I had no clue what to do.

Finally, through the inspiration of desperation, I had an idea. I am an introvert by nature, but I am also a "morning person." I wake early each day and I find the early morning hours the best times for me to be reflective. My spiritual practice, therefore, has long been to do my prayers, light my candles and sit in Zen meditation, early in the day, usually before the sun comes up.

It struck me that during those times I have many thoughts and emotions that arise from my prayers and meditation. I have images and feelings that surface and linger in my heart and mind.

I decided to simply try to capture those impressions, whatever they might be, and write them down spontaneously on my Facebook page.

And so I did. I did not take a long time to try to formulate my thoughts. I did not try to control what I wrote. I put it down just as it came to me in only a minute or two. I jotted down my morning meditation and posted it for what it was worth.

That was how it started. I will not belabor the rest of this story other than to say that from these humble origins some wonderful things began to happen.

One of the realities of post-modern media is that it is like playing a connect-the-dots game. If one person sends something to another person, and that person sends it on to two more people, and those two send it to four more, then exponentially, organically, a network begins to form.

This is one of the fundamental realities of social media: it is crystalline. It grows. It adds on, ever building on itself, ever expanding with an intentionality of its own.

That was my experience because, one-by-one more and more people came to ask if they could be my Facebook friend to read my daily meditations. I always said yes, so little-by-little the number of people on my friend's list grew. As more people told more people a community began to form. I remember my amazement when the number hit the 100 mark . . . then the 500 mark . . . then 1,000 . . .

It went on and on. And not only were people joining me on my own page, they were sharing my words on their pages, so the number of people reading my meditations, people I might never know were doing so, also continued to proliferate. In time, so many people were part of this process that they asked me to collect my meditations and publish them so they could be maintained in a different form.

Red Moon Publications is the publishing house I created to do this, although that was not my original intention either. When the expanding number of people began to ask me to publish my writings I first went to some established publishers to see if they would accept my meditations in book form. They said no. But even in that "no," in that rejection, I learned something else about the power and dimensions of post-modern communications.

The traditional publishing business that people of my age still remember has long gone. The gate-keeper quality of a few national outlets that exercise the right to say what can make it to print has dissolved under the insistently democratic force of technology. Today, the definition of what "publishing" means has altered forever. People can publish themselves easily in a host of formats from print books to e-books, on blogs and You Tube, even in streams of their own consciousness on Twitter.

Faced with a rejection from the old school publishing system, I went to Barnes and Noble, bought a book called "The Idiot's Guide To Self-Publishing", followed the directions and printed my first collection of meditations from 2011 under the title *Hope As Old As Fire*.

It sold out in a matter of weeks.

And what is interesting to me is not just this sudden success in an end run around the tradition of old-style publishing, but the strange combination of electronic media and print media. My first book was not an e-book. It was what the people online wanted: something not online.

We sometimes imagine post-modern technology to be the destroyer of print. We conjure up images of future generations who will never hold a book in their hands but read in their brains through a chip implanted under their skin, but I am not so sure if that will be the case.

What I discovered with my publishing experiments was that there is a subtle, very human and very nuanced relationship between the old and the new. People were gathering around my writing because it was accessible to them in the immediacy of electronic media, but they were also expressing a desire to "touch" those words, to "hold" them for themselves.

I believe this is part of our spiritual instinct. The sacred is not just a cerebral exercise; it is not quantified as information for us; rather it has a tangible quality, an intimate quality and, therefore, people wanted to not only read the words on a screen, but have them in a form they could keep by the bedside, carry in the purse, hold in their hands when they were thinking or praying.

Electronic media is not necessarily the death of tactile media. It may be a companion, a door way, a counter-balance. I am not sure, but I believe this relationship deserves more thoughtful attention. We must not jump to conclusions about the triumph of any one form of communications because ultimately the sources of communication, those points of both transmission and reception, are human spiritual synapses. The vagaries, the comfort needs, the romantic imagination of who we are will hold the technical in balance and determine how different forms both emerge and interact.

As things continue to evolve with how my writing is passed on, I suspect new combinations will emerge. Very soon my meditations will come out in e-book format. A blog-radio format is in the works. And since my words are being shared in distant cultures and different religions, I know they are being translated into a variety of languages.

How do I plan to keep a handle on all of that?

The answer is: I don't. While I am both proud and humbled by what has happened with my meditations, I have no sense of a need to control their distribution. The core Facebook community that reads and disseminates them has grown to over 5,000 people now and adds new members each day. I have been told that we are one of the largest congregations in the Episcopal Church. We meet each day. Every Saturday we have a time for prayer requests and hundreds of people participate, not only in asking for prayer, but in praying for others. People exchange messages with me and with one another. The focus for our daily devotion is passed on in other branches of the congregation, far out into numbers I cannot guess or count.

So we are a large congregation, but not actually just an Episcopal congregation, or even a Christian congregation, because we are a community of women and men from every walk of life. There are members from every form of Christian tradition (Catholic, Protestant, Orthodox); there are Jews, Buddhists, Muslims, Jains, Hindus and Wiccans; there are people who follow their tribal religions; there are agnostics, seekers, doubters and people who tell me they are there for reasons they cannot explain other than it seems to keep drawing them back. We are from age ranges between 10 and 98. We live on every continent except Antarctica. We are from every political persuasion. We are ethnically diverse. We encompass all economic classes.

One of the profound learnings of my experience in social media . . . and this cannot be stressed enough . . . is that true community is possible. In an age when religious conflict is endemic we are a small proof that people of all faiths (and of no faith) can gather in peace and harmony for a shared purpose, and more importantly . . . in fact, astoundingly . . . gather for a shared *spiritual* purpose.

This is not a case of people coming together to do something pragmatic for the common good while leaving their spirituality at the door, as if bringing their religious convictions with them would automatically imply breakdown and dissent; no, this is an example of people gathering for a clear spiritual focus and doing so with their own religious views intact and apparent.

That, I believe, is something to celebrate. That is a minor miracle, especially in these days.

The sheer diversity of religious opinion in our community, coupled with the constancy with which all of these people continue to share in the meditations together demonstrates a critical hope for our future. We may not completely understand why it is happening, but it is happening and that fact alone should intrigue us and urge us to continue the invitation to this type of world without borders.

So let me now offer some more substance to my lecture by drawing out what I would characterize as "observations" based on my experience. If I am trying to understand what has happened over these last few years, if I am wanting to comprehend how social media has shaped spirituality, if I want to describe how a global electronic community came into being and continues to grow: these are some of the points to ponder. I welcome you all to join me in taking these home with you for further prayerful study and action.

I offer them in no specific order. I will state the observation and make a few comments to stir your own thinking.

1. *The spiritual community that I just described was created in the electronic culture of Facebook in a way that is counter-intuitive to our sense of religion.* A religious community is often formed by identifying the parameters which circumscribe it: the borders of faith, the articulation of creeds, the rules and rituals that become the container for a culture. Once people either self-select or are recruited into this paradigm, they become a community. In the experience of our Facebook congregation, just the reverse process has taken place; over time people have entered in without any sense of structure; we have no litmus test for belonging, not even the need to believe in a higher power. Instead, an unspoken consensus of hospitality has developed. We have welcomed people to come and read the meditations and say nothing at all; we have members who like to remain anonymous (I know this because privately they tell me so); we have people who like to engage with others through comments; and we have the weekly open invitation for people to ask for prayer and share in prayer with no central definition of what that means. In effect, this community has evolved a culture of acceptance in an almost effortless way. On only three very rare occasions over three years have I ever had to excuse someone from the community for negative behavior. These were individuals who attempted to enter into the community, bringing their very judgmental religious attitudes with them. They lasted less than a day and were no disruption to the larger community at all. Therefore, one observation is that it is possible to create a cohesive spiritual community, living out very apparent spiritual values (such as compassion, pastoral care, prayer, and study) by simply allowing people to express themselves in their own way without censure or control. Somehow, the permeable character of the virtual culture is conducive to this kind of positive behavior. It does not require policing; it does not need hierarchy. It is an exercise in a golden rule that seems instinctive to those who are drawn to it. And it manifests itself across the board, meaning that persons of all or no religious affiliation are more than capable of living in spiritual relationship with others when given the chance. What this implies for the nature of religion in the future is both intriguing and positive. For one thing, it means that we may have more electronic "islands" of spirituality emerging online: inter-religious, international, inter-cultural communities coalescing around a common desire to be together in peace and shared learning. In essence, the simple value of shared kindness may be starting to appear in the connecting links between people who regularly use social media for spiritual reasons.

2. Let's take a moment and consider these good people in a second observation. We have often heard it said that "people in this digital age are hungry for spirituality". I think some of us say that and adhere to it because we are hoping it is true and that it will bring these folks back to church. But I am not certain if this statement is completely correct. *Based on my learnings*

from the online spiritual community I have been describing, I would say that people are wanting to share their spirituality . . . not necessarily just receive it. There is a difference. For example, what is it exactly that draws people every morning to read my simple little meditations? Of course part of me would like to say that it is the startling brilliance of my prose, but honestly I know it is something else, something that people express in our community over and over again: the most important thing about my online presence is not that it "gives" something to people they don't have or know, but instead, that it "releases" something within them that has always been there. Social media seems to have the effect of releasing the human "voice". It gives permission for people, even people who say they are shy or introverted like me, to claim a place at the electronic table and express themselves. My daily meditations are a catalyst online, not a product. They seem to touch a generic vein of spirituality in a wide range of people that they recognize, affirm and embrace as their own. Technology has given human beings an enhanced sense of capability; it allows us to believe that information is always there for us and that we have only to select the format to receive what we want; therefore, we are not so much "hungry" to get spiritual content since we are forever standing at a buffet of religious data, but rather, we are wanting to do something with that experience. We want to share it. We want to engage it. We want to make it a living part of who we are. And not just at a Sunday service. The interesting thing about the online congregation to which I belong is that it gathers daily. When theologians say that religion should be a part of daily life, they are describing the actual practice of the people who interact on my Facebook wall. And I think what brings people back each day is not that they are empty vessels waiting to be filled, but full spiritual beings overflowing with the desire to connect with others who have a need for spiritual insight. If we are sincere about wanting to understand a "ministry of all believers", an egalitarian congregation or community where every person can feel empowered to participate and be who they are, then we need to observe the lessons of online spirituality, because that is precisely what is happening. In many ways, my Facebook page is a spiritual pit stop for people on a daily basis, a place where they come to read my few words, draw energy from the recognition that these words speak to their own life situation, and then launch out into the real world. Therefore, another valuable lesson for us is that social media is not an "escape" from reality. It is a reflection of reality, a place of contact for human beings who are wanting more out of reality than just business as usual. If these folks are hungry for anything, they are hungry to do more than a once a week religion may offer them.

3. I think there is a corollary to this sense of engagement that people have online that we ought to flag as a third observation. In essence it is that *people perceive information online to be more reliable than other forms of traditional communication.* Consider this as an example of what I mean: both the Fox network and CNN are suspect to different audiences for different reasons. There-

fore, their information stream flows only to a particular community. But in this vacuum of objective information, people turn to online sources and invest them with the confidence they once reserved for people like Walter Cronkite. When we see network news, we think of it as "filtered" news, but when we see a cell phone photo or a tweet from a demonstrator in Cairo or Kiev, we believe it is authentic. Social media embodies a similar phenomenon. Part of the egalitarian nature of online spirituality is that it is instantly "criticizable". If I write something in my meditations that are offensive, insensitive or just plain wrong in people's minds, they have an immediate recourse to object; they can do so instantly; they can do so without regard to credentials, hierarchy or institutional sanction; they can, in effect, stop the sermon at any point and take the floor for their own opinions. On my Facebook wall, people make any comments they wish to share. They can either affirm or reject what I have to say. The integrity of my message, therefore, is on the line every day. The fact that people seek out sources like mine, because they believe they are receiving an unfiltered, genuine expression of faith, is borne out by the positive way they respond on a regular basis. One of the implications of instant digital media for the future of religion is the same as the implications for politics: there is a levelling influence at work here, a shift in confidence away from official pronouncements, a shift in attitude away from the hierarchs and managers of information, and toward the electronic grapevine that offers a vision from eye-level, from the street, from the common citizen or common believer. This new paradigm is already a powerful force for rallying people to a cause; in the days to come it will be an equally authoritative medium in creating new "Reformations", reformations far more sweeping than the ones we experienced in the 16th century because these reform movements in spirituality will emerge from the rapid congealing of a public opinion spread out over continents and under no control or coercion of the religious leadership. My few daily words are words of support and encouragement, but one day, in some distant time of need and change, other writers may rally people in a different way; their words will be words of a revolutionary nature, a call to religious reform, and that will change the face of global religion forever.

4. *A fourth observation is that we may doubt that digital evangelism . . . for any cause . . . could have the power to make such sweeping changes because we think of digital communication as being too abbreviated to be consequential.* I entitled my lecture "OMG" to symbolize this. Digital speak is compressed speak. It is, quite literally, changing the way we talk, the way we think, and therefore, the way we are. It is popular today to describe how people accustomed to online communication adapt to ever more concise symbols of meaning. "LOL" means laugh out loud . . . "BTW" is by the way . . . "BRB" is be right back. We all know that now; it is part of our global language system. These quick, shorthand messages may seem trivial to us, but it is my contention that they are signaling something important to us, something that will shape the gospels of a new age. Consider this: before there were written gospels like Matthew,

Mark, Luke and John, we believe there were collections of the sayings of Jesus being circulated among those who wanted to hear and follow his message. These were "sound-bites" of his sermons, pieces of his thoughts that were remembered, copied down, passed around. They were not long written documents. They were not formal theological works. In fact, they were the kinds of information that would fit easily into a digital format. I think it is worth remembering that the original sources for religions, the words of the Koran, the Gospels, and the Sutras, were abbreviated thoughts that carried deep meanings. Therefore, the medium is the message, as Marshall McLuhan put it. In effect, digital communication, even in its most abbreviated form, is an ideal delivery system for the basic building blocks of a spiritual faith. We should not imagine that the fingers of the future will only be tapping out short signals of no consequence; we need to understand that among their messages will be compressed religious realities for a "culture of the concise"; as technology morphs the mind of communication, as it trains us to both send and receive even our most critical thoughts in abbreviated symbol systems, spirituality and religion will be equally re-made in the image of the Word. The "Q Document" of the next generations will begin circulating and, by so doing, energizing the next incarnation of spiritual community.

An emerging, global spiritual community without borders . . . a gathering of human beings highly motivated to express their beliefs and ideas . . . a system for doing so at their fingertips that they trust more than institutions . . . a new paradigm of religion written in the short-hand of everyday experience . . .

Last year, I wrote a science fiction novel about the future of the Episcopal Church. It is called THE BISHOP OF MARS.

Is what I imagine here, in my four "observations" about spirituality in the digital age just that, science fiction, or are there hints here of the trajectory we are already committed to, not by our own design, but by the crystalline unfolding of the technology we have set in motion?

I will leave you to ponder that for yourselves. But I will offer my own closing thoughts.

Spirituality is a message.

It is a message we give to ourselves. It is that deeply internal, deeply intimate communication between what we perceive, what we feel, and what we believe. When we meditate, when we observe, when we are mindful: we are messaging ourselves in a spiritual symbol system that forms our individual faith.

This is the same message we share with others when we find other human beings who want to hear what we have to say about what we believe. Spirituality is this conversation. It is this exchange. And community is the by-product. When we mingle our messages, compare them and collate them, we begin the ongoing process of creating religion.

Finally, spirituality is a message that many of us believe we receive from somewhere else, from Someone else, from a source and a power far beyond our own intellect or comprehension. We believe we have experienced these messages; we believe we have heard the voice of God; perhaps only in snippets, in sound bites, in digital flashes of intuition in our brains, but we are convinced it is there and it is real.

These three core qualities of human spirituality are what we are learning to communicate in the "digital age", in this brief transition in our history that will soon take us to places we cannot now describe. The brave new world, far from being devoid of faith, will be immersed in it. The spiritual will be the common. The sacred will be on every screen. The holy will be carried in the pocket or the purse or perhaps even under the skin.

As I have tried to suggest in this lecture, there is a process at work here, an ancient process, that is now appearing in a new form through digital communications. The same elements are at play in this process because they are the ways in which human beings have developed religion in the past. The core teachings of a faith are being shared among people who are drawn to coalesce around them like planets being formed by particles of matter, the substance of a teaching, the building blocks for new communities of like-minded people that are taking shape all over the world through the Internet.

What is different is that these communities are being formed across many of the old lines of demarcation between us. Spirituality in the digital age is porous. It is flexible. It is highly democratic and non-institutional. That image of planets coming into being, of a new solar system of spirituality being formed around us, is a good one because it reminds us that this transformation is far from complete. We can only now see the outlines of what the future of spirituality and religion will be, but they are clear outlines.

For one thing, the technology itself will continue to mutate the mind of believers. We will be very accustomed to living in a wide and instant marketplace of spiritual ideas; we will trust what we see arise from this free and open forum, not just what institutional structures tell us; we will be used to adapting messages to our own needs, criticizing what we don't like, accepting what we want, even if in so doing we are creating an amalgam of ideas, a hybrid spirituality of many parts and pieces. It may even be likely that this formative process will one day lead to a global redefining of religion: a "Digital Reformation" that will articulate a post-postmodern vision of what religion is for a great many people around the world.

My own small experience on Facebook is only a fraction of this reality. It is a sample, a bit of bone from which we can extract the DNA of the digital age to infer what the whole may look like. I do not think my experience is in any sense definitive, but it is descriptive. It is what H.G. Wells might have called, "The Shape Of Things To Come."

And what about "church"? What does this mean for those of us raised in and committed to the spiritual communities we call church?

Again, I don't know, none of us know, not yet, but I am betting on the process, on what we have seen occur in all of the past generations and all of the past technologies that brought human beings together in religious community. I am believing that these same forces will be at work in ways that follow a pattern familiar to our spiritual history:

First, that the seeds of a faith, the small sound-bites of a religious impulse will spread out for people to grasp, one-by-one, individually, just as people came to my Facebook page one at a time.

Then, from these "plantings" of new spiritual visions, more and more people will seek one another out; they will self-structure a community, a "tent of meeting" called the Internet where they will develop their identity and design their meaning.

Finally, I think this process will not stop in virtual space any more than our solar system remained a flying pinwheel of dust. It will take a more concrete form. Over time, the online spirituality will produce just what my little Facebook page produced; what began as sayings online became words in print; it happened because, in the end, people wanted it to happen; they wanted to make the virtual the tangible; they wanted to engage that creative process.

Therefore, the digital spirituality of tomorrow may be the essence of the formation of a new sense of "church" for tomorrow. As local people discover one another, not only online, but nearby, in proximity, in the same geography, they will be drawn to put a face to what they have seen and heard. They will want to "touch" the ideas they have shared and, therefore, they will begin to create physical communities from the ether of online ideas. In a few more generations, the church may be social gatherings of local online "friends", like my Facebook friends, who have reached critical mass, been inspired by their own visions of spirituality, and taken the step out of the water of the electronic ocean onto the dry land of a physical embodiment of the next evolution of religion in human history.

And in the end, the *source* for all of that spirituality . . . that strange and mysterious impulse that has been with us since we once sat by firelight . . . will laugh and dance before us, winding its way around our human invention, always just beyond our reach, always beckoning us on to new discoveries and new ways to share our story . . . a vision of the next horizon…an impulse to belong . . . a longing for the Other that changes to adapt to any and every age . . . precisely because it never changes.

Thank you.

Focus

What does the writer mean when he says, "Spirituality is a message"?

Respond

Bishop Charleston observes that the community forming around his meditations posted on Facebook is "*an emerging, global spiritual community without borders . . . a gathering of human beings highly motivated to express their beliefs and ideas . . . a system for doing so at their fingertips that they trust more than institutions . . . a new paradigm of religion written in the short-hand of everyday experience. . . .*"

If you use Facebook or other social media platforms, think about your experience there with spirituality, with groups centered on spiritual or religious topics or themes, and with groups centered on other topics such as politics, local community, or family life. Where does your experience seem congruent with some of Bishop Charleston's observations of his Facebook experience? Where have you experienced significant differences? What are some of the best and worst aspects of using social media to form communities?

If you do not use social media platforms, what is your impression of them? What has contributed to your impression? Do you think you draw more from personal experience or culture? Reflect on reasons you would or would not consider joining a social media community focused on spirituality after reading this essay.

In what ways is the institutional Church being affected by digital life? How do you envision "church" in the future?

Practice

THEOLOGICAL REFLECTION BEGINNING WITH A TEXT (CULTURE SOURCE)

Identify a statement in the essay that seems especially strong to you. What kind of a picture could represent the position represented by that statement?

Find an essay statement or idea that you want to reflect on and create an image to capture something of that statement.

What seems to be the essence of the statement and/or the image you developed?

Explore the image from one or more theological perspectives based on terms used by Bishop Desmond Tutu: Wholeness/goodness (Creation), Brokenness/Separation from God (Sin), Recognition (Judgment), Reorientation (Repentance), and/or Restoration to wholeness (Redemption). Choose any one or more of the following questions to pose to your picture.

What wholeness or goodness does the image or statement reflect?

What demonstrates brokenness in the image/statement?

What represents recognition of the brokenness in the image/statement?

What reorientation is possible in the image/statement?

How would restoration come about for those in the image or statement?

What seems to be at the heart of the consideration at this point?

Connect

Bishop Charleston's essay presents his personal position about the future of spirituality, drawn from his personal experience.

What do you believe about the central matter of the image or statement you chose to explore?

Compare and contrast Bishop Charleston's position with your own. What seems to be "at stake" in the comparing and contrasting?

How does your personal experience connect with the image or statement you are exploring?

What spiritual practices do your faith tradition/background teach that support and sustain your spiritual life?

What do you see or understand in a new way?

Apply

What does your new (or reaffirmed) understanding suggest for your ongoing life in Christ?

In light of the reflection, name some implications for ministry in your life. Think especially of how this reflection contributes to living faithfully in a multicultural world.

Week Seventeen

YEAR ONE

Read

1 Samuel

2 Samuel

Collins, Chapter 11, "1 Samuel," and Chapter 12, "2 Samuel"

Note: Next week there also will be substantial reading.

Focus

First and Second Samuel paint a sweeping picture of the formation of the Jewish faith. Identify ideas, images, and actions that were vital to that faith community's spiritual life.

Create a chart in three columns that identifies concerns at the time of Samuel–concerns of Samuel, of the religious community, of the political constituent.

Describe Samuel's relationship with God.

YEAR TWO

Read

Powell, Chapter 11, "New Testament Letters," and Chapter 12, "Paul"

Focus

Terms and names to note: Pastoral Epistles; Prison Letters; Catholic Epistles; *cuneiform; ostraca; papyrus; amanuensis*; structure of epistles; Gamaliel; chiasm; pseudepigraphy; Muratorian Fragment; gospel (*euangelion*); Jesus' death, resurrection, and ascension; life after death; being made right with God (justification); new age of God; nature of Jesus

Using the material in Powell's Chapter 12, construct a first-person spiritual autobiography of Paul's life. For example, identify ten to twelve events that cover his entire life, such as, "I was born and raised as a member of the people of Israel within the tribe of Benjamin"; "I lived as a Pharisee observing the Jewish law"; "I studied at the feet of Gamaliel." Read through the events of Paul's life to get a sense of the flow of his life as a whole.

Note the context(s) of Paul's ministry and how different experiences shaped his spirituality–how he prayed and worshiped; revelations and/ or visions he reported; and other experiences that formed his relationship with God.

YEAR THREE

Read

MacCulloch, Chapter 11, "The West: Universal Emperor or Universal Pope"

Focus

Terms and names to note: Monastic revival in England; Cluny Abby's legacy, especially noting the agrarian economy, pilgrimage piety, origin of purgatory, and the Peace of God movement; universal monarchy; marriage as sacrament; rise of papacy–from Vicar of Peter to Vicar of Christ; clerical celibacy; dividing lay and clergy

Describe the growth struggles of the church in the West during this historical period.

What were the costs and promises of separating lay and clergy?

YEAR FOUR

Read

McIntosh, Chapter 1, "Mysteries of Faith," and Chapter 2, "The New Encounter with God: The Mystery of the Trinity"

Focus

Terms and names to note: mystery and meaning; three moments on the theological journey; Logos; habitus; communion; Trinity as mutual relationships; the *relationality* of God; becoming a person; Trinity vs. "tri-theist"; mutuality vs. subordination; mathematical vs. organic unity; interdependence; Herbert McCabe; Simone Weil; Elizabeth Johnson

Looking back over your life, when and where have you been aware that God is speaking? How are you cultivating a habit of theology? In what ways can you see your developing theology as a conversation with God? What is the relationship between your theology and your prayer life?

What role has Christian community played in your spiritual life? How have liturgy and sacraments shaped your identity as a person who seeks to live faithfully?

ALL YEARS

Respond

Gustavo Gutiérrez was born and raised in Peru. His academic work helped create the twentieth-century theological movement known as liberation theology. His theological writings emerged out of living in the midst of slum poverty in Rimac, Peru. The following excerpt from *We Drink from*

Our Own Wells helps clarify the relationship between theological reflection and spirituality.

> A spirituality is a walking in freedom according to the Spirit of love and life. This walking has its point of departure in an encounter with the Lord. Such an encounter is a spiritual experience that produces and gives meaning to the freedom of which I have been speaking. The encounter itself springs from the Lord's initiative. The scriptures state this repeatedly: "This is why I told you that no one can come to me unless it is granted him by the Father" (John 6: 65). "You did not choose me, but I chose you" (John 15: 16). A spiritual experience, then, stands at the beginning of a spiritual journey.[31] That experience becomes the subject of later reflection and is proposed to the entire ecclesial community as a way of being disciples of Christ. The spirituality in question is therefore not, as is sometimes said, an application of a particular theology. Let me begin by clarifying this point.

Spirituality and Theology

The adoption of a spiritual perspective is followed by a reflection on faith (therefore, a theology) as lived in that perspective. This sequence is clear from the historical course followed in all the great spiritualities.[32]

I Believe in Order to Understand

Spiritual experience is the terrain in which theological reflection strikes root. Intellectual comprehension makes it possible to carry the experience of faith to a deeper level, but the experience always comes first and is the source. St. Anselm (1033–1109) reminds us of this in a well-known passage:

> *Lord, I do not attempt to comprehend Your sublimity, because my intellect is not at all equal to such a task. But I yearn to understand some measure of Your truth, which my heart believes and loves. For I do not seek to understand in order to believe but*

---

31. The theme of an experiential Christology in Mark has been deepened by the recent work of Edward Schillebeeckx.

32. Many years ago, in a well-known book that was much misunderstood at the time, M. D. Chenu wrote as follows about doing theology: "The fact is that in the final analysis theological systems are simply the expressions of a spirituality. It is this that gives them their interest and grandeur. If we are surprised by the theological divergences found within the unity of dogma, then we must also be surprised at seeing one and the same faith give rise to such varied spiritualities. The grandeur and truth of Bonaventuran and Scotist Augustinianism is entirely derived from the spiritual experience of St. Francis, which inspired his sons; the grandeur and truth of Molinism derives from the spiritual experience of the Exercises of St. Ignatius. One does not get to the heart of a system via the logical coherence of its structure or the plausibility of its conclusions. One gets to that heart by grasping it in its origins via that fundamental intuition that serves to guide a spiritual life and provides the intellectual regimen proper to that life" (Le Saulchoir: *Una scuola di teologia* [Casale Monferrato: Marietti, 1982], 59; the French original dates from 1937).

I believe in order to understand. For I believe even this: that I shall not understand unless I believe.[33]

I believe in order to understand. The level of the experience of faith supports a particular level of the understanding of faith. For theology is in fact a reflection that, even in its rational aspect, moves entirely within the confines of faith and direct testimony. "This is the disciple who is bearing witness to these things, and who has written these things; and we know that his testimony is true" (John 21: 24).[34]

Study can become a spiritual discipline when learning arises out of an integration of experience and reading content. Theological reflection becomes a spiritual discipline whenever it allows a person "to carry the experience of faith to a deeper level." Reflection provides substance for spiritual growth whenever a person connects the wisdom of the past to the realities of present experience.

Often if a person is asked to identify times when they have encountered God, they go blank. The God-encounters that Gutiérrez points to are those that result from reflecting on things that matter to a person. Experiences that have existential import to the individual hold the potential for finding the work of "the Spirit of love and life." Too often "spiritual experiences" are confined to dramatic on-the-road-to-Damascus occurrences. As people give their studied attention through the discipline of theological reflection to incidents that matter, they can discover the "encounters with the Lord" as God's dwelling among humanity in most daily circumstances.

Develop the practice of noticing what matters to you; things that interest you; things that excite or disturb you; that you want to know more about. List three or four of such experiences. These can be beginning points for theological reflection either in a group or individually.

Use ABCD as you prepare what you will share in the seminar.

Practice

In the opening essay of this unit (page 101 above), Bishop Charleston writes:

When theologians say that religion should be a part of daily life, they are describing the actual practice of the people who interact on my Facebook wall. And I think what brings people back each day is not that they are empty vessels waiting to be filled, but full spiritual beings overflowing with the desire to connect with others who have a need for spiritual insight. If we are sincere about wanting to understand a "ministry of all believers", an egalitarian congregation or community where every person can feel empowered to participate and be who they are, then we need to observe the lessons

---

33. Proslogion 1, Anselm of Canterbury (New York: Edwin Mellon Press, 1974), vol. l, 3.

34. Gustavo Gutiérrez, *We Drink from Our Own Wells* (Maryknoll, NY: Orbis Books, 1985), 35–36.

of online spirituality, because that is precisely what is happening. In many ways, my Facebook page is a spiritual pit stop for people on a daily basis, a place where they come to read my few words, draw energy from the recognition that these words speak to their own life situation, and then launch out into the real world.

Use the four movements of EfM theological reflection to guide you in reflecting on spirituality and ministry in your life.

Identify

Consider the various contexts of your life, e.g., work, friends, family, times of leisure, study, physical life. How have you experienced a desire to connect within those various contexts and other contexts you might name?

Explore

What metaphor or image expresses what it is like to have a desire to connect in any of those contexts? What questions do you have for the image-world? What questions explore the "snapshot" from the standpoints of sin, judgment, repentance, or redemption?

Connect

Make connections between the image and our Christian tradition; our society or the culture we inhabit; and personal values or beliefs about openness to relationship. Write belief/value statements.

Apply

In terms of desire to connect, what do you see that you have not seen before? What contributes to and has implications for ministry in your daily life and for developing a spirituality that sustains and supports you in that ministry?

Week Eighteen

YEAR ONE

Read

1 Kings
2 Kings
Collins, Chapter 13, "1 Kings 1–16: Solomon and the Divided Monarchy,"
and Chapter 14, "1 Kings 17–2 Kings 25: Tales of Prophets and the End of
the Kingdoms of Israel and Judah"

Focus

Prophets speak God's truth and frequently have the most to lose. Difficulties arise when prophetic voices do not agree on what the "truth" is. Possible
responses to uncertainty are to wait to see which choice leads to the most
life-giving outcome, to decide what is correct for one personally and act
accordingly, or to view the variations as each addressing something of truth.
    How do you discern truth in the midst of uncertainty?

YEAR TWO

Read

The Letter to the Romans

Focus

The letter to the Romans likely contains verses you know as familiar quota-
tions. Note any changes in your perception of the meaning of these familiar
verses when read in their context.
    How is the letter structured? Name the key aspects of the case Paul builds
in the letter.

YEAR THREE

Read

MacCulloch, Chapter 12, "A Church for All People?"

Focus

Terms and names to note: Waldensians; *scholae* educational model; Peter
Abelard's *Theologia Christiana*; Dominic and Dominicans (Blackfriars); Fran-
cis, Franciscans, and Francis's *Testament*; Carmelites; Fourth Lateran Council;
transubstantiation (Real Presence); Thomas Aquinas; *Summa Theologiae* (Sum
Total of Theology); Anselm; Abelard; Hildegard of Bingen; *The Cloud of
Unknowing*; Meister Eckhart; Bridget of Sweden; Catherine of Siena

Consider how mysticism and other spiritual movements of this period were responses to prevailing contexts in society and the church.

YEAR FOUR

Read

McIntosh, Chapter 3, "The Splendor of God: The Mystery of Creation," and Chapter 4, "The Voice of God: The Mystery of Revelation"

Focus

Terms and names to note: to be something vs. to be; "creation out of nothing"; revelation through the Books of Nature and Scripture; concern for certainty; early modern scientific approach to knowing; Jesus as God's revelation; church as the eucharistic Body of the Word; Thomas Aquinas; Hadewijch of Brabant; Dorothy Sayers; Thomas Traherne; William Temple; William of Ockham; Francis Bacon; René Descartes; Austin Farrer; Richard Hooker; Hans Frei

What is the relationship between God's revelation and personal transformation?

How can knowing God come through practice?

ALL YEARS

Respond

Philip Sheldrake, in a 2009 article, links the practice of contemplative prayer to public action:

> A number of recent writers also suggest that contemplative spirituality is vital to the public realm. The Spanish theologian Gaspar Martinez notes that modern Catholic theologies engaged with public or political life also focus sharply on spirituality. He cites in particular Johannes Baptist Metz, Gustavo Gutierrez, and David Tracy—inspired in different ways by the Jesuit Karl Rahner.[35] Rahner himself defined prayer fundamentally in terms of relationship rather than merely as practices and went on to say that: "All positive religious acts which are directly and explicitly related, both knowingly and willingly, to God may be called prayer."[36] So, it is possible to think of our committed Christian lives as prayer and formal moments of meditation or common liturgy as explicit articulations of our larger business of living for God.[37]

---

35. Gaspar Martinez, *Confronting the Mystery of God: Political, Liberation and Public Theologies* (New York: Continuum, 2001).

36. Karl Rahner, "Prayer," *Encyclopedia of Theology* (London: Burns & Oates, 1975), 1275.

37. Philip F. Sheldrake, "Spirituality and Social Change: Rebuilding the Human City," *Spiritus: A Journal of Christian Spirituality*, vol. 9, no. 2, (Fall 2009), 139.

Identify several experiences that you have witnessed or lived that might be considered "positive religious acts which are directly and explicitly related, both knowingly and willingly, to God. . . ."

Additionally, how might you understand the spiritual disciplines of study, prayer, and worship as part of "our larger business of living for God."

Practice

THEOLOGICAL REFLECTION BEGINNING WITH THE CHRISTIAN TRADITION

Identify a focus.

Select something that caught your attention from your study this week. This can be a piece of scripture or something you read in your textbook that may have produced responses in you either of affirmation or disagreement or confusion.

Review the selected passage carefully.

Write three paragraphs about your response to that passage. Summarize/ focus your work with a statement or image of what you believe is the central idea of your response.

Explore your response.

Read through your paragraphs again, looking for any of the following:

Wholeness/goodness—What does your writing reveal about wholeness or goodness of creation?

Brokenness/Separation from God—What does your writing recognize as threats to wholeness or goodness or as brokenness or separation from God?

Recognition—How does your writing show that there is a threat to goodness or to a relationship to God? How would you recognize such a threat?

Reorientation—How is a reorientation to relationship with God discussed in what you wrote? How would you discuss that if you see no evidence of that reorientation in your writing? What would such a reorientation cost? What would it promise?

Restoration to wholeness—How does your writing express a possibility of restoration to wholeness?

Connect with the voices of our other three sources of wisdom (Culture, Position and Experience).

Again, drawing on your writing, mark places where you referred to personal experience or to something you have come across in the world around you, such as a reference to an author, a news story, or a television/movie presentation.

Your summary statement represents a personal position, something you believe. In what ways has the reflection affected that statement?

Apply this exercise to your life.

Write a prayer or litany, drawing from your reflections above.

To whom do you pray?

What do you offer?

What do you ask?

For whom do you pray?

How do you close your prayer?

Be prepared to offer what you are comfortable sharing at your seminar meeting.

Week Nineteen

YEAR ONE

Read

Yee: Chapter 2, "Intersections of Ethnicity, Gender, Sexuality, and Nation" by Vanessa Lovelace

Focus

Terms and names to note: covenantal relationship; identity defined by exclusiveness; gendered nationalism; exogamy; gendered boundaries; metaphors of cities and territory as women; masculine performativity; ritual purity; circumcision as sign of the covenant; women as keepers of purity; women and their sexuality as commodities; foreign wives; judges in the Book of Judges; female figures in Judges; womanist; "text of terror"; misogyny; necromancer; corvée; sex workers and widows; from exogamy to apostasy; image of black women as "jezebels"; the politics of belonging; Anne McClintock; Walter Brueggemann; Rahab; Musa Dube; Deborah; Jael; Wil Gafney; Delilah; Carol Meyers; David's wives; Solomon's foreign wives; Jezebel; Huldah; Asherah

What is your response to the violence toward women in these biblical stories?

What is your response to Lovelace's feminist analysis?

YEAR TWO

Read

Powell, Chapter 13, "Romans"

Focus

For Western Christianity, the Pauline teaching on justification, being in right relationship with God, is highly influential and formative. Which model or combination of Powell's "Models for Understanding Justification" best clarify the "justification issue" for you?

YEAR THREE

Read

MacCulloch, Chapter 13, "Faith in a New Rome"

Focus

Describe three or four characteristics of Orthodoxy.

Name distinctive qualities of Byzantine spirituality.

Name one or two reasons that understanding the iconoclastic controversy is important to you as you live in today's world.

In a nutshell, describe Photios's missionary strategy and the significance for Christianity in the twenty-first century.

YEAR FOUR

Read

McIntosh, Chapter 5, "The Humanity of God"

Focus

Terms and names to note: Incarnation; desire; God and humanity are not mutually exclusive; objections to the idea of incarnation; Chalcedonian Definition; "person"; John Neville Figgis; Frederick Denison Maurice; Charles Gore; Michael Ramsey; John Henry Newman

McIntosh says that transformation is painful because of distorted desire. How do you respond to that assertion?

What is your understanding of Incarnation? What in McIntosh's chapter surprised, challenged, or encouraged you?

ALL YEARS

Respond

James K. A. Smith, a philosophy professor at Calvin College in Grand Rapids Michigan, writes as a Christian who is at home in the Reformed tradition. He has begun a trilogy on the power of liturgy, especially practices that he calls cultural liturgies.

> If historic Christian worship and ancient spiritual disciplines carry the Story that seeps into our social imaginary, this is in no small part because liturgical practices are also intentionally aesthetic and tap into our imaginative core. It is no accident that the poetry of the psalms has long constituted the church's prayerbook, nor is it mere coincidence that the worship of the people of God has always been marked by singing. In these and countless other ways, the inherited treasury of formative disciplines has been characterized by an allusivity and metaphoricity that means more than we can say. There is a reason to our rhymes—a logic carried in the meter of our hymns and the shape of our gestures. Worship innovations that are inattentive to this may end up adopting forms that forfeit precisely those aspects of worship that sanctify perception by

forming the imagination.[38] Hence wise worship planning and leadership is not only discerning about content—the lyrics of songs, the content of a pastoral prayer, the message of a sermon—but also discerning about the kin/ aesthetic meaning of the form of our worship. We will be concerned not only with the what but also with the how, because Christian faith is not only a knowing-that but also a kind of know-how, a "practical sense" or *praktognosia* that is absorbed in the "between" of our incarnate significance. Because meter and tune each *means* in its own irreducible way, for example, the form of our songs is as important as the content. It is in this sense that to sing is to pray twice.[39] [40]

Summarize Smith's thoughts in a sentence or two.

How do Smith's thoughts relate to the material you studied this week?

What do Smith's thoughts contribute to the work of building a sustaining spirituality in the context of living faithfully in a multicultural world?

Use ABCD as you prepare what you will share in the seminar.

Practice

THEOLOGICAL REFLECTION BEGINNING WITH A PERSONAL POSITION

Identify a focus.
Begin with a focus on the value of music and poetry in worship and prayer.

Explore the focus.

Make a statement or image that reflects a connection between music and poetry and prayer or worship. For instance, someone might express that he only likes a certain type of music in worship because another kind destroys the sense of peace and beauty. Or another person might create an image that depicts people singing or playing instruments and the music notes floating outward towards God and the world.

---

38. This is not to say that there is no room for innovation or improvisation in Christian worship or that affirming the formative wisdom of historic Christian worship requires merely repeating status quo forms. The point is rather that improvisations and innovations of worship form need to be attentive to the narrative arc of the form and the unique "incarnate significance" of worship practices. Innovations that are "faithful" will preserve the plot of that narrative arc and deepen the imaginative impact of worship. Unfaithful and unhelpful innovations will be developments that are detrimental to the imaginative coherence of worship.

39. See Brian Wren's unpacking of this famous epigram in *Praying Twice: The Music and Words of Congregational Song* (Louisville: Westminster John Knox, 2000), particularly his discussion of how hymns "work" as "poems of faith," 253–94. My thanks to Kevin Twit for pointing me to this resource.

40. James K. A. Smith, *Imagining the Kingdom (Cultural Liturgies): How Worship Works* (Grand Rapids, MI: Baker Publishing Group), 174.

Explore your statement or image theologically, using a few of the questions provided, or create your own questions for the image:

How does the overall statement or image reflect wholeness or goodness?

What view of the world is contained in your statement or image?

What view of the relationship between God and creation exists in your statement/image?

How would someone experience God in that statement/image?

What might disrupt someone's relationship with God and others in that focus?

What view of restoration to wholeness is contained in the focus?

Connect to other sources.
State your personal belief that undergirds your initial image or statement.

How do your personal belief and the exploration above coincide and how do they conflict?

What troubles you about the comparison? What comforts you about the comparison?

Find one or two scripture references to the place of music and poetry in liturgy and worship. Or, select one or two hymns to connect to. How do those hymns relate to your focusing image or statement and to your position? How do they relate to the exploration?

What view of the world around you is contained in your personal belief statement, in the image, in the hymns you chose?

Apply what is learned to daily life.
Once a person takes a stance or affirms a position, implications for ministry begin to emerge.

What do you see for your ministry as you live day to day?

Close by composing a prayer adapting the structure of Jewish prayers:
Blessed are you, O Lord God, _____
(description of God),

for you _____

and make us _____

through _____. *Amen.*

Week Twenty

YEAR ONE

Read

Amos
Hosea
Collins, Chapter 15, "Amos and Hosea"

Focus

Terms and names to note: prophecy; royal archives of Mari; the essence of prophecy; focus of Amos's prophecy; Amos's themes of social justice and of condemnation of the cult; the day of the Lord; metaphor of marriage to a promiscuous woman; Gomer; two crucial differences between Amos and Hosea's messages; Hosea's basic critique

What contemporary prophetic statements like those of Amos or Hosea can you identify?

What themes or images in Amos and Hosea do you find troubling or challenging?

YEAR TWO

Read

1 Corinthians and 2 Corinthians
Powell, Chapter 14, "1 Corinthians," and Chapter 15, "2 Corinthians"

Focus

What is the context of the letters to the Corinthians?

Paul addresses a number of issues he has heard about the church in Corinth. What does he say about the spiritual life, prayer, worship, and faithful living?

YEAR THREE

Read

MacCulloch, Chapter 14, "Orthodoxy: More Than an Empire"

Focus

MacCulloch uses a sweep of eight centuries of history to show how Orthodoxy became more than an empire's religion. Describe the profile of Orthodoxy that comes through to you from the chapter. What key figures, ideas, and events contributed to what Orthodoxy became?

YEAR FOUR

Read

McIntosh, Chapter 6, "The Glory of Humanity: The Mystery of Salvation"

Focus

Terms and names to note: the nature of evil; baptismal renunciations; Orthodox and feminist critiques of Jesus suffering to appease God's wrath; Thomas Hobbes; Peter Abelard; *Christos Yannaras*; William Temple

McIntosh asks, what do we need to be saved from? How do you respond? What is your understanding of sin? What is your understanding of salvation? From what sources do you draw in forming your position on these key topics in theology?

ALL YEARS

Respond

Consider the following,[41]

> We are what we love, and our love is shaped, primed, and aimed by liturgical practices that take hold of our gut and aim our heart to certain ends. So we are not primarily *homo rationale* or *homo faber* or *homo economicus*; we are not even generically *homo religiosis*. We are more concretely *homo liturgicus*; humans are those animals that are religious animals not because we are primarily believing animals but because we are liturgical animals—embodied, practicing creatures whose love/desire is aimed at something ultimate.

Describe how liturgy relates to what you have been studying this week or over the past several weeks. How would you describe the value and meaning of liturgical or spiritual practices? How do such practices support a faith community's relationship to God?

Use ABCD as you prepare what you will share in the seminar.

---

41. James K. A. Smith, *Desiring the Kingdom (Cultural Liturgies): Worship, Worldview, and Cultural Formation* (Grand Rapids, MI: Baker Publishing Group, 2009), 40.

Practice

THEOLOGICAL REFLECTION BEGINNING WITH A PROVOCATIVE WORD

Identify: Select a word that has impact. For the purpose of this reflection and the practice, try the word "DESIRE."

What revelations on the meaning of the word do you have? Anything it denotes or connotes?

Explore: Next, ask the six "journalist's questions" about the feeling the word conveys:

WHO was involved when you were feeling DESIRE?
(Action . . . tell the stories from your life)

WHAT image comes to mind about the feeling DESIRE?
(Image . . . explore the metaphor—its reflection of wholeness, brokenness, recognition, reorientation, and/or restoration)

Connect
Go to the other sources we use to help explore meaning.

WHERE does this feeling come from and WHERE is it found in society?
(Source/Culture)

WHEN does this feeling come up in the Bible, lives of saints, hymns, and so forth?
(Source/Tradition . . . explore the world of tradition)

WHY is this feeling manifest in our lives? (Source/Position)

HOW might God redeem any negatives in this (Hope in Christ)

Consider insights and implications.

WHAT have you learned for the next time you feel DESIRE?

Apply
Write a collect using the outline:

Dear God . . .	(naming of God's aspects)
You . . .	(connect situation of the image to that aspect)
We pray that . . .	(petition of our hearts)
So that . . .	(result we desire)
Amen.	

Week Twenty-one

YEAR ONE

Read

Micah

Isaiah 1–39

Excerpt: "Micah," Supplemental Readings, pages 253–256, in Part II of this Guide

Collins, Chapter 16, "Isaiah"

Focus

Collins does not include some of the minor prophets (Micah, Nahum, Zephaniah, Obadiah, and Habakkuk) and some of the deuteron-canonical books (Tobit, Judith, Baruch) in this abridged edition of his *Introduction to the Hebrew Bible*. Since Micah is read in the Episcopal Daily and Revised Common Lectionaries and is often quoted in Episcopal circles, the commentary on Micah is excerpted from the longer work and printed in Part II of this Guide as a supplemental reading.

What does Micah 6:6–8 say to you about liturgy and worship?

Describe how imagery from Isaiah has contributed to Christian theology and worship.

Micah and First Isaiah contain familiar and often-quoted passages. Identify key verses from both prophets that speak to relationship with God.

YEAR TWO

Read

Galatians

Powell, Chapter 16, "Galatians"

Focus

What does Paul have to say to the Galatians about cultural differences? What does this letter contribute to developing a spirituality that sustains us in service to others?

YEAR THREE

Read

MacCulloch, Chapter 15, "Russia: The Third Rome"

Focus

Note the markers of Orthodox spirituality that developed in this period: church architecture; kenotic emphasis on Christ's example; the Holy Fool; monastic communities; hermits; Rublev's icon of the Trinity; liturgy; popular piety

Find a color image of Rublev's icon of the Trinity if you can and try using it as a focus for prayer. Describe your experience.

YEAR FOUR

Read

McIntosh, Chapter 7, "The Drama of the Cosmos"

Focus

Terms and names to note: Pentecost; persona; personhood at individual, communal, and cosmic levels; *apostello*; unlocking desire; "re-membered into God's Body"; the Trinitarian self-giving of God; baptismal moment; eucharistic moment; Augustine; Rowan Williams; Simone Weil; John Polkinghorne; Herbert McCabe

What role has the church played in your spirituality? How is communal life "sealed by the Holy Spirit in baptism and marked as Christ's own forever"? Connect if you can with an experience of this communal life that grounds your spiritual life.

ALL YEARS

Respond

Contemporary society is replete with challenges and opportunities, difficulties and delights, fear-fed violence and astonishing compassion—all set within the complexities of living in a multicultural world. Disciplines of study, prayer, and worship along with others lead Christians into a sustaining spirituality that supports and encourages ministry in daily life. Consider the following collect and its implications for ministry in a multicultural environment.

O God, who created all peoples in your image, we thank you for the wonderful diversity of races and cultures in this world. Enrich our lives by ever-widening circles of fellowship, and show us your presence in those who differ most from us, until our knowledge of your love is made perfect in our love for all your children; through Jesus Christ our Lord. Amen.[42]

---

42. Collect "For the Diversity of Races and Culture," *The Book of Common Prayer* (New York: Church Hymnal Corporation, 1979), 840.

Practice

Create a Rule of Life: Collaboration between Washington National Cathedral and the Friends of St. Benedict resulted in a Community of Reconciliation to provide an "ecumenical network of individuals seeking radical balance in life and a deepening commitment to reconciliation in the world." [43] This EfM *Guide* will draw from the booklet produced by the Community that provides guidance in creating a Rule of Life, a guide toward the journey of the reconciling life.

For the EfM community, a Rule of Life could be a balance of prayer, study, action, and reflection. Key elements in developing a Rule of Life are first listening—listen to what your life has revealed to you; listen to what voices of your family, friends, church, and society have revealed to you; listen to the still, small voice within your soul that reveals, prods, calls you. Second, commitment—be willing to open this gift for yourself and then to accept it. Third, time—make the time to create the beginning of the Rule, knowing that it is a lifelong activity. Fourth, reflection—take time to reflect on experience and to make a renewed commitment to the Rule. Fifth, hospitality—be open to God, to others, and above all to self, our humanness with all the glory and strength and weakness that encompasses.

Keep in mind that the term "Rule" used in this manner is a synonym for teaching, training, education, coaching. A Rule of Life serves as a guide to help an individual or group learn to attend to their relationship with God and others.

---

43. *Creating a Rule of Life*, Washington National Cathedral and The Friends of St. Benedict, 2009.[Washington, DC]

Creating a Rule of Life

The following will help to prepare the soil of your life for the activity of strengthening your spiritual muscle through a Rule of Life.

Listen

Review your spiritual autobiography. Be aware of when you "heard" God in your journey. Note what you have learned from others in your life that has been of significance to you regarding your spiritual growth. Consider what the world around you has been making known to you.

Commit

Make yourself available to God's Holy Spirit. Decide how you will do that.

Express your availability to God.

Time

Decide on how much time you are willing to give to focused spiritual practice of prayer, study, action, and reflection. What will you need to do to set time aside for creating a Rule?

Hospitality

Identify what you are going to have to "befriend" in yourself, to make room for, as you move into a more conscious life of prayer, study, reflection, and action. How will you make room for hospitality inside yourself? Think about what you will need to welcome from others.

Reflection

This may mean keeping a journal so that you can review aspects of your life as you encounter others and the circumstances of daily living and study and prayer. Taking time to reflect helps to deepen an understanding of how God is moving in a life and of how any of us might be allowing other distractions to pull us away. Reflection will include reviewing these five preparations regularly.

Create the Rule

Keep this simple to start. When you are ready (or at least willing), begin by writing, "With God's help I will . . . " and continue by making statements regarding the practices of:

Prayer

Study

Action

Reflection

UNIT FOUR

Integrating Belief, Behavior, and Doctrine in a Multicultural World

Week Twenty-two

ALL YEARS

Read

EfM provides resources and processes that are intended to support a person in living authentically as a Christian. Authenticity involves coherence, wholeness, integrity, and honesty. Something is incoherent whenever a dissonance occurs between thought and actions or even between two incongruent ideas. For example, a person receiving the benefits of twenty-first-century technology, whether received through medicine, transportation, or communication, may well hold beliefs that contradict or even deny the science that gave rise to the technological innovations. In addition, a person can easily fall into judging others by a double standard, by instituting a restrictive policy that is to be universally applied—that is, except for good friends. Beliefs (positions) and behaviors (actions) easily can become fragmented and separated from one another.

Integration brings the fragments of a person's life into conversation with one another so that the person moves toward wholeness in a process of continual growth that brings disparate fragments together. What does it mean to flourish in relationship with God as a human being, both as an individual and as a member of the human community? In traditional theological language, integration includes the theological process known by various terms: sanctification, deification, *theosis*, and participation in God. The integrative process at its deepest level is none other than the movement into communion with God. A. M. Allchin, in *Participation in God: A Forgotten Strand in Anglican Tradition*, concluded his introduction with:

> To become fully human, to realise our human potential, we need to enter into communion with our Creator. . . . There is nothing static about this communion. It is the beginning of a process which will lead us through death into life, life in this world and life in the world beyond this one, "an eternal process into the inexhaustible riches of the divine life."[44]

This unit in modest ways begins the process by focusing on gaps that exist between:

• beliefs and behavior;

• Christian teaching (doctrine) and personal beliefs;

• and behavior and doctrines.

---

44. A. M. Allchin, *Participation in God: A Forgotten Strand in Anglican Tradition* (Wilton, CT: Morehouse–Barlow, 1988), 6. The end of the quotation includes a phrase from John Meyendorff's *Byzantine Theology* (New York: Fordham University Press, 1974), 225–6.

As a person becomes aware of multicultural forces that shape the world, the gaps take on different nuances. In a homogeneous community, the belief and behavior gaps grow out of familiar tensions. In a multicultural world the tensions grow out of the soil of unfamiliarity and ignorance.

The tension between behavior and beliefs has a long history in Christianity. The technical theological terms that have developed are "orthodoxy" and "orthopraxis." Both, in their purest expressions, seek wholeness. Right belief (orthodoxy) is to bring wholeness and health. That same is to be said of right action (orthopraxis). However, history is replete with examples of how orthodox positions, separated from concerns about orthopraxis, wrought destruction and death.

The next several weeks call EfM participants into the work of integration. Integrating requires awareness, attention, and intention: awareness of one's beliefs, attention to one's actions, and a commitment to acting in ways that reflect core beliefs as much as human frailty and faithfulness allow. Such integration, congruency, and consistency are desirable in any context, multicultural or otherwise. Clarifying one's beliefs helps a person take action but also permits that person to adjust those beliefs in light of God's revelation through personal experience. However, clarity alone, without the humility to leave room for God's ongoing revelation through the Holy Spirit, can foster rigidity and lifelessness; there is no breath. Education for Ministry encourages ongoing examination of beliefs and behavior, and openness to revelation through study, reflection, group interaction, and prayer.

A diverse, multicultural world has long been a given. Encounters between differing cultures and their consequent differences in beliefs and practices are the "stuff" of history books. Conflict has frequently emerged in those encounters. The current reality of travel over highways both real and virtual makes the truth of our multicultural context even more evident and imminent. How can one know the truth? How can personal beliefs that differ permit peaceful coexistence and humble openness? How can "the holy" be worshipped? How can integration and wholeness be achieved?

The following excerpt from Diana Butler Bass's *Christianity after Religion: The End of Church and the Birth of a New Spiritual Awakening* provides a careful examination of what "believing" means. Her essay supports integration by increasing awareness of the dimensions of belief, both individual and doctrinal.

Believing[45]

The gym was packed for the baccalaureate service, not only with people, but also with anticipation, because a respected Christian scholar would be preaching on this happy academic occasion. Like everyone else, I looked

---

45. Diana Butler Bass, *Christianity After Religion: The End of Church and the Birth of a New Spiritual Awakening* (New York: HarperOne, 2012), 103–136.

forward to hearing his words of wisdom. Glancing through the program, I read the scripture passage chosen for the occasion:

> **Let the same mind be in you that was in Christ Jesus,**
> **who, though he was in the form of God,**
> > **did not regard equality with God**
> > **as something to be exploited,**
> **but emptied himself,**
> > **taking the form of a slave,**
> > **being born of human likeness,**
> **And being found in human form,**
> > **he humbled himself**
> > **and became obedient to the point of death—**
> > **even death on a cross.**
> **Therefore God also highly exalted him**
> > **and gave him the name**
> > **that is above every name,**
> **so that at the name of Jesus**
> > **every knee should bend,**
> > **in heaven and on earth and under the earth,**
> **and every tongue should confess**
> > **that Jesus Christ is Lord,**
> > **to the glory of God the Father.**

The sermon text is from the New Testament book of Philippians, ascribed to the apostle Paul (2:5–11). The unusual arrangement of the words indicates that the author is quoting a hymn, one most likely used in early Christian worship. It is an ancient and beautiful text.

It is also a rich theological passage. These words form the basis of the doctrine of kenosis, or the "emptying" of Christ. Jesus surrendered aspects of divinity in order to become human. Although there are many theological complexities regarding this idea, the spiritual intent of the passage moves from the humility of God toward a triumphant Jesus lifted up in glory.

The preacher mounted the pulpit dressed in the scarlet regalia conferred upon him by a prestigious university, thus reminding the audience of his authority to interpret the Bible's deeper meanings. As expected, he spoke of kenosis and humility. But then his tone changed. He told us that the word "Lord" used in the passage was the same word used for Caesar in the Roman Empire. Hence, "Jesus Christ is Lord" was to say "Jesus Christ is Caesar." This, of course, is true. He, however, proclaimed that one day Jesus—like Caesar of old—would exert his imperial will across the world and "force every living thing to its knees" to confess his name. At the end of time, God would make everyone worship him, just as everyone subject to Caesar had to pay homage to the Roman emperor—crawling backward to the imperial throne.

He continued likening Jesus to an imperialist warlord whose triumph over recalcitrant sinners, doubters, discontents, and rebels was assured. Emphasizing Jesus's regal glorification, he turned God into a vengeful king out to get those who had killed his son. Oddly enough, his tone was not that of a hellfire-and-brimstone evangelist. Instead, the entire lecture was delivered with stern intellectual certainty and detached professorial authority. "You will confess Jesus is Lord someday," he stated coolly. "Believe and confess this now."

I wanted to run out of the gym. Instead, I quietly slipped from my seat and stood shaking outside on the balcony. A friend, who was equally as distraught, joined me.

"How could he do that?" I exclaimed. "He turned Jesus into Caesar, a hierarchical and tyrannical monster!"

My friend draped her arm around my shoulder and said, "I think that's what he honestly believes. That's what many people believe."

I looked at her and replied hopelessly, "How could I believe that Jesus is like Caesar? That's not my God, and if that's what Christianity is, I don't want any part of it."

The Belief Gap

That sermon marked the moment in which I fell into the belief gap. I may have been walking near the edge for some time, but this sermon pushed me over. What once made sense no longer did. It was not a case of rejecting everything; rather, it was more like seeing from some angle you never imagined. Like slipping off a wet rock and finding yourself in the river rather than above it. There are lots of questions when you slip. Will I stop falling? Will I regain my footing? Will I reach solid ground? Where will the current take me?

That baccalaureate service was twenty years ago. I admit that through the haze of middle-age memory, I cannot recall the preacher's words verbatim. But I remember the increasing alarm I felt as he preached, and I wondered, "Is this what Christians really believe?" At an earlier time in my own life, I would have approved of the professor's sermon. On that evening, however, I heard Jesus presented in a deeply discomforting way, a way that made me understand why others might not like Jesus, embrace Christianity, or want to go to church. Up until then, I could not fathom the hurtful side of Christian faith. It was the first (but it would not be the last) time that I felt horrified by a presentation of Christian doctrine. A gap of belief opened before me. I knew that Christians believed as the professor did, but I just could not believe it anymore myself.

A few months later, I was preaching in a small, rural Lutheran church. The church was charming and old-fashioned, mostly older people with only a few young families; their weekly bulletin announced a quilting bee and plans for members to pave the parking lot the next Saturday. About seventy people gathered for church in a cozy sanctuary where we listened to the Bible being read and sang hymns together. After my sermon, we all shared a potluck lunch. A young woman sat next to me and shared her story of being in the belief gap.

She was a student at the nearby university, one of the only young and single members of the church. "I love this congregation," she said. "The people have become my family." She paused, and her voice dropped to a confessional whisper. "But I don't know what to say to my classmates when they ask me what I believe. Whenever I say 'I believe in Christianity,' they look at me as if I'm crazy. Besides, I don't even know if I believe 'in' Christianity or Lutheran doctrine or anything like that. I just experience how to love God and how God loves me through these people, by learning how to quilt and singing these hymns. I don't know what to call it, but it is less about believing and more about living. Does that still count as being Christian?"

Her confession remained with me, because it was one of the first gap stories that anyone shared with me. In the two decades since, the gap has widened, and the confessional whisper is gone. The gap is everywhere, and people are not afraid to share the news. On November 9, 2010, I was sitting at O'Hare airport and opened *USA Today*. A large advertisement trumpeted the gap:

> What some believe: "A woman should learn in quietness and full submission. I do not permit a woman to teach or to have authority over a man; she must be silent" (1 Timothy 2). What humanists think: "The rights of men and women should be equal and sacred" (Robert Ingersoll).

It was an ad for an atheist group. Between the time of the student's confession and that November day, hundreds of people have trusted me with their stories of not believing–not believing that wives must submit to their husbands, not believing in the virgin birth, not believing in an inerrant Bible, not believing in hell, not believing that Jesus is the only way to salvation, not believing that only one religion is true, not believing that the institutional church is important, not believing in Jesus, not believing in the resurrection, not believing that God cares or heals or loves, not believing that God exists. They don't believe in Christianity anymore. When many people slip from believing into not believing, they find it difficult to regain their footing. Maybe because they are trying to climb back on the same rock. Or maybe because they know they cannot go back to the path that landed them in the drink in the first place.

Despite the differences of detail in testimonies, almost all of them share an important assumption about belief. "Belief" is the intellectual content of faith. Typically, belief entails some sort of list–a rehearsal of ideas about God, Jesus, salvation, and the church. What to believe? If I am slipping, do I hold on tighter or let go? If I no longer believe, am I still a Christian? Am I spiritual, but not religious? An agnostic? An atheist?

Belief, especially Christian belief, has entered a critical stage in Western society. Masses of people now reject belief. For many centuries, Christians have equated faith with belief. Being faithful meant that one accepted certain ideas about God and Jesus, especially as articulated in creedal statements. Denominations specified what adherents must believe about the sacraments, salvation, and authority. Confirmation in faith entailed memorization and recitation of doctrine or facts about the Bible. Some groups even insisted that true Christians must further believe particular ideas about drinking, women, science, the end times, or politics. Layers of beliefs, stacked through the centuries from the apostles to our own times. Alongside this weighty pile of beliefs, it often seems as if Christians actually live their beliefs less—beliefs like "God is love" or "Blessed are the peacemakers" or "Love your neighbor as yourself"—thus leading to often heard charges of hypocrisy.

With this accretion of beliefs, a corresponding incredulity spread through Western culture, leading to doctrinal boredom, skepticism, agnosticism, and atheism. As science, history, and psychology offered ever more sophisticated understandings of the universe and human experience, some Christians became increasingly hostile to secular knowledge, building museums to creationism, proclaiming that America is a Christian nation, and excommunicating those who would question the existence of hell. Put simply, as they reacted to unbelief, certain Christians asked for more belief about increasingly unbelievable things.

Meanwhile, other Christians began to wonder if belief was even the point. At the college where the professor who delivered the baccalaureate sermon taught, for example, the majority of younger faculty signed the institution's doctrinal statement with crossed fingers and a knowing wink to their friends, telling sympathetic souls that they "agreed in spirit" with the statement, even if the exact words rang hollow. Eventually, they revised their statement of faith to be more open and inclusive. It is not only the case that the Western world has grown weary of doctrine, but that Christianity itself is changing—shifting away from being a belief-centered religion toward an experiential faith.

Many philosophers, scholars, and theologians have explored the shift in Western culture away from beliefs toward experience, a move from rationalism toward practice. Harvey Cox proposed that Christianity reflects this broader transformation regarding human knowledge and experience by dividing church history into three ages: the Age of Faith, the Age of Belief, and the Age of the Spirit. During the first period, roughly from the time of Jesus to 400 CE, Christianity was understood as a way of life based upon faith (i.e., trust) in Jesus. Or, as Cox states, "To be a Christian meant to live in his Spirit, embrace his hope, and to follow him in the work that he had begun." Between 300 and 400, however, this dynamic sense of living in Jesus was displaced by an increasing emphasis on creeds and beliefs, leading Professor Cox to claim that this tendency increased until nascent beliefs "thickened into catechisms, replacing faith *in* Jesus with tenets *about* him. . . . From an energetic movement of faith [Christianity] coagulated into a phalanx of required beliefs."[46] Cox argues that the Age of Belief lasted some fifteen centuries and began to give way around 1900, its demise increasing in speed and urgency through the twentieth century. We have now entered into a new phase of Christian history, which he calls the Age of the Spirit.

If the Age of Faith was a time of "faith *in* Jesus" and the Age of Belief a period of "belief *about* Christ," the Age of the Spirit is best understood as a Christianity based in an "experience *of* Jesus." The Age of the Spirit is nondogmatic, noninstitutional, and nonhierarchical Christianity, based on a person's connection to the "volatile expression" of God's Spirit through mystery, wonder, and awe. "Faith is resurgent," Cox claims, "while dogma is dying. The spiritual, communal, and justice-seeking dimensions of Christianity are now its leading edge. . . . A religion based on subscribing to mandatory beliefs is no longer viable."[47] When questioned by an interviewer about his thesis, Cox further explained:

> What I see, and what a lot of others see too, is that people frequently want to refer to themselves now as not really "religious," but "spiritual." I used to be very suspicious of that. But I began asking questions and finding out what the dimensions of the term are. . . . What I think it really means is that people want to have access to the sacred without going through institutional and doctrinal scaffolding. They want a more direct experience of God and Spirit. And I don't think it's really going to go away. This is an increasing tendency across the board.[48]

Accordingly, Christianity is moving from being a religion about God to being an experience of God. In a real sense, both the baccalaureate speaker and the student questioning her faith at the Lutheran church I preached at were right. The professor's world of "belief about" God was eroding, leading him to reassert ideas he believed necessary to faith; and the student's intuition regarding an experiential future has been coming to pass, leading her to question the older definitions of "Christian." Although I have no idea what happened to the young woman, the professor has called for a new fundamentalism, writing books that few people read, arguing that what is old is better, and defending narrow understandings of belief and piety, something clearly evident in his sermon two decades ago. If one believes that Christianity is about belief, taking refuge in fundamentalism is logical. On the face of things, it sometimes seems as if fundamentalism may be the only vibrant form of faith. As Harvey Cox argues, however, "Fundamentalisms, with their insistence on obligatory belief systems, their

---

46. Harvey Cox, *The Future of Faith: The Rise and Fall of Beliefs and the Coming Age of the Spirit* (San Francisco: HarperOne, 2009), 5–6.

47. Ibid., 213, 221.

48. Nathan Schneider, "Age of Spirit: An Interview with Harvey Cox," October 30, 2009, blogs.ssrc.org/tif/2009/10/30/age-of-spirit-an-interview-with-harvey-cox

nostalgia for a mythical uncorrupted past, their claims to an exclusive grasp on truth . . . are turning out to be rearguard attempts to stem a more sweeping tidal change."[49] The professor's "Jesus/Caesar" was like Romulus Augustus, the last ruler of a collapsing Roman Empire.

The Religious Question: What Do I Believe?

Despite such obvious changes, most religious institutions act as if the gap does not exist and that the questions have not substantially changed in recent decades. Conservative or liberal, evangelical or mainline, Protestant or Catholic, denominations and churches still provide answers to questions *about* God. Most assume that dogma and doctrine are the right approach to holy matters, differing only on the details of their preferred answers. Religion answers *what* questions: What should one believe? What do Christians believe?

This is bad news for Christianity. The *what* questions are the very questions causing people to slip into the gap. Doctrine is seen as not only divisive, but as contrary to the message Jesus himself taught. Many people stumble on the creeds, thinking them to be a sort of doctrinal test for church membership, and are unable to recite them in full or even part. As a pastor asked me, "Can we stop reciting the creed now? I'm tired of it driving people away from church." Theologian Dwight Friesen puts it bluntly—and speaks for many—when he says that Jesus had no interest in orthodoxy, but rather offered his followers "a full and flourishing human life."[50] At an event I was leading recently, an Episcopal priest inquired, with a sense of hopeful anticipation, "Isn't it true that belief-oriented faith is disappearing?" His colleague chimed in, "My generation doesn't really care about doctrine; that's just not the way we think." Indeed, even among Christians, there is a sense of mild relief, maybe even quiet jubilation, that the Age of Belief is giving way to something else.

The erosion of belief has occasioned many a new jeremiad from those who, like the professor, feel threatened by the current situation. The college faculty who fudge the truth about the doctrinal statement or the clergy who wish they could get rid of creeds are, both in my experience and as surveys seem to point out, fairly typical. Yet they fear someone finding out—that they might lose their jobs in religious institutions that continue to mark their boundaries with such beliefs *about* God. It is not only loss of employment or community that they fear, but the cultural ridicule that comes upon people pondering such questions. The media scorn them as "cafeteria Christians" and "spiritual consumers" who pick and choose what they like about faith, while conservative pastors accuse

---

49. Cox, *Future of Faith*, 2.

50. Dwight Friesen, "Orthoparadoxy: Emerging Hope for Embracing Difference," in Doug Pagitt and Tony Jones, eds., *An Emergent Manifesto of Hope* (Grand Rapids, MI: Baker, 2007), 204.

them of vacuity and spiritual shallowness and use them as scapegoats for all that is wrong in religion.

It may be easy to dismiss anxiety about belief as anti-intellectualism or as a theological problem associated with Western religious decline. But something else is at work. On the face of it, *what* questions should be benign. After all, *what* is a fairly objective question, a request that seeks information. "What time is it?" "What color is the sky?" "What day does school start?" "What would you like for dinner tonight?" Even more philosophical questions, like "What is art?" or "What do you want to do with your life?" assume a well-formed opinion, if not a conclusive answer.

During the last few centuries, to ask "What do you believe?" in the religious realm was to demand intellectual answers about things that cannot be comprehended entirely by the mind. Thus masked as objective truth, religion increasingly became a matter of opinion, personal taste, individual interpretation, and wishful thinking. People became quite militant about the answers they liked the best. The *what* questions often divided families and neighbors into rival churches, started theological quarrels, initiated inquisitions, fueled political and social conflict, and led, on occasion, to one losing one's head.

It's time to face up to the truth: an increasingly large number of people are experiencing the *what* questions in profoundly negative ways. In the minds of many, dogma deserves to die.

SPIRITUAL QUESTION I:
How Do I Believe?

"You're a Christian?" quizzed my acquaintance. "How do you believe in that? I don't know how I could ever believe that."

Belief is not going to disappear, and it will not become a relic of the religious past. Rather, as religion gives way to spirituality, the question of belief shifts from *what* to *how*. People generally assume that they know the *what* of religion. For example, they may know that Christians believe that Jesus died and was raised, that Jews believe that Moses freed the slaves from Egypt, or that Buddhists believe that the Buddha achieved Enlightenment. Indeed, in many years of discussing faith in public, few have ever asked me, "What do Christians believe?" *What* is not the issue—the world of religion is a world full of *what*. Instead, they have asked *how*. Belief questions have become, "How do you believe?" "How could I ever believe?" "How does this make sense?" "How would believing this make my life different?" or "How would this change the world?"

How differs from *what*. "How do I get to your house?" "How would that move change my family's life?" "How do I love?" *How* is the interrogator of direction, of doing, of curiosity, of process, of learning, of living. When we ask *how*, we are not asking for a fact, conclusion, or opinion. Rather, we are seeking a hands-on deeper knowledge of the thing—a neighborhood or city, a craft or recipe, an open possibility, an idea, a sense of ourselves or of a relationship. *How* moves us around in the question. Instead of being above the information, giving an expert opinion about something, *how* weaves our lives with the information as we receive, review, reflect, and act upon what we sought. *How* provides actionable information; we can choose to act upon the answer or not, and we choose the extent of our action. *How* is a question of meaning and purpose that pushes people into a deeper engagement in the world, rather than memorizing facts. Parker Palmer refers to the shift from *what* to *how* as part of the "inner search" that enables individuals to develop the "habits of the heart" necessary to forming both a grounded moral life and a caring community. He asserts that inner-life questions are the sort of questions Americans ask most regularly, and the *how* questions are the ones our schools and churches often fail to address. Institutions cannot "dictate" answers to *how* questions. Instead, spiritual communities must open space to engage the inner search: "*How can I connect with something larger than my own ego?*" This, Palmer insists, involves going "beyond teaching the *what* of things into the labor-intensive process of teaching the *how* of things."[51]

From *what* to *how* is a shift from information *about* to experience *of*. *What* is a conventional religious question, one of dogma and doctrine; how is an emerging spiritual question, one of experience and connection. We have lived through many generations of *what* and have nearly exhausted ourselves by doing so. But *how* opens the question of belief anew: How do I believe? How do we believe? How does belief make a difference? How is the world transformed by believing? Belief will not entirely go away. Rather, "believing *about*" appears to be going away. Belief itself is being enfolded into a new spiritual awareness as belief questions morph from *what* to *how*, from seeking information about God to nurturing experience of the divine.

SPIRITUAL QUESTION 2:
Who Do I Believe?

Several years ago, I asked students in a seminary class a question: "To whom do you turn when you have an ethical or spiritual concern?" One quickly said, "I ask my friends." Another laughed, saying, "I ask Google." For the next few minutes, they came up with a variety of answers, mostly those involving personal relationships, the media, or the Internet. Interestingly enough, none of these future pastors said that they asked a bishop, priest, or seminary professor about their religious questions, much less read a book of canon law or turned to a creed.

The question is, of course, a question of religious authority. Who provides trustworthy answers to difficult questions? Once upon a time, Americans would have deferred to the clergy, a teacher, or a parent on issues of

---

51. This paragraph follows the argument laid out by Parker J. Palmer, *Healing the Heart of Democracy: The Courage to Create a Politics Worthy of the Human Spirit* (San Francisco: Jossey-Bass, 2011), 119–150.

belief. When it comes to questions of meaning and purpose, however, it no longer seems adequate to say, "The church teaches," "Christians have always believed," or "the Bible said it, so I believe it." External authorities do not carry the weight they once did. Thus, questions of belief have not only morphed from *what* to *how*, but they necessarily include the secondary dimension of *who*. My seminary students did not look to conventional institutional authorities for answers. Instead, they looked to relationships and online sources and social networks. Who is trustworthy in the search for meaning?

As the question of *how* is experiential, so is the question of *who*. In the early twenty-first century, trustworthiness is not simply a matter of an expert who holds a degree or a certain role in an institution. Rather, authority springs from two sources: one, relationship, and two, authenticity. People trust those with whom they are friends or feel they could be friends—thus the presidential election question, "With which candidate would you rather have a beer?" Authority comes through connection, personal investment, and communal accountability, rather than submission to systems or structures of expertise. Related closely to friendship is the test of authenticity. Something is true and trustworthy because it springs from good motives and praiseworthy intentions, with results that prove to increase happiness and make peoples' lives better. Practicing what one preaches is a mark of spiritual truth, and humanity and humility foster trust. Although certain people will always hanker for authoritarian or charismatic leaders, there is a much broader longing for authentic leaders in these times—those whose message and actions validate their deepest beliefs. In the emerging spiritual culture, *what* matters much less than who is sharing the news, and the messenger has become the message.

This is a very interesting development in terms of faith. After all, Christians, Jews, and Muslims consider God to be personal and truthful, the Messenger of Good News to humankind. Thus, religious organizations, ordained leaders, and conventional creeds recede in importance as mediators in favor of direct friendship with God through prayer and discernment as means to spiritual understanding. Friendship with God can be mystical and individual, but it is also communal and corporate—every major faith asserts that friendship with God is strengthened through friendship with our neighbor. Ultimately, spiritual authority rests in the voice of God, the voices of community, and in our own voices. It is a harder path to hear answers than to ask someone to give us an answer, but it is the path that many people have embarked upon.

Spiritual Insight: Belief as Experience

As demonstrated in the polling data, about 9 percent of Americans understand themselves as "religious" only. They are probably still greatly concerned with the *what* of faith. About a third of Americans describe themselves as "spiritual" only. They have embarked on a quest of *how* to relate to transcendent things. But half of all Americans claim to be "spiritual and religious." For them, *what* is not necessarily being replaced by *how*; the *what* of religion is being redefined by the *how*. When belief springs from and is rewoven with experience, we arrive at the territory of being spiritual and religious: experiential belief.

Understanding belief-as-experience is not a new concept. Actually, it is much closer to the original definition of believing than the popular definitions we have inherited from more recent centuries. In his essay "Believing: An Historical Perspective" (first published in 1977), Wilfred Cantwell Smith argues for a distinction between "faith" and "belief" based upon the etymologies of the terms. Although the words overlapped at one time, he says, the "English word 'believe' has, in usage, connotation, and denotation, undergone an arresting transformation" in recent centuries—one that has had an unprecedented negative impact on Western religious life.[52]

"To believe" in Latin (the shaping language for much of Western theological thought) is *opinor, opinari*, meaning "opinion," which was not typically a religious word. Instead, Latin used *credo*, "I set my heart upon" or "I give my loyalty to," as the word to describe religious "believing," that is, "faith." In medieval English, the concept of *credo* was translated as "believe," meaning roughly the same thing as its German cousin *belieben*, "to prize, treasure, or hold dear," which comes from the root word *Liebe*, "love."[53] Thus, in early English, to "believe" was to "belove" something or someone as an act of trust or loyalty. Belief was not an intellectual opinion. As Smith says:

> The affirmation "I believe in God" used to mean: "Given the reality of God as a fact of the universe, I hereby pledge to Him my heart and soul. I committedly opt to live in loyalty to Him.". . . Today the statement may be taken by some as meaning: "Given the uncertainty as to whether there be a God or not, as a fact of modern life, I announce that my opinion is 'yes.' I judge God to be existent."[54]

In previous centuries, belief had nothing to do with one's weighing of evidence or intellectual choice. Belief was not a doctrinal test. Instead, belief was more like a marriage vow—"I do" as a pledge of faithfulness and loving service to and with the other. Indeed, in early English usage, you could not hold, claim, or possess a belief about God, but you could cherish, love, trust in, or devote yourself to God.

From a historical perspective, the misidentification of faith-as-experience and belief-as-opinion also involved the translation of the Bible from Greek

---

52. Wilfred Cantwell Smith, *Believing: An Historical Perspective* (Oxford: One World, 1998), 40. First published as *Belief and History* (Charlottesville: Univ. of Virginia Press, 1977), Marcus Borg has written about the shift of the language of belief. See his *The Heart of Christianity: Rediscovering a Life of Faith* (San Francisco: HarperOne, 2003), chapter 2, 26–42; and *Speaking Christian*, chapter 10.

53. Ibid., 41.

54. Ibid., 44

(the other theology-shaping language of Christian thought) into English. In Greek, there is a verb for the experience of beloving God: "to faith" (i.e., *pist-*). In English, however, "faith" is a noun and not a verb. With no equivalent active word, English translators rendered the Greek verb "to faith" in English as "to believe." The verb "to believe" (meaning "to belove, prize, or treasure," as explained above) appears frequently in the English Bible. It typically occurs without a direct object, in the forms "I believe" or "I believe you" (or "him," "her," or "God"). This reinforces its original meaning of "belove" as a general confession of trust or a specific disposition of trusting someone—it is a personal and relational action initiated by love. In only 12 percent of scriptural cases does "to believe" appear as "I believe that. . . ," an impersonal affirmation about something.

To read the Bible with this understanding orients our attention away from cognitive speculation about God toward the state and direction of our hearts. For example, John 3: 16 might be the most well-known Bible verse across North America as a result of signs held up by evangelistically minded Christians at sporting events: "For God so loved the world that he gave his only Son, so that everyone who believes in him won't perish, but will have eternal life" (CEB). If we think that "believe" means doctrinal truth, then the verse means "everyone who agrees that Jesus is the Son of God won't perish" or "everyone who thinks that Jesus is the Second Person of the Trinity won't perish." According to its more ancient rendering, however, the verse would better read, "everyone who trusts in Jesus" or "everyone who directs his or her heart toward Jesus" will not perish. You may or not may want to trust in or incline your love toward Jesus, but it is an entirely different, and more spiritually compelling, invitation than an offer of debate about Jesus. And it is a fresh way of understanding a widely misused text.

Smith demonstrates how belief shifted away from "trusting the beloved" toward being a word that is "increasingly technocratic and thing-oriented," outside the realm of personal relationships.[55] The shift occurred gradually in the eighteenth century, mostly through the work of the influential philosopher David Hume. When people use the word "believe" today, it is often for factually erroneous opinions, disconnected from any aspect of interpersonal trust or love: "I believe that dinosaurs walked the earth at the same time as human beings," or "I don't believe in global warming." No wonder people can no longer "believe" in Christianity. For masses of contemporary people, to believe in Christianity is like believing in aliens or that President Obama was born in Kenya, since "the word [belief] denotes doubt, and connotes falsehood."[56] Thus, Smith claims, "The idea that believing is religiously important turns out to be a modern idea. . . . [A] great modern heresy of the Church is the heresy of believing. Not of believ-

---

55. Ibid., 58.
56. Ibid., 65.

ing this or that, but of believing as such."[57] Christianity was never intended to be a system or structure of belief in the modern sense; it originated as a disposition of the heart.

From an ancient perspective—whether of Latin or Greek, of the creeds or the Christian scriptures—the words "belief" and "believing" implicitly carried within them relational and lived dimensions.

Accordingly, you cannot "believe" distinct from trust, loyalty, and love. Wilfred Cantwell Smith, analyzing this history some forty years ago, had a dim view of the future of belief. He writes:

> The English "belief," which used to be the verbal sign designating allegiance, loyalty, integrity, love, commitment, trust, and entrusting, and the capacity to perceive and to respond to transcendent qualities in oneself and one's environment—in short, faith; the Christian form of God's most momentous gift to each person—has come to be the term by which we designate rather a series of dubious, or at best problematic, propositions.[58]

Smith clearly wished this were not the case, but held little hope that it might change.

A surprising thing has happened, however. In those same forty years, in some quarters at least, there has been a return to the older understanding of belief-as-trust. Half of the American population now claims to have had "a mystical experience," a statistic that suggests we are in the process of returning to the idea of faith as an encounter with God. As religion in the modern sense fails, we appear to be busily restitching the ancient fabric of belief. It seems we may have entered a new (or perhaps very old) theological door, the way of experiential belief.

Spiritual and Religious: Experiential Belief

The Priority of Experience. I spend most of my work time with mainline, liberal, and progressive Protestants, religious groups with high educational attainments and little patience for faith without reason. They are doubters and skeptics (that is, indeed, their spiritual gift) and downright skittish regarding experience. Despite the fact that many of them share the cultural anxiety about the creeds (worrying that the creeds are not factually true), they are not entirely comfortable with the shift toward experiential faith either. Put the words "experiential" and "belief" in the same sentence, and you are asking for trouble.

At a United Church of Christ clergy education day, I explained Harvey Cox's chronology, saying: "Professor Cox argues that the 'Age of the Spirit' began around the turn of the twentieth century with the modern Pentecos-

---

57. Ibid., v.
58. Ibid., 69.

talism movement. That was the first expression of the turn toward experience." Silence filled the room.

Then one pastor said, "You mean we're all going to become Pentecostals? My congregation would rather die first! Faith isn't about feelings. It has to have intellectual content."

Her reaction is not unique. When Americans think about religious experience, the first thing that often comes to mind is some form of religious enthusiasm—a fulminating revivalist, a frenzied faith healer, or a fainting congregant. A significant tension in American religious identity is shaped by two enduring images—one, the orderly parish church, and the other, the exuberant tent meeting. Since the First Great Awakening, Americans have often felt forced to choose: the pew or the anxious bench, the prayer book or the praise chorus, restraint or revival, mind or heart? Or, as one of my Facebook correspondents bemoaned, "Why is it that the choice among churches always seems to be the choice between intelligence on ice and ignorance on fire?"

Religious experience and the Spirit are often associated with Pentecostalism, the global form of Christianity that emphasizes the work of the Holy Spirit in and through religious ecstasy, miraculous gifts, and healing. In the 1880s and 1890s, an intense and radical form of evangelical religion took hold in the form of healing revivals and holiness meetings emphasizing the power of the "Holy Ghost baptism." On January 1, 1901, Agnes Ozman, a Topeka Bible school student, prayed to receive the gift of the Holy Spirit. After her friends laid hands on her to pray, she began to speak in tongues— thus began the modern Pentecostal movement.

An African-American evangelist named William Seymour heard Agnes's story and embraced the new teaching. He moved in 1906 from the American heartland to Los Angeles, where his preaching sparked the Azusa Street revival and thence spread around the world.[59] For Pentecostals, the experience of speaking in tongues validated and confirmed true faith and empowered believers to do God's will. For them, faith, feeling, action, and experience were a tightly woven cloth of Christian life, the threads of which could not be pulled apart. This experiential rendering of faith made sense to the poor, the deprived, working-class people, and rising middle-class folks, many of whom felt marginalized by liberal elites and their restrained religion. In Pentecostalism, many outsiders discovered a new sense of self and God and a sort of spiritual land of opportunity. By the end of the century, Pentecostalism had given birth to scores of new denominations, claiming hundreds of millions of adherents in nearly every country on earth.

Pentecostalism developed, however, within a larger historical context—one increasingly fascinated with the territory of human and divine experience. Grant Wacker, a leading expert on Pentecostal history, points out the similarities between Pentecostalism, Protestant liberalism, and Roman Catholi-

---

59. Grant Wacker, *Heaven Below: Early Pentecostals and American Culture* (Cambridge, MA: Harvard Univ. Press 2001), 4.

cism at the turn of the twentieth century. Despite the "vast gulf" between Pentecostals and liberals, Wacker suggests that both traditions emphasize "the nearness and salvific power of God's Spirit in history," while Roman Catholics "evince unprecedented interest in the Holy Spirit's sanctifying presence."[60] As the "Age of the Spirit" dawned, radical evangelicals, liberal Protestants, and Roman Catholics alike were caught up in a quest for transforming religious experience–they wanted to know how God's Spirit made a difference in their lives and the world around them.

This was certainly fostered by a more general, and even secular, impulse toward understanding the nature of human behavior–how experiences molded human personality, thought, and action and how personality, thought, and action were shaped by experience. As the Pentecostal movement began in the early years of the twentieth century, Sigmund Freud published the first of his books exploring the connection between conscious and unconscious experience and its relationship to human development.

With enthusiastic Pentecostals on one side and secular Freud on the other, liberal Protestants also opened up issues of religious experience as a way to protest spiritual ennui in organized religion. The most influential of these was American Transcendentalism, a movement that appeared some fifty years before Pentecostalism and Freud, replete with its rejection of church in favor of nature mysticism, poetry, and spiritual solitude. Although not every Protestant embraced Transcendentalism, the movement created a yeasty spiritual environment in which experiential religion could eventually grow. By the time Protestant liberalism emerged in the late 1800s, its most thoughtful proponents argued that experience was central to vital faith.

The insight regarding experience was partly the result of the American religious environment and partly the result of the theological influence of the first liberal Protestant theologian, Friedrich Schleiermacher, who wrote:

> Religion is the outcome neither of the fear of death, nor of the fear of God. It answers a deep need in man. It is neither a metaphysic, nor a morality, but above all and essentially an intuition and a feeling. . . . Dogmas are not, properly speaking, part of religion: rather it is that they are derived from it. Religion is the miracle of direct relationship with the infinite; and dogmas are the reflection of this miracle.[61]

There are many ways to criticize Schleiermacher, but if you read these words simply and directly, you intuit that there is something to them. Religion is not its accretions of dogma; rather, faith is a divine encounter. Experience needed to be the starting place to engage a skeptical, dogma-weary world. Belief is "derived" from a "direct relationship with the infi-

---

60. Wacker, *Heaven Below*, 4.

61. Friedrich Schleiermacher, *Addresses on Religious Experience* (1799), quoted in Kedourie, Elie, *Nationalism* Praeger University Series, 1961, 26.

nite." Beliefs gain credibility insofar as they spring from rightly directed human experience.

William James wrote of this impulse in his *Varieties of Religious Experience* in 1902, an essay on the "feelings, acts, and experiences of individual men in their solitude, so far as they apprehend themselves to stand in relation to whatever they may consider the divine."[62] James discussed saints and mysticism and philosophy. In the end, James concluded that religious experience is useful even if not provable. Experiences connect human beings with an "altogether other dimension of existence" and enable people to live more meaningful lives.[63]

Thus, at the beginning of the twentieth century, Pentecostalism and liberal Protestantism—as well as various streams of mystical Catholicism—came together in a quest for an experience of God. The Age of the Spirit dawned not only with Pentecostal fervor, but experiential faith also arrived with the reflections of William James at Harvard and in the candle-lit prayer of Roman Catholics to their saints. And it was not only Christians exploring the realm of the Spirit—restless seekers appeared across the landscape with new spiritual practices and formed new communities.[64] These groups competed with each other, to be sure, and often did not think the adherents of other ways would find salvation. But they all shared the traits of experiential belief—a practical spirituality that transformed beliefs about God into a living relationship with the divine. The impulse toward experience grew, developed, and deepened throughout the twentieth century, leading to increasing awareness that the nature of Christianity itself was changing. Mysticism and religious experience were no longer limited to a spiritual elite in a monastery or a forest cabin. As once predicted by the ancient Hebrew prophet Joel, the Spirit was poured out on all flesh (2:28).

The Need for Reason. "But anyone can have a religious experience," protested a minister during a question-and-answer discussion. "The members of the Taliban have religious experiences; Hitler might have had mystical experiences. Experience can't be the basis for religion, because you can't say what counts as a valid experience. Creeds and doctrine have to be the test."

Experiential religion is not a new phenomenon; it is an ancient one. And the question as to the validity of religious experience is about as ancient as the experiences themselves. Although many people in a tribe may have had spiritual experiences, only one arose as the shaman or wise woman. Thus, even primitive people recognized that some religious experiences were more profound than others and set up authorities to help others achieve certain kinds of experiences. People adjudicated between experiences, discerning

---

62. William James, *Varieties of Religious Experience* (London, New York, and Bombay: Longmans, Green, 1911), 31.

63. James, *Varieties of Religious Experience*, 515.

64. Leigh Schmidt, *Restless Souls: The Making of American Spirituality* (San Francisco: Harper San Francisco, 2005), 170–171.

which ones nurtured the tribe and which ones might not foster group prosperity. Meaningful religious experiences were shared through story and ritual in an attempt to enable other people to participate in a sense of the divine. Occasionally, an independent mystic would challenge the authority of established religious leaders or rituals by claiming a new experience, leading the tribe to either accept the new insights or reject the messenger. History is rife with accounts of experiential religious figures facing the wrath of institutional doubters–Jesus, Joan of Arc, and Oscar Romero, to name only a very few.

Although Western Christianity turned toward the rational and away from the mystical in the seventeenth and eighteenth centuries, the question of religious experience actually remained important. In the 1740s, a group of religious protesters called "evangelicals" argued against established Christians by claiming that an experience of being "born again" was necessary to faith. Their experiential religion wreaked havoc in English and colonial churches, where revivalists interrupted worship services, led people to psychological breakdowns, and undermined the social order. Women preachers and unlettered male evangelists roamed the land and stirred up the religious rabble, inciting everyone to believe that their experiences of God were equal to any theological insight proclaimed by the educated clergy. In the midst of revival fervor, Jonathan Edwards, a philosopher and pastor deeply shaped by an experience of God, tried to discern true religious affections from delusion.

Edwards condemned both intellectualism and emotionalism in religion, arguing instead that "true religion, in great part, consists in holy affections." Although some of his learned colleagues said that "affections" were "inferior animal passions," Edwards oriented true religion toward what he called "the heart," a unitary faculty of will and love. "The Holy Scriptures do everywhere place religion very much in the affections," he wrote, "such as fear, hope, love, hatred, desire, joy, sorrow, gratitude, compassion and zeal."[65] Affections were not only emotions, however. Affections were the capacity of the heart willing and acting upon that which was good or generous or lovely. How is one's will directed toward beauty? Edwards insisted that true religious experience emanated from a divine source that opened human beings to sensing the unity of God's love and beauty in all things. Put simply, human beings apprehend the spiritual dimension of the universe from beyond themselves through a transformative experience of what Edwards called "a divine and supernatural light."

The experience of divine light reshaped men and women in the virtues of humility, mercy, and justice. An experience of the divine leads people toward greater "tenderness of spirit. . . and a readiness to esteem others better than themselves."[66] True religious experience manifested itself in "beauti-

---

65. George Marsden, *Jonathan Edwards: A Life* (New Haven, CT: Yale Univ. Press, 2003), 285.
66. Ibid., 284.

ful symmetry and proportion" in one's character. Edwards argued that this culminated in a well-ordered and disciplined life: "Gracious and holy affections have their exercise and fruit in Christian practice."[67]

Of his own argument, Edwards claimed, "As that is called experimental philosophy, which brings opinion and notions to the test of fact; so is that properly called experimental religion, which bring religious affections and intentions to like test."[68] Edwards may sound like a rationalist here, as if he needed a scientific experiment to prove the goodness of religious experience. What counted as evidence for Edwards? The quality of one's life. Quite simply, truthful religious experience started with the affections and deepened one's character, one's love of God, and service to neighbor; it unified and balanced head and heart. In turn, the movement toward love served as the test for valid religious experience. Spiritual experience initiates the well-lived life; the well-lived life confirms the nature of one's spiritual experience.

Jonathan Edwards was both a mystic and a philosopher. At the time he lived, it was fashionable to speak of the "beauty of reason." For vast numbers of Christians, reason was an experience, and it was a powerful, life-changing one at that. Although difficult to remember now, *reason* had not yet hardened into *rationalism*. Reason was a capacity of deep understanding, not a set of opinions; it was a journey, a practice, and an inner adventure of soul, not a finished philosophical or theological product.

European Christianity was just moving out of a time when religious passion had resulted in schism, excommunications, exile, witch hunts, inquisitions, and wars of religion. Critical thought provided welcome relief from religious excess; reason, thankfully, muted the fervor of theological hubris and wild spiritual speculations. Reason was the gift of individuals to think for themselves, the ability to judge rightly, to make good choices. Reason sowed seeds of freedom and human rights. It was the philosophical twin of political democracy and the economic engine of an emerging middle class.

Reason did not oppose religion or religious experience. Rather, reason softened religion's sharp edges by providing balance, harmony, and order in a supernatural world too often ruled by a seemingly capricious God. Reason was beautiful. And it was mystical. Literature is full of accounts of people transformed by words, ideas, and books—as a growing industry of popular novels taught both men and women that logic and literacy opened the way to full humanity. Priests and professors wore the same garb; the church and the college embraced a common mission. In early modern depictions of reason, angels often accompany reason, crowning it with laurels of wisdom and justice. Often personified as a god or goddess, reason bestowed divine gifts on humankind. Indeed, people were tempted to worship reason as she had opened for them a new way of understanding themselves and ordering society.

---

67. Ibid., 288.
68. Ibid., 288.

Our own age has conflicted views of reason, because we understand its limits, feel its inhumane touch, and doubt the power of pure reason to solve our problems (indeed, we have witnessed how it has created quite a few). Long gone are the angels casting crowns; we now speak of the overly rational as "cold and calculating," possessed of "unyielding logic," people who "follow their ideas to the bitter end." As a result, education is devalued, and anti-intellectualism has taken hold. Experts are eyed with suspicion. Those who care about facts are derided as part of a "reality-based community." People make decisions "from their gut" or opine that something "just felt right" as they appeal to experience as the arbiter of personal, professional, and political choices. As our own age turns toward the authority of experience, it is good to remember that reason is not bad. Reason is part of human experience, often considered a reflection of God's image in humankind. To be spiritual *and* religious is to call for a new wholeness of experience and reason, to restitch experience with human wisdom and to renew reason through an experience of awe. Thus, the path of Christian faith in a postreligious age must be that of experiential belief in which the heart takes the lead in believing. As Parker Palmer writes,

> "Heart" comes from the Latin *cor* and points not merely to our emotions but to the core of the self, that center place where all of our ways of knowing converge—intellectual, emotional, sensory, intuitive, imaginative, experiential, relational, and bodily, among others. The heart is where we integrate what we know in our minds with what we know in our bones, the place where our knowledge can become more fully human.[69]

Experiential belief is integrated belief, that which brings back together capacities of knowing that modernity ripped apart. It is only in the territory of the heart where faith makes sense.

The Creed Revisited

More than a decade ago, I was part of an Episcopal congregation that loved asking questions. Indeed, many people made their way to that particular church because the community valued questions. We felt free to question everything—the creeds, the prayers, the scriptures. A member once moaned to me, "I just wish we could get everyone together on this monotheism thing."

On another occasion, we were having an argument about the resurrection, whether or not it had happened and whether or not it could be proved. One of my friends shared the story of how she had asked a liberal bishop if he actually believed in the resurrection. "Believe it?" he answered incredulously. "I've seen it too many times not to!"

---

69. Palmer, *Healing the Heart of Democracy*, 6.

The question "Do you believe in the resurrection?" often results in long, often tedious, explanations of creeds and councils, of texts and evidence, of arguments about historic and scientific facts and in disputes between liberals and conservatives. Few, however, stop and ask what the real question might be. The question is not "What do you believe about the resurrection?" The question is simpler and more profound: "Do you trust in the resurrection?" The bishop was not interested in a doctrinal test, proving a historical event that happened many years ago. He believed–that is, he trusted and was loyal to–the resurrection, because he had witnessed it himself. "Do you trust in the resurrection?" is a much harder question than "Do you believe that Jesus was historically and scientifically raised from the dead?"

The bishop was pointing toward the same sort of belief that Jonathan Edwards suggested in the eighteenth century. He pushed the question out of the realm of scientific speculation toward experiential validation: How does the resurrection make things different in a discernable, practical way here and now in our lives, in our communities? Anyone can believe that a resurrection happened; the real question is whether one trusts the resurrection. The test for the bishop, as for Edwards, was a transformed heart and ethical action.

The bishop, however, pushed it one step farther than Edwards. Edwards was attempting to validate spiritual experience by appealing to the affections, but the bishop was trying to explain a theological idea, a classical Christian belief appealing to the heart. Edwards would have thought the resurrection a fact of history, one that needed little or no validation or explanation. It simply was. The bishop, however, lived in radically different times–when only a few question spiritual experience, but many question Christian doctrine. Although the two made the same links between Christian faith, character, and experience, the historical situation is inverted. The bishop needed to validate the central Christian idea of resurrection with an appeal to experiential belief.

Although some spiritual experiences appear as random insights or miraculous encounters, most are shaped by prayer. In stories, memoirs, and testimonies, saints, mystics, and ordinary people recount how speaking with God opened the way for an experience of God. It is in words, and in the territory immediately beyond our words, that human beings meet the divine. As John the Evangelist says, "In the beginning was the Word, and the Word was with God, and the Word was God" (1:1). The Jewish philosopher Martin Buber suggests that spirituality–a deep encounter with God–begins with trust-filled conversation. Prayer is not talking about God "in the third person," rather prayer means speaking to God as "You," a subjective person with the capacity for relationship. Buber claims that "in true prayer, cult and faith are unified and purified into living relation."[70] Prayer transforms religion, doctrine, and dogma into vital spirituality.

---

70. Martin Buber, *I and Thou*, trans. R. G. Smith, 2nd ed. (London and New York: Continuum, 1958), 88–89.

The ancient Christian tradition *Lex orandi, lex credendi*, or "The law of prayer is the law of belief," means that praying shapes believing. The first Christians prayed and worshipped for several generations before they had a written creed, and they prayed for several hundred years before they had a canon of scripture. The liturgy of the Jesus communities and the prayers early followers uttered nurtured Christian theology, doctrine, and creeds.

"I don't want to be part of your church, because I don't believe in the Nicene Creed" is a common objection of those considering Christianity—or those considering leaving Christianity. But Christians do not worship a creed. The Nicene Creed was written some three centuries after Jesus taught his followers to love God and their neighbors. For the first three hundred years of church history the followers of Jesus worshipped God, served others, preached, taught, baptized, and evangelized the world without the benefit of a formal, universal doctrinal statement. The creeds developed in the context of a living, transformative, prayer-filled, risky, and active spiritual life—not the other way around. Indeed, a creed is considered a "symbol" of faith, not the faith itself. The words function as an icon, a linguistic picture of a divine reality beyond the ideas and concepts, a window into the world beyond words. Creeds are not unimportant; they are important only in the right order.

Creeds are essentially prayers of devotion that express a community's experience of encountering God. Indeed, the first creeds emerged from the Jewish experience of Jesus. The earliest Christians were Jews, men and women raised in a strictly monotheistic faith: "Hear, O Israel: The Lord is our God, the Lord alone" (Deut. 6: 4) and "You shall have no other gods before me" (Exod. 20: 3). Yet these same Jews worshipped Jesus as God, functionally making them bi-theists. Their experience of Jesus led them to rethink their understanding of God the Father and God's relationship to Jesus the Christ. The "rethinking" in context of experience took a very long time and eventuated in what we now know as creeds.

The experiential nature of the creeds can be seen in the Apostles' Creed (ca. 390), which begins with the words *Credo in Deum patrem*, translated into English as "I believe in God the Father." For those who read this through the modern lens of "belief," it seems as if this is an idea *about* God to which one must assent in order to join a Christian group—a question to answer correctly for entrance into heaven. But, if we grasp that the ancient sense of "believe" means "trust" or "devotion," the creed might be better translated thus:

> I trust in God the Father Almighty, Maker of heaven and earth. And [I trust] in Jesus Christ, his only Son, our Lord, who was conceived by the Holy Ghost, born of the Virgin Mary, suffered under Pontius Pilate, was crucified, died, and was buried. He descended into hell; the third day he rose again from the dead. He ascended into heaven, and sitteth on the right hand of God the Father Almighty. From thence he shall come to judge the quick and the dead. I trust in the Holy Ghost, the holy catholic church, the communion of saints, the forgiveness of sins, the resurrection of the body, and the life everlasting. Amen.

Notice that when we insert ourselves as the ones who must trust, the tone changes and the Apostles' Creed takes on the quality of a prayer. Instead of factual certainty, the creed evokes humility, hope, and a bit of faithful supplication. It moves the action of the creed from the brain to the heart. Changing a single word, "believe," to its original sense of "trust" transforms the text from a statement of dogma to an experience of God.

Since all creeds derive from the spiritual experience of the community, it is occasionally necessary and appropriate to rewrite them. Using the experiential language of belief, the Apostles' Creed could be rendered:

> I give my heart to God the all-powerful One, who created the universe, and Jesus Christ, God's Son, the Christ, who through the power of the Holy Spirit was born of the Virgin Mary. . . . And I give my heart to the Holy Spirit, devoting myself to the church and the communion of saints, trusting in the forgiveness of sins, the resurrection of the body, and life everlasting. Amen.

Notice that not all the intellectual problems of Christian doctrine are solved here—the language remains sexist and hierarchical, and we are still stuck with a virgin birth and a sin-filled church. You and your skeptical friends may not want to devote yourselves to this particular God.

But the emotional thrust is different from the one in the creeds recited in church. This no longer expresses philosophical ideas about God; rather, these words turn the affections toward what the early Christians experienced. They had found God, the One they called Father, Son, and Holy Spirit, to be the trustworthy Creator, Savior, and Sustainer of the universe, the beloved of their hearts. Through these words, contemporary followers continually remind themselves of the early Christian experience of God and Jesus, humbly dedicating themselves to a path of devotion and of beloving their God.

For people who have long recited the traditional creeds of the church, it can be hard to think of reinterpreting them or rewriting them. However, as Christianity expanded in the twentieth century, new believers found it necessary to rewrite the creeds in words and images that meshed with their cultures and their own experiences of God. In 1960, the Maasai people of East Africa, aided by Catholic missionaries, revised the creed in light of their encounter with Jesus:

> We believe in the one High God, who out of love created the beautiful world and everything good in it. He created Man and wanted Man to be happy in the world. God loves the world and every nation and tribe on the Earth. We have known this High God in darkness, and now we know Him in the light. God promised in the book of His word, the Bible, that He would save the world and all the nations and tribes.
>
> We believe that God made good His promise by sending His Son, Jesus Christ, a man in the flesh, a Jew by tribe, born poor in a little village, who left His home and was always on safari doing good, curing people by the power

of God, teaching about God and man, showing the meaning of religion is love. He was rejected by his people, tortured and nailed hands and feet to a cross, and died. He lay buried in the grave, but the hyenas did not touch him, and on the third day, He rose from the grave. He ascended to the skies. He is the Lord.

We believe that all our sins are forgiven through Him. All who have faith in Him must be sorry for their sins, be baptized in the Holy Spirit of God, live the rules of love and share the bread together in love, to announce the Good News to others until Jesus comes again. We are waiting for Him. He is alive. He lives. This we believe. Amen.

The Maasai creed invites us to go on a safari with Jesus. These are not just words about God; rather, these words welcome us into a story of God's hope for human happiness and healing.

Indeed, the word "doctrine," a word fallen on hard times in contemporary culture, actually means a "healing teaching," from the French word for "doctor." The creeds, as doctrinal statements, were intended as healing instruments, life-giving words that would draw God's people into a deeper engagement with divine things. When creeds become fences to mark the borders of heresy, they lose their spiritual energy. Doctrine is to be the balm of a healing experience of God, not a theological scalpel to wound and exclude people.

Rowan Williams, the Archbishop of Canterbury, pointed out in a recent book that the Christian creeds are similar to the Three Jewels of Buddhism, the vows that shape a Buddhist way of life: "I take refuge in the Buddha; I take refuge in the Dharma (Teaching); I take refuge in Sangha (Community)." The creed reminds us that Christians take refuge in God the Creator, take refuge in Jesus's teaching (forgiveness, love, and justice), take refuge in the life-giving Spirit, and take refuge in the church (the community). A vow. A prayer. An invitation. A living experience. Spiritual and religious. The heart of faith.

Focus

Write a summary of Diana Butler Bass's considerations. What hope does she express? What does her writing indicate she "believes," i.e., trusts, loves, takes refuge in (her personal position)?

Respond

Write your responses to Diana Butler Bass's assertions. What hope do you express? What does your writing indicate you "believe," i.e., trust, love, take refuge in?

Practice

The diagram attempts to visualize something of the swirl of motives, intentions, beliefs, and actions alive in someone at any given time. The following exercise is designed to increase awareness of the belief, practice, and congruence gaps a person has experienced. Identify the different gaps you presently experience or have known sometime in your life:

Belief Gap: the separation between orthodox teachings and personal belief

Practice Gap: the separation between orthopraxis and personal behavior and practices

Congruence Gap: the disjunction between personal beliefs and personal action

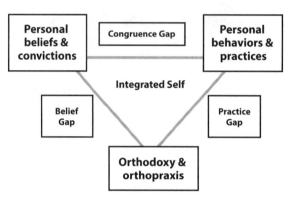

Belief Gap: Beliefs may be individually held or official positions held within a community (doctrines). Separation of personal belief and official doctrine can fragment a life and a community. A pastor of a church denomination that holds the belief that salvation is exclusively through Jesus Christ became ostracized when the pastor preached universal salvation. The gap between the pastor's belief and the denominational doctrine fragmented the community. A "belief gap" can disrupt harmony and force a decision for conformity or expulsion.

Practice Gap: A "practice gap" surfaces whenever a faith community advocates prescribed behavior and an individual does not conform to that behavior. A gap emerges as the mores of a community clash against individual actions and interests.

Congruence Gap: The gap phenomenon becomes internal when a person values something and behaves in conflict with that value. For example, honesty and truth-telling might be a high value but the person may habitually lie. The "congruence gap" generates internal conflicts that can become psychologically and spiritually destructive.

Wholeness, health, and holiness are closely related. Congruence intimates integrity. Living faithfully as a Christian, especially in a multicultural environment, entails facing and addressing the variety of "gaps" present. Unit Four directs attention toward wholeness by identifying and addressing the different "gaps" present in a person. Initially, you will be asked to become aware of the way you experience the different gaps. In subsequent weeks the gaps will be taken up one at a time to more carefully consider them.

Theological reflection is an important process of awareness, the first step toward wholeness, congruency, and integration. Often, those incidents that represent an occurrence "in the gap" are the ones most fruitful for theological reflection.

Review your writing in the preceding Respond section. Where are your "gaps"?

In the coming days and weeks, become mindful of those moments when you do/say something that goes against what you think you really believe. If there is such a moment that you can recall at this time, make note of it if you wish.

Week Twenty-three

YEAR ONE

Read

Jeremiah
Lamentations
Ezekiel
Collins, Chapter 17, "The Babylonian Era" and Chapter 18, "Ezekiel"

Focus

What beliefs sustained the people of God during the Jeremiah/Lamentations time period as they strove to live spiritually grounded lives?

What vision of wholeness or goodness do Jeremiah and the writer(s) of Lamentations hold up? What sense of brokenness are they responding to?

State some noteworthy elements that distinguish the book of Ezekiel. Identify the two traditions that combine in Ezekiel's opening vision. How does symbolic action figure into Ezekiel's prophetic work?

Describe the impact of Ezekiel's prophetic work on your personal beliefs.

YEAR TWO

Read

Ephesians
Powell, Chapter 17, "Ephesians"

Focus

Locate Ephesus and state its significance in Paul's journeys.

What are some of the opinions about the authorship of the letter to the church at Ephesus?

What does it mean to you to "lead a life worthy of the calling to which you have been called" (Ephesians 4:1)?

YEAR THREE

Read

MacCulloch, Chapter 16, "Perspectives on the True Church"

Focus

With this chapter, MacCulloch returns to Western Christianity. Events, especially tragic ones, impact how people think about and know God. Describe how the Black Death influenced behavior and belief.

YEAR FOUR

Read

Sedgwick, Preface, Introduction, and Chapter 1, "Describing the Christian Life"

Focus

Given Sedgwick's presentation, reflect on how the study of ethics contributes to the formation of a theology.

What are the creative aspects of Sedgwick's views? What choices do his views present to you?

Reflect on how his views of ethics relate to what you see in the culture in which you live.

ALL YEARS

Respond

Read a couple of good online or printed magazine or news articles about something that you care about in the field of history, theology, literature, politics, or science.

Use the following outline to build the skill of reflecting theologically on something you read (or perhaps watch on TV) from the culture/society source.

Use ABCD as you prepare what you will share in the seminar.

Practice

As a way to reflect theologically from several sources, use a "wide-angle lens" to find a common thread in the articles or reports you identified in the Respond section above.

Why this title? Instead of the usual first step to **Identify** a focus from one of the four sources, the wide-angle lens is a pre-**Identify** step that begins with a variety of perspectives, then isolates a thread/theme/idea/image that connects them, which in turn becomes the focus for the reflection. A theological reflection beginning with a wide-angle lens can begin in any of the four sources. The key is that it requires initiation from something that could produce several themes or ideas. There are innumerable options. An individual can begin with movies, assigned readings, incidents from one's life, or several personal positions. In an EfM group, the beginning point can be themes from the spiritual autobiographies, themes from the week's reading, themes from any on-board time of the group, or some other starting point from which a variety of perspectives can be elicited. The initial step always is to list themes and find a thread that runs through several of them.

THEOLOGICAL REFLECTION BEGINNING WITH A WIDE-ANGLE LENS

This particular reflection begins in the Culture/Society Source. Start by finding the threads or themes present in several personal incidents drawn from the Respond section above, several incidents that indicate a gap between belief and behavior.

Identify
FIND A COMMON THEME OR THREAD

Begin with the articles chosen for the Respond section above.

What are the common themes or elements that emerge? Is there a central question, struggle, or issue contained in the articles?

A theme may be expressed as a simple statement, an image, a metaphor, or an issue.

Select one thread that connects various themes. For instance, a review of several articles could reveal themes of challenge of the status quo, support of a particular view, and/or revelation of something new. Asking "What ties some of those themes together?" yields a thread that may have run through the articles.

Explore
REFLECT ON SOME THEOLOGICAL PERSPECTIVES

What image could paint a picture of the thread identified from the articles?

What questions does your image or statement raise?

What questions does that image or statement answer?

Describe or draw that image. Examine the image for what's going on in it. Write about what's going on in that image.

Ask theological perspective questions to explore the focus. Which theological perspective in terms of wholeness, brokenness, recognition, reorientation, or restoration comes first to mind? Consider several. For example, what would reorientation look like in that image? Or restoration?

Connect

Bring other sources into the conversation to help find meaning in matters of daily life and ministry.

CONSIDER THE CHRISTIAN TRADITION

Identify biblical passages or other elements from Christian Tradition in which this common thread is evoked or brought to mind. Provide time to find and read passages. Select one text that seems to speak most clearly to the thread that was evoked.

Examine the passage with these questions: What do you know about the meaning of the text in its original setting? How have others interpreted this text? What does this text mean to you? Note how the passage offers insight into the focus. Note how the passage challenges the focus.

COMPARE AND CONTRAST CONTEMPORARY CULTURE AND CHRISTIAN TRADITION

From the perspectives of Culture and Tradition, what kind of a world emerges?

Where do these perspectives join or compete? Where do they clash or contrast?

Note what seems to be "at stake" as you compare and contrast your Culture and Tradition connections.

Use one or two theological perspectives— wholeness, brokenness, recognition, reorientation, or restoration—to consider how the perspectives of Culture and Tradition compare and contrast.

CONNECT TO PERSONAL EXPERIENCE

When have you experienced something that relates to what seems to "be at stake" above?

CONNECT TO BELIEFS, POSITIONS, AND AFFIRMATIONS

What positions or affirmations do you hold in relation to what is at stake?

Identify how that belief formed for you. Was it from personal experience, from something you learned in your faith tradition, or from the cultural messages you have inherited or encountered?

What "gaps" are there for you between what you believe and how you act in relation to the theme considered in this reflection?

Apply

IDENTIFY INSIGHTS AND PERSONAL IMPLICATIONS

What have you learned about coherence of belief and behavior?

What are you personally called to do differently, to affirm, or to change?

What skills did this reflection help you learn in thinking theologically about something you read or watch?

DECIDE ON SOCIAL AND CIVIC CONSEQUENCES

What actions will you take to carry out the implications you have discovered?

Week Twenty-four

YEAR ONE

Read

Isaiah 40–66
Haggai
Zechariah
Malachi
Joel
Jonah
Collins, Chapter 19, "The Additions to the Book of Isaiah" and Chapter 20, "Postexilic Prophecy"

Focus

Prophets speak God's truth to those in power and generally have the most to lose in speaking. Difficulties arise when prophetic voices do not agree on what the "truth" is. Two possible responses to the contradiction are either to wait to see which was speaking truth or to decide, in the midst of the uncertainty, which is correct and act accordingly. Reflect on how uncertainty impacts the consistency of belief and behavior.

What do the terms "major prophets" and "minor prophets" mean?

YEAR TWO

Read

Philippians
Colossians
Powell, Chapter 18, "Philippians" and Chapter 19, "Colossians"

Focus

What are issues of behavior and/or belief in these two communities?

Note what passages Powell highlights from Philippians and/or Colossians. Which passages did he not include in his discussion, but that you thought were important?

Identify any issues related to multicultural encounters that might have been present in the Philippians' and Colossians' experience.

YEAR THREE

Read

MacCulloch, Chapter 17, "A House Divided"

Focus

Describe the values that drove the actions of reformers. Think about how those values shape doctrines of God, humanity, and creation. How do those values relate to your personal experience and values? How are those values reflected in our contemporary society? What challenges or support are there for you in living faithfully with your values in a multicultural world?

YEAR FOUR

Read

Sedgwick, Chapter 2, "An Anglican Perspective"

Focus

Faith as a way of life, the theological tradition, and theology and ethics are the three sections in this chapter.

Name one key idea in each section.

State your own beliefs around those ideas.

ALL YEARS

Respond

Rushworth Kidder, an ethicist, wrote *How Good People Make Tough Choices: Resolving the Dilemmas of Ethical Living*, in which he defined a dilemma as a choice between two "goods." The gap between a belief and behavior can be framed within the conflict between two values in a specific situation.

Identify an incident or two in which you were in a dilemma of conflicting values, perhaps between two good choices. For example:

> I had looked forward to my best friend's wedding for months and had my plane ticket and my new outfit. We had plans to enjoy the sights and catch up and just have fun. And then my surviving parent got sick, but told me I could go ahead with my plans. I felt so torn. There was no one else there.

What's the dilemma? What are my choices? What beliefs do I use to sift and decide among choices?

Use ABCD as you prepare what you will share in the seminar.

Practice

Reflecting theologically on dilemmas can move a person toward integrating beliefs and behaviors. Building a theology relies on the integration of beliefs with doctrines as experienced in the actions taken in everyday life. Building a theology also relies on the ability to reflect through a variety of theological lenses. How do I know I have made a faithful decision or choice?

Theological perspective questions can be drawn from many parts of the Christian tradition, such as themes from the scriptures or from the work of theologians. Those drawn from systematic theology may be most familiar: creation, sin, judgment, repentance, and resurrection, but in this Guide you have also encountered theological perspective questions drawn from Bishop Tutu's work: wholeness, brokenness, recognition, reorientation, and restoration. You can compile your own set of theological perspective questions over time as you draw from your readings over the four years in EfM and beyond.

The practice reflection below draws its theological perspective questions from Eric Law's Cycle of Gospel Living found on pages 342–343 of this Guide. Please read it before beginning the reflection.

Law's Cycle is an exploration of power dynamics viewed through the lens of crucifixion and resurrection. Through it Law encourages us to remember that Jesus offered power to the powerless through the Holy Spirit (symbolized by resurrection and the empty tomb) and called the powerful to humility in giving up power to others (symbolized by death and the cross). The key to this cycle is that it is dynamic and continuous. We are called to keep moving around the circle. As we move from powerless to powerful we are called to service that bestows power on others, rendering us powerless again, at which point we move in faith toward receiving the power of the Holy Spirit once more. Wholeness comes from moving through the cycle and not remaining only on one side or the other.

Explore a theological reflection that begins either with a belief (Position Source) or a behavior (Action Source). Use the example below, which begins in the Action Source, as a guide if you prefer to begin with a belief (Position Source). Set aside an hour or so if you can to work through the process and take your work to the seminar session. What might you share in the seminar about your experience of reflecting on a dilemma?

THEOLOGICAL REFLECTION BEGINNING WITH A DILEMMA

Identify

DESCRIBE an incident for reflection, an experience in which you felt pulled in at least two directions over something, and for which there are no decisions pending. The incident is over.

NAME the turning point in the incident. What is the central moment of the incident? Where is the tension greatest? What was happening? What were you thinking and feeling at that moment? Record the central moment in a short sentence.

STATE the dilemma. Try to state what is at stake or what the central issue is at the moment of greatest tension. To help clarify the dilemma, list declarative statements about what you wanted at that moment or what interests were at stake at that moment. Select a pair of statements that best represent the central tension, identifying what is at issue or at stake in that tension. Record the primary pair of tension statements as

"I wanted _____ and I wanted _____."

Remember that this is a difficult choice between two good things.

Example, as in the Response section above:

> *I wanted to attend my best friend's wedding and I wanted to stay to take care of my ailing parent.*

> Note the central issue/what is at stake. Example: *Personal fun conflicting with caring for another*
> [Note: In a group reflection, others would now be invited to recall a time when each experienced a similar dilemma.]

Explore

EXPLORE the dilemma.

What is it like to live in that tension? Contrast the cost/promise of the dilemma.

Record your responses to the questions using either cost/promise or theological perspectives:

COST OF EACH SIDE OF THE TENSION	PROMISE OF EACH SIDE OF THE TENSION
Ex., Plans: caught off guard, decisions made that are hard to change	Ex., Know what is coming

OR use one or two theological perspective questions adapted from the Cycle of Gospel Living, developed by Eric Law (please review pages 342–343 in Part II of this Guide).[71] This cycle focuses on power, loss or yielding up of power, and re-empowerment, and moves through four phases.

- Give up power, choose the cross–This is a point of entry for the powerful

- Cross, death, powerless–This is a point of entry for the powerless

- Empowerment, endurance or faithful waiting

- Empty tomb, resurrection, powerful

Here are examples of asking questions of the dilemma or image. Use only one or two when exploring your image or dilemma:

Give up power, choose the cross: What are the power dimensions of the dilemma or image? Who has power? What has to be yielded?

Cross, death, powerless: What sacrifice(s) might be called for? What are the temptations of accepting death, the cross, or powerlessness? To whom or what is power yielded?

---

71. Law, *The Wolf Shall Dwell with the Lamb*, 74.

Empowerment, endurance: How is power transmitted to the powerless party? What is required in order to enter the cycle that leads to empowerment? What builds endurance?

Empty tomb, resurrection, powerful: What is left behind in the image or dilemma? How does resurrection occur in the image or dilemma? What is the hope of the power received?

Connect

CHRISTIAN TRADITION: Identify some stories from scripture or church history that relate to the dilemma. Or perhaps some prayers or hymns come to mind. Compare and contrast what the Christian tradition has to say about that dilemma. What choices would the tradition support? Not support? Why?

CULTURE: Where is this dilemma experienced in our culture? Have there been news stories about it? Have you read a book or seen a movie that dealt with the dilemma? Is there a political dimension to the dilemma?

POSITION: What do you believe about the dilemma? How is your belief in conflict in the issue? What do you hope for regarding the dilemma?

[*Note: If your reflection began in the Position Source, the connecting questions here would be focused on the Action Source. "What personal experiences can you recall that are related to this dilemma concerning belief?" or similar questions about personal experience will work.*]

Apply

INSIGHTS and QUESTIONS: What do you see in a new way now? What have you learned from facing this dilemma? What questions do you have about the dilemma in your life?

IMPLICATIONS: What do you want or need to do about similar dilemmas when they arise? Are there social implications? Are there actions you could take? Is there something more to learn? What support would help? Where will you find that support?

Week Twenty-five

YEAR ONE

Read

Yee: Chapter 3, "The Challenge of Violence and Gender under Coloniza-tion" by Corinne L. Carvalho

Focus

Terms and names to note: unhelpful modern assumptions about the role of the prophets; highly rhetorical, literary texts; gender stereotypes; invisibility of the marginalized; intersectionality; unrecognized androcentrism; not prediction but persuasion; literary conventions; trope; blurred boundaries between history and metaphor; polygamous; hypermasculine view of God; feminine images of God; warrior goddesses; symbolic role of women; pro-phetic guild; professional female mourners; "cows"; elite women; widows, orphans, and resident aliens; social fragility; poverty; cultic prostitution; rape as a tool of conquest; gender identity as social construct; binary view of gender; gender fluidity; prophet at the edge of society; eunuchs; sexual acts and procreation; contextual theologies; *mujerista* theology; womanist theology; second wave feminism; liberation theology; *praxis*; Black theol-ogy; hermeneutics of suspicion; hermeneutic of listening; Daughter of Zion; Ishtar; Mary Daly; Queen of Heaven; Ada María Isasi-Díaz; Cheryl Kirk-Duggan; Renita Weems; Elisabeth Schüssler Fiorenza

In what ways have the cultural and literary conventions about women in the prophetic writings been used to define the role of women in the history/cul-ture of the Christian church?

How might feminine images of God in the prophetic writings and a more developed understanding of the cultural context of images such as the Divine Warrior help challenge modern cultural assumptions about God in the Hebrew Bible?

What do the various liberation and intersectional lenses bring to reading a theological text?

YEAR TWO

Read

1 Thessalonians
2 Thessalonians
Powell, Chapter 20, "1 Thessalonians," and Chapter 21, "2 Thessalonians"

Focus

Note which doctrines are either implicitly or explicitly mentioned in the two letters to the Thessalonians. What light does Powell shed on the doctrines?

YEAR THREE

Read

MacCulloch, Chapter 18, "Rome's Renewal"

Focus

Often, reforming led to examination and renewal among those to whom the protestations were leveled. As you read through MacCulloch's account of the catholic counterreformations, consider what this renewal disclosed about the church's understanding of the nature God.

YEAR FOUR

Read

Sedgwick, Chapter 3, "Incarnate Love"

Focus

In Chapter 3 Sedgwick uses sexuality, idolatry, and hospitality as elements to sketch a picture of incarnate love. What do you find challenging in this chapter? What can this chapter contribute to your own reflection on the nature of incarnate (or human) love? You may find the Roberts–Sedgwick document on the EfM Resources page helpful.[72]

ALL YEARS

Respond

Christian theologians over the centuries have developed a long list of doctrines. The table of contents of most theological textbooks reflects an author's arrangement of important doctrines. Often an author devotes an entire chapter to a particular doctrine or doctrines.

Each historical period prioritizes doctrines in response to the social and intellectual environment. For example, in the nineteenth and early twentieth centuries, most systematic organizations of theology began with the doctrine of God; the characteristics and actions of God. By the end of the twentieth century, Anglo-American theologians began by discussing the doctrine of human nature; what are the characteristics of humankind–how we act and who we are. John Macquarrie, a Scottish theologian who taught at Union Theological Seminary in New York City and at Oxford University, consistently asserted that contemporary theology must begin from the ground up.

---

72. efm.sewanee.edu/resources/resources, "On Chapter 3 of Sedgwick's *The Christian Moral Life.*"

Thus, his *Principles of Christian Theology* begins with theological anthropology (i.e., the doctrine of human nature).

As a way to build a theology, create a list of fifteen or more doctrines. A denominational catechism would be a good place to start. For example, the Episcopal Book of Common Prayer (1979) beginning on page 845 presents "An Outline of the Faith." Each boldface heading names a doctrine.

Once you have collected a list of doctrines, arrange them in an order that reflects your interest in the doctrine, beginning with what interests you the most. Using the first three or four doctrines, review the reading assignments over the past few sessions, noting how the author dealt with one or two of the doctrines of interest.

Use ABCD as you prepare what you will share in the seminar.

Practice

Try to locate doctrinal statements of several denominations (Anglican, Methodist, Christian Science, or any others) or faith traditions (Judaism, Islam, and so forth). Constructive theology is essentially a conversation among Christian doctrines and an individual's beliefs and actions (behaviors). Select one doctrine from your list, for example, the doctrine of God. Find a statement from the Catechism (Outline of the Faith) of the 1979 Book of Common Prayer that addresses the doctrine. Then make your own statement of your belief relative to the chosen doctrine. Finally, recall your behavior that revealed a stance relative to the doctrine.

Example:

Question from the Book of Common Prayer: What are we by nature?

Answer from the Book of Common Prayer: We are part of God's creation, made in the image of God.

An individual's statement: I believe that we are all equal.

Behavior (action) that reveals an understanding of human nature: I cheered for my high school basketball team, shouting "We're Number One!"

Write about how the three statements support, challenge, or contradict one another. Reflect on images, emotions, or concepts that contribute to the threefold conversation. What other doctrinal statements from the Christian tradition speak to the conversation? What other position statements have you said or heard? Describe how different actions contribute to the conversation.

What are the implications for exploring doctrines in a multicultural setting?

Week Twenty-six

YEAR ONE

Read

Ezra
Nehemiah
1 Chronicles
2 Chronicles
Collins, Chapter 21, "Ezra and Nehemiah" and Chapter 22, "The Books of Chronicles"

Focus

Sometimes a reform movement is tied to strengthening a community's sense of identity. Why would this be important to the returning exiles? Where today do you see reform movements aimed at establishing or setting boundaries around religious identity?

The two books of Chronicles tell the history of the kingdoms from a slightly different perspective from how that history is related in First and Second Samuel and First and Second Kings. Collins notes that David and Solomon are idealized as cultic figures in the Chronicles. Where do you see evidence of this? For those who have returned from exile, what does the chronicler have to say about their relationship to the past? What might God's promises to David and Solomon mean for them in their new life as a restored community?

YEAR TWO

Read

1 Timothy
2 Timothy
Titus
Philemon
Powell, Chapter 22, "The Pastoral Letters: 1 Timothy, 2 Timothy, Titus," and Chapter 23, Philemon

Focus

Think about Paul's struggle against "false teachings" while advocating "sound doctrines." Compare how the same issues play out in the contemporary church.

The letter to Philemon is the shortest book in the Christian Bible, but is the subject of varying interpretations. Consider how Philemon has figured in the history of Christianity and the institution of slavery in the United States and other places. What light does Powell shed on differing scholarly interpretations of Paul's attitude toward slavery? What sources do you draw on in forming your own understanding of how biblical interpretation is used in controversial questions today?

What do these books—First and Second Timothy, Titus, and Philemon—have to say about the nature of Christian identity in relationship to culture?

YEAR THREE

Read

MacCulloch, Chapter 19, "A Worldwide Faith"

Focus

How might well-crafted histories aid in understanding the social and intellectual period in which contemporary theology has developed? What does a knowledge of the church's past contribute to forming a theology that supports you in living faithfully in your world?

YEAR FOUR

Read

Sedgwick, Chapter 4, "Love and Justice"

Focus

Chapter 4 brings an important discussion of love and justice to the table. Note how these themes are addressed in the theology you are building. What does Sedgwick offer in this chapter that you might want to consider more closely? What do you find challenging in his chapter?

ALL YEARS

Respond

Prayer, worship and study open one's heart to God. Ideally, all three frame theological reflection and all three contribute to developing a theology that stands one in good stead in the midst of life. Building an awareness of the theological "gaps" in one's life—and accepting that some will likely always exist for any given person—helps the Christian sojourner to walk with more steadiness in daily life. In this unit, Diana Butler Bass's work provides a frame for looking at aspects of believing and identifies some of the gaps that exist for individuals and institutions, both sacred and secular.

Use the scheme laid out in Week 21 to organize the material you studied this week in terms of the kinds of gaps that you might discern.

Belief Gap: the separation between orthodox (institutionally accepted) teachings and personal belief.

Where did those gaps appear in what you studied?

Where did they appear in how you responded to some of the ideas you encountered in your study?

Practice Gap: the separation between orthopraxis (institutionally accepted behavior) and personal behavior and practices

Where did this gap occur in the material you studied and where has it occurred in your own experience?

Congruence Gap: the disjunction between personal beliefs and personal action

Where did this gap occur in your personal experience?

Use ABCD as you prepare what you will share in the seminar.

Practice

THEOLOGICAL REFLECTION BEGINNING WITH A WIDE-ANGLE LENS

Identify
After describing the gaps in the Respond section above, pick one gap and identify themes or threads that run through that gap.

What kinds of things does that gap seem to be about? Is it about civil disobedience, or punishment, or resistance—or something else?

Choose one thread (theme) as the focus for reflection.

Explore
The theme is descriptive of some kind of world, where "that's how things are." For example, the focus may be about an act of civil disobedience that represents personal behavior in the gap between orthopraxis and personal action. Deepen your reflection on the theme using two or three perspective questions to ask the focus:

- What temptations or dangers are present in such a world (of civil disobedience, or whatever the focus is about in your incident)?

- What is shown about human nature in this gap?

- What would wholeness look like?

Connect
Consider any or all of the following in any order:

- What's at the "heart" of the selected gap?

- Note your personal positions or beliefs about the matter under consideration. On what ground is your belief resting? What contributed to the formation of that belief?

Identify how the ground of your belief is watered by a faith tradition, by the world around you, or by personal experience.

Apply

What new ideas or understanding do you have now?

What are the implications for ministry in daily life in a multicultural environment?

Journal about living with your Rule of Life. Where have you encountered God?

Week Twenty-seven

YEAR ONE

Read

Psalms
Song of Songs
Collins, Chapter 23, "Psalms and Song of Songs"

Focus

Don't try to read each psalm in depth, but read quickly through, pausing on a specific psalm as your attention is captured and noticing how the psalms are grouped. What strikes you about their arrangement? Which psalms are most familiar to you?

Identify a psalm that illustrates each of the following categories:

- complaints

- hymns of praise

- royal psalms

- thanksgivings

Psalms tell of the kingship of God, the human situation, the character of God, and the nature of human kingship. Notice two or three features of these found in the Psalms.

Given that the Song of Songs does not mention God, why would the compilers of the Bible include it as a sacred text? Make a case for why or why not the Song of Songs conveys a theology.

Reflect on when you have heard the Song of Songs read in church. What did you think?

YEAR TWO

Read

Hebrews
Powell, Chapter 24, "Hebrews"

Focus

Powell notes that "persistent Christians have found real substance in this [Hebrews] letter: teaching that not only reveals who Christ is but also discloses who they are (and can be) in relation to him." What significance does knowing who Christ is and who people are in relation to him have for developing a theology that undergirds the work of ministry in daily life? Notice especially the role faith plays in fostering ministerial identity.

YEAR THREE

Read

MacCulloch, Chapter 20, "Protestant Awakenings "

Focus

Terms and names to note: covenant in the establishment of the church in North America; John Winthrop; congregational; Anne Hutchinson; Roger Williams; Quakers; John Eliot; John Locke; William Penn; Non-Jurors; pietism; Moravians; August Hermann Francke; place of hymnody and music; Count Nikolaus Ludwig von Zinzendorf; Methodism; John Wesley; evangelicals; George Whitefield; Gilbert Tennent; Great Awakenings

What aspects of North American Christianity's growth are most evident in your religious heritage?

YEAR FOUR

Read

Sedgwick, Chapter 5, "The Practices of Faith," and Chapter 6, "The Call of God"

Focus

Terms and names to note: kataphatic; sacramental acts; sacrifice

Note any ways in which your reading of Sedgwick's book has contributed to the building of your own theology.

Reflect on your answer to Sedgwick's question, "What has been most significant in your experience of worship, and what has been most difficult?"(page 103).

ALL YEARS

Respond

Throughout this constructive theology unit, you have worked with various facets of building your own theology. Such work always is enriched when done within a learning community. Mark McIntosh, in *Mysteries of Faith*, notes three movements that a person or a community undergoes in building a life-giving theology: 1) seeing differently; 2) developing a habit of life; 3) ongoing conversation with God.[73]

Regularly practicing the discipline of theological reflection allows people to see things differently. Fresh visions, in turn, lead to developing a "habit of life" in which thinking theologically becomes routine. In McIntosh's words, "Learning to see the mystery of God's plan, to see in a way that illuminates the meaning of the world, requires you to develop some habits of mind and heart."[74]

EfM presents opportunities to develop habits of mind and heart—ways of seeing God's mystery and presence. McIntosh notes that "when theology becomes a habit, it becomes part of your character, a fundamental having and holding of who you are."[75] Theology opens a person to knowing about God and knowing God, and at the same time allows people to know more *about* themselves and, more importantly, to *know* themselves. The two-fold practice of knowing God and knowing oneself embodies the incarnational process. It is an interactive, dynamic, dance-like reality in which a person intentionally develops a "God-knowing" habit and simultaneously develops a *habitus* of self-knowing.

Review the work you have done throughout the unit and note what you have learned about yourself and about God. Assess where you are in the theological practice of knowing God and yourself.

Use ABCD as you prepare what you will share in the seminar.

Practice

Review your spiritual autobiography and your Rule of Life, considering how you would express your experience of God in terms of wholeness, broken-ness, empowerment, and/or resurrection.

Who are your theological or spiritual wisdom figures, drawing from the scriptures, your study of church history, and your life?

On what basis do you consider any of those figures to be sources of wisdom for you?

---

73. Mark McIntosh, *Mysteries of Faith* (Cambridge, MA: Cowley Publications, 2000), 5–20.

74. McIntosh, *Mysteries of Faith*, 12.

75. Ibid.

SECOND INTERLUDE

Christian-Muslim Vision and Practice

Week Twenty-eight

ALL YEARS

Read

Heaney, Sayilgan, and Haymes, Foreword and Chapters 1–4
Note: Chapter Three outlines the basic methodology and results of a survey regarding interfaith engagement. You do not need to read this chapter deeply, but you may want to skim the results, especially the "Key Results" listed on page 41 and the final pages, 60–64.

Focus

Terms and names to note: "yacht dialogue"; "the almost comprehensive list"; ontological; *missio Dei*; missional acts of God; Five Marks of Mission; proselytism; contextualization; personal, cultural, political, and religious reconciliation; Sunnis; Shiites; Qur'an; *sunna*; *ijim*, *qiy s*; "Constitution of Madina"; *jinn*; twenty-eight messengers; "People of the Book"; *basmala*; *Allahu akbar*; *indaba*; Dodoma Statement; Miroslav Volf; John S. Mbiti

Respond

Chapters One and Two set up arguments for interfaith engagement. What is your response to these statements? Is there anything you would add to Heaney's argument? What new or surprising information do you find in Sayilgan's argument?

What is your experience of engaging those of other faiths? Does your congregation participate in any intentional engagement with congregations of other faiths? What opportunities are there in your local area for intentional interfaith engagement?

Use the ABCD schema to decide what you want to share in the seminar.

Practice

Each chapter in Part Two ends with questions for discussion and suggestions for further steps. Look over the "Further Steps" at the ends of Chapters Three and Four. Choose one from each to follow to the best of your ability. How easy is this for you? What barriers do you need to overcome? What resources would make following these suggestions easier? What steps do you need to take to overcome the barriers and/or develop the resources?

Week Twenty-nine

ALL YEARS

Read (All Years)

Heaney, Sayilgan, and Haymes, Chapters 5–9 and Resources

Focus

Terms and names to note: Ramadan; "*hislam*"; *hijab*; *Alhamdullilah*; PBUH; Baptismal Covenant; *Risale-i Nur*; Ottoman Empire; *hilf al-fudul*; Abyssinians; Hare Krishna; "interstate bridging"; "intrastate bridging"; xenophobic; comity; dinner dialogues; grassroots dialogue; assimilation; ecumenical/Ecumenism; National Council of Churches; World Council of Churches; constructive interfaith conversation; Peter Gomes; Bediuzzaman Said Nursi; Pope Pius XII; Robert Putnam and David Campbell; Robert Wuthnow

What chapter in this book did you find to be the most inspiring or encouraging? What chapter offers the most practical help?

Respond

With pluralism, contemporary American religion reveals a shift away from institutions and toward faith community, away from doctrine and toward personal encounter with the sacred. Faith is now distinct from belief. Trust has to be built; authority must arise. Tradition is distinct from institutions. Religious identity is less passed from generation to generation than it is created anew of disparate elements and personal searches. Membership in religious institutions is declining while participation in local congregations is increasing. Many Americans are as charmed by "spirituality" as they are wary of "religion."[76]

What from your own experience resonates with or pushes back against the passage above?

What do you see or hear in your culture/society that affirms or denies this assertion? What from a global perspective speaks to this?

Practice

Consider initiating an interfaith meal or gathering to provide a space for constructive conversation. A small event is probably best to start. Who will you invite to help you? How will you invite participants?

Remember the description of constructive conversation in Chapter Nine:

---

76. M. Imad Damaj and William L. Sachs, "Local Diversity and Interfaith Initiative: Going Global Hits Home" in *Faithful Neighbors: Christian-Muslim Vision and Practice*, ed. Robert S. Heaney, Zeyneb Sayilgan, and Claire Haymes (New York: Morehouse, 2016), 140.

- A journey of self-discovery

- Relational

- Generous

- Affirms difference

- Takes account of power relations

- Contextual

- Marked by humility

After the event assess whether there is opportunity for another gathering.

UNIT FIVE

Vocation

Week Thirty

ALL YEARS

Read

"It is a continual theme of Christian theology that every new generation must take up the task of 'faith in search of understanding' with fresh vigor and creativity."[77] The essay selected to introduce this unit on vocation comes from a book that is the work of a group of theologians who set about the task of doing theology in today's multicultural world. They describe themselves as "a committed, diverse group of theologians who stand at the beginning of a new millennium and in the center of the world's most powerful empire and ask again: How should the Christian faith be understood today, here and now, in this place and time?"[78] The book covers the classical theological themes of God, human beings, sin and evil, Jesus Christ, church, and spirit. Their work on the theology of the church (ecclesiology) culminates in presenting a theology of mission (missiology).

Paul Lakeland is the "Aloysius P. Kelley, S. J., Professor of Catholic Studies" at Fairfield University in Connecticut. Among his works are *The Liberation of the Laity: In Search of an Accountable Church* (Continuum, 2003) and *Postmodernity: Christian Identity in a Fragmented Age* (Fortress Press, 1997).[79]

Lakeland's essay sets a context for discerning one's vocation in a postcolonial, multicultural world. It provides a launching point for a discussion of Christian mission and vocation, intended to provoke discussion and raise basic questions that push EfM participants to examine their theological foundations and to think through their own understandings of the relationships between Christology, missiology, and ecclesiology. Carefully read and note your own responses: disagreement, challenge, or agreement.

The Mission of the Church[80]

Mission means "sending" or "being sent." The mission of the church is thus that for which it is sent, those purposes for which Christ commissioned it. To understand the full complexity of the term *mission*, however, we have to approach it from at least three different perspectives. First, *who* is sent?

---

77. Serene Jones and Paul Lakeland, eds., *Constructive Theology: A Contemporary Approach to Classic Themes.* A project of The Workgroup on Constructive Christian Theology (Minneapolis: Fortress, 2005), 1.

78. Ibid., 1.

79. Ibid., xii.

80. Ibid., 230–238.

Second, *to whom* is the church sent? Third, *what* is the church sent to do? In actual fact, the questions need to be asked in reverse order. That being said, there is a preliminary question that we need to address: What is the relationship between the mission of the church and the larger question of the *missio dei*, "God's mission," or what we might better understand as the divine purpose or creative will of God? These four questions will guide our examination of the mission of the church.

God's Mission and the Mission of the Church

God's purposes in and for the world are revealed to us through the Bible, but also through looking around us at the world. The world, in its goodness, is the expression of God's creative will, filled with the Spirit and offering glory to its Creator. Of course, there is abounding sin, suffering, and evil in this world, but the person of faith cannot see these as God's responsibility. In the Book of Genesis, God looks upon the creation and sees that it is good. As the early chapters of Genesis unfold, it becomes clear that God's purpose for the world is precisely that it shall be itself, a created reflection of divine goodness. God wills that all creatures, including human beings, be fully what they are—no more and no less. In the case of human beings, being fully what they are, made in the image of God, is made clear in God's commission of Adam and Eve for stewardship. On God's behalf, human beings will cherish creation. In a sense, they are commissioned as "cocreators" and "copreservers" of God's handiwork. Their tragedy, and that of creation, of course, is that they are not equal to the task. Moreover, it is apparent from the very beginning that their principal failure is their inability to recognize that their freedom does not mean autonomy. Their success in carrying out their mission is directly connected to their awareness that they depend on God, not on themselves, for their achievements.

From the beginning, then, God's mission and human purposes are closely intertwined, though there is tension between them. God's commission to human beings to share in the divine creativity is addressed, too, to the whole human race. Adam and Eve are not Hebrews, still less Christians. They represent all humankind. Their failure is our failure. Their task is our task. The Hebrew scriptures tell the story of God's continuing faithfulness to the task of creation and the new initiative that God takes with the covenant people. It is as if God is trying again to enlist human beings in the task of cocreation, this time choosing Abraham and his descendants. Once again, as in the Genesis account, human beings take up the task and are unequal to it. Time after time, the heroes of the Hebrew scriptures reveal their prideful egos; Moses, Saul, and David are good examples of the failure to do what God has called them to do, while Israel itself is another.

Christian scripture sees God's initiative in and through Jesus Christ to be a further effort to engage the human race in God's mission. Jesus is sent into the world to show the way in which a human being can conform his or her life to God's mission. The way of the cross is the way of conformity to the will of God. Jesus Christ is the perfect instrument of God's mission. He proclaims the kingdom of God. But he is also the perfect exemplar of the one who is called to mission. Discipleship, then, is mission, but only because discipleship is, like Christ, outwardly directed in response to God's call to share in God's mission. Discipleship, in other words, is commitment to the mission of Christ, which is in its turn carrying out God's mission. And God's mission is expressed in the creative will as it shows itself in the world. Thus, to complete the circle, the divine creative will is to a degree dependent on the faithfulness of human beings to the divine purpose. For Christians, this means faithfulness to their discipleship of Christ.

What Is the Church Sent to Do?

Given that God invites all human beings to cooperate in the work of cocreation, what is the specific mission of the disciples of Christ, the community called church? Formally, of course, there is no difference. That is, all human beings take up their mission insofar as they live out lives that respect and foster the integrity of God's creation, whether they know it or not, whether they know God or not. Through revelation, all the children of Abraham know more about God's purposes and are aware of their call to mission in ways that others are not. This is both a privilege and an enormous responsibility. However, there is a material specificity to the call of Christ to his church, one that historically Christians have understood as a more perfect revelation of truth but that might better be expressed as a clearer call to participation in the mission of God. When Jesus commissions the disciples to go out like sheep among wolves, when he calls his apostles, when he charges his followers to "preach the gospel to all nations," his commission to them is to spread the Good News of the gospel, to proclaim the imminence of the reign of God.

To talk of the mission of the Christian community, then, is to talk about being called to further the reign of God. But this calling is one that is always subject to historical conditioning and that must be asked and answered anew for every generation. Alongside the scriptural message that we have so far focused upon, there is also the need to "read the signs of the times." Reading the signs of the times is a vital dimension of contemporary religious reflection. It is a kind of lectio divina that focuses not upon the text of scripture but upon creation and human history as texts, in which the call of God and the challenges of meeting that call are always there to be seen. It is also a hazardous enterprise, since it requires an attention to the prejudices and ideology that we may bring to the reading through our own social location, gender, race, and so on, and that may distort our reading or lead us to find exactly what we are looking for. But it is a necessary activity, since without this prayerful and spirit-filled act of divination, the mission of the Christian community will be pursued naively, and thus ineffectually.

The Christian tradition, like other religions, cherishes a specific vision of what it is to be a human being and, since "ought" follows "is," sees itself as called to foster and protect that vision. To read the signs of the times, then, is to search our moment in history for all that seems to threaten the human and for those special people and places where the defense of the human and the world in which we live has been especially promoted. The anti-human will be the challenge that defines mission today. People and movements that struggle against the anti-human are our resources and our guides in the struggle.

There are many candidates for the label of "anti-human" in our world today: world poverty, disease, malnutrition, drugs, violence, terrorism, military and corporate greed, environmental collapse, and so on and so on. These are all signs of the anti-human. Reading these signs is a challenge, but one very persuasive contemporary reading of them unifies the problems under the heading of globalization. Readings of the phenomenon of globalization range from canonizing it to demonizing it, with many shades between. But there can be little doubt that the phenomenon of globalization offers the possibility of ameliorating the condition of the world's hopeless masses on the one hand, while apparently exacerbating their misery on the other. It may very well be the case that globalization is an unstoppable social force, if we mean by it the collapse of distance and the homogenization of values, which seem to follow inexorably in the wake of the miniaturization of the world brought about by the communications explosion in general and the World Wide Web in particular. But if we simply acquiesce in its inexorable advance, we abandon the Good News of the gospel. The gospel, of course, stands against evil, not against globalization. But it must stand today against those antihuman forces that gain power and momentum through the communications explosion, whether they be "savage" capitalism, power politics, or the contempt for the human that all forms of violence evince.

Mission will never stop being partially about little things, binding up the wounds of those close to hand, comforting the dying, visiting the sick. But in the face of globalization we also need to be aware that so much of what we are called to attend to close at hand is occasioned or intensified by much grander and less visible forces. The "wretched of the earth" and the "masters of the universe" are linked together. In the gospel vision, the linkage is one of a love that does justice. What are the concrete changes to which we must be committed if that relationship is to be marked by love, justice, and solidarity? Answering that question is a way of defining the face of mission today, not the whole of mission, perhaps, but that part of the mission of the church that is distinctive of our moment in history.

To Whom Is the Church Sent?

This question can be answered in fairly traditional terms. The church is sent to "all the nations," to preach the Good News. But given the nature of the contemporary mission as we have determined it above, the way in which it is sent differs remarkably from past understandings. In traditional understandings of mission, the church is the body that possesses the truth, and it is divinely commissioned to preach that truth to the ignorant of all other religions and none. This work of evangelization is successful when those who hear the message are moved to accept it and to become part of the body that proclaims it. The conversion of the world to Christ is the objective of Christian mission traditionally understood. In our contemporary approach, these assumptions have to be challenged.

If the core of the Christian gospel is the message that God loves and cares for the divine creation and wills human fulfillment, then the church is called to proclaim this truth and to struggle against everything in our world that militates against it. However, the other great world religions also maintain this same truth in their different ways, and while Christians find Jesus Christ to be the exemplar and guarantor of God's love of the world, Jews and Buddhists and Hindus have other ways of expressing their commitments to the project of human liberation from all forms of bondage. The need for mission to be effective would suggest, then, that in addressing those of other faiths, it is the message of Jesus rather than Jesus as the message that ought to be stressed. In the end, the Christian claim that Jesus is savior means that through discipleship of Jesus, the church is led to faithfulness to God's call. Successful mission needs to be measured by its effectiveness in leading people to faithfulness to the call of God as they hear it in their lives, not by its success in persuading people to abandon their own faiths and choose Jesus as the one who is exemplar and guarantor of God's love. Thus is the mission of the church fulfilled, while the integrity of the great world religions is respected.

If Christian mission can be conducted in an atmosphere of respect for the wisdom of the world's religions, then a posture of solidarity and indeed of listening can and should be adopted. Mission today has to be collaborative and humble. In the face of globalization, a solidarity of those who will work to protect the human race and our world is a necessity. But once we understand that God wills the salvation of human beings more than God wills the worldly success of Christ's church, it is also a theological responsibility. If the mission of the church is to succeed through alliances that lessen the sense that the church is privileged, and through a humble posture of listening to the wisdom of the world that is not the church, it can only conform the church more fully to Christ, who is its head, the one who was faithful to God in and through apparent human failure.

Who Is Called to Mission?

Different branches of the Christian church have answered this question in different ways, some stressing that mission is primarily the responsibility of ministers or clergy, others seeing mission at least as witness as a responsibility of the whole church. Typically, however, across the denominational divides, Christians have tended to distinguish between mission narrowly understood, which is conducted primarily through preaching the gospel, and mission more broadly construed as the exemplary lives of Christians in the world.

Today we have to rethink this division of responsibilities. If mission is primarily conducted through the church's active concern for God's world and in a struggle against the forces of the antihuman, then "preaching the gospel" in the narrow sense is more properly to be understood as a responsibility of "internal mission." Preaching the gospel is above all the way that Christians are reminded of their responsibility to mission and inspired to the cost of discipleship. The work of priests and ministers, in other words, is instrumental to the mission of the church, but not itself the mission of the church. The mission of the church is the work of the whole community, as it engages in a praxis of defense of the human, the contemporary proclamation of the Good News. In traditional categories we could call this "witness." But it is not so much witness to discipleship as it is witness that discipleship entails solidarity with suffering humanity, in the cause of faithfulness to God's love for the world. In the ancient world, those outside the young Christian community marveled at their praxis, exclaiming, "See how those Christians love one another." In our world, our mission will be successful if the world beyond the church looks at us and says, "See how those Christians love us!"

Focus

Use the ABCD method to identify points that caught your attention or challenged you in this reading.

Respond

Consider your entire time in EfM and name some views that you have discovered in your study of the EfM material regarding the mission of Israel or of the church.

Locate what your denomination or faith tradition says is the mission of the church or of people of faith, corporately or individually.

What do you believe God is up to in the world, the nation, the region, and the neighborhood in which you live, and/or in your personal life?

Practice

Reflect on your beliefs about the mission of the church and of your individual mission in the world.

THEOLOGICAL REFLECTION BEGINNING WITH A PERSONAL POSITION

Identify

From whom is the church's mission or your mission received?

How is Christ associated with the church's mission? With your understanding of your mission?

Name one context where you especially feel a sense of mission in your life.

Explore

Draw on the variety of theological perspective questions we have considered this year (systematic theology doctrines/Bishop Tutu's schema/Eric Law's Cycle of Gospel Living), choosing one to reflect on a Personal Experience or Belief, a scripture passage or other article from a faith Tradition, or messages and actions of the Culture in which one lives.

Creation/Wholeness/Powerful:
What is good or creative in the statements? How do your statements reflect or reveal a notion of wholeness or goodness? Who is empowered in this world?

Sin/Brokenness/Powerlessness:
What do your statements indicate is broken or may be a cause of separation from God? How might acting on your statement cause or support brokenness? Who is powerless? How might your statement keep someone powerless?

Judgment/Recognition/Endurance:
How would action on your stated belief(s) about a personal or corporate mission in faith provide opportunity for a change of direction? How might endurance/faith lead to empowerment?

Reorientation/Repentance/Choose the Cross:
What would need to change if you carry out the mission you believe you or the faith community has? What power may need to be relinquished? Who might need to relinquish that power?

Resurrection/Restoration/Powerful:
How might the mission you assent to contribute to restoration of wholeness between God and creation or between human beings and our world? How might the powerless receive power and the powerful take on humility?

Connect

Who, what, when, or where are the contributing factors to your beliefs about personal and corporate mission? How did those beliefs come into being? Does your belief conflict with something you learned through experience or the world around you?

Apply

What or whose freedom is possible if your mission is fulfilled in any aspect of your life?

What do you need to learn in order to better live out your sense of mission?

What has already helped to prepare you to take up that mission?

Week Thirty-one

YEAR ONE

Read

Proverbs
Job
Ecclesiastes (Qoheleth)
Collins, Chapter 24, "Proverbs" and Chapter 25, "Job and Qoheleth"

Focus

Proverbs mainly consists of ancient aphorisms, or wisdom sayings. Notice the passages from Proverbs that appeal to you as well as passages that do not appeal to you.

What do you notice about the portrayal of wisdom in Proverbs 8?

Choose some of the wisdom sayings from Proverbs that ring true for you. Read your selections aloud, noticing what stirs in you. Reflect on how the passages you selected reveal something of your deeper self: your hopes, your concerns, your experience. What position statement would you like to make?

Like Proverbs, the books of Job and Qoheleth (Ecclesiastes) are considered Wisdom books in the Jewish tradition. What is their role in relation to the book of Proverbs?

What picture of God emerges in the story of Job? What challenges or supports your own theology of God? Put yourself in the story in the place of Job; what do you say to your friends and family about God's part in what has happened to you?

In what ways does Qoheleth challenge Proverbs? What supports or challenges your own theology of creation/the world and the human condition?

YEAR TWO

Read

James
Powell, Chapter 25, "James"

Focus

Terms and names to note: wisdom literature; dispersion; purpose of the Letter of James

What view of God and of Christian community does James promote?

YEAR THREE

Read

MacCulloch, Chapter 21, "Enlightenment: Ally or Enemy?"

Focus

The Enlightenment produced a sea change in Western Christianity that continues well into the contemporary social and intellectual context. In what ways has the Enlightenment revolutionized the understanding of human nature? Think about the positive and negative impact the altered views of humanity have had on understanding vocational development.

YEAR FOUR

Read

Peace, Rose, and Mobley, Foreword, Introduction, and "Part I: Encountering the Neighbor"

Focus

In the Foreword to *My Neighbor's Faith*, Joan Chittister aptly describes what the book intends and why: "In this book all the languages of God are spoken—Hindu, Buddhist, Jewish, Christian and Muslim—so that we can learn from one another."[81]

Much is to be learned in this book about God's "commonwealth of love and justice," also known as God's reign or the kingdom of God. Identify ways the essays in "Part I: Encountering My Neighbor" contribute to developing a theology of mission and ministry in a pluralistic world. Also, what specific ideas, images, or stories foster vocational development?

ALL YEARS

Respond

Read "The Cycle of Gospel Living" by Eric Law, found on pages 342–343 in Part II of this Reading and Reflection Guide.

What personal experiences can you recall that correspond to the various points on Law's diagram of the cycle?

---

81. Jennifer Howe Peace, Or N. Rose, and Gregory Mobley, eds., *My Neighbor's Faith: Stories of Interreligious Encounter, Growth, and Transformation* (Maryknoll, NY: Orbis Books, 2012), xii.

Practice

THEOLOGICAL REFLECTION BEGINNING WITH THE CHRISTIAN TRADITION

Identify

Eric Law guides men and women to reflect on their perceptions and actions in light of increasing multicultural dynamics in much of the world. His work in the Kaleidoscope Institute presents a model of human community and interaction that may be useful in theological reflection as a means of encouraging deeper insights and implications for ministry. His Cycle of Gospel Living considers human relationship in terms of the dynamics of power viewed through a theological lens. This reflection begins with the diagram from "The Gospel Cycle of Living."

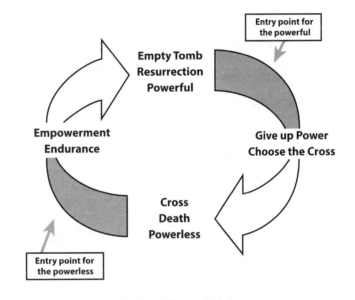

Cycle of Gospel Living

Explore

Imagine Law's model as an overlay on the EfM material you studied this week:

Where or how does the model fit?

Who had power?

Did anyone relinquish power? How?

Was anyone empowered? How did that empowerment occur?

Where is brokenness in the model? Where is restoration? At what point(s) might there be recognition that something needs to change?

Connect

Relate the model to your life and make notes about your connections from personal experience.

What aspects of your societal dimension relate to the model?

Apply

In what ways are you sent into the world to participate in Law's dynamic?

What is the relationship between the mission of the church and the larger question of the *missio Dei*?

Make notes for discussion in the seminar.

Week Thirty-two

YEAR ONE

Read

Ruth
Esther
    Collins, Chapter 26, "The Hebrew Short Story"

Focus

Imagine Ruth and Esther as stories in a volume of fictional short stories.
Now consider them as nonfiction stories that are to be taken as literally and
historically true.

    Notice what happens to the stories when read as fictional prose or as history. What contribution does each reading bring to a sense of identity and
purpose/call/mission?

YEAR TWO

Read

1 Peter
2 Peter
Powell, Chapter 26, "1 Peter," and Chapter 27, "2 Peter"

Focus

What do 1 and 2 Peter contribute to developing a theology of vocation that
can sustain you in difficult times, such as when a ministry that once brought
joy now feels unrewarding?

    What does Powell have to say that enhances your understanding of these
letters and the world in which they were written?

YEAR THREE

Read

MacCulloch, Chapter 22, "Europe Re-enchanted or Disenchanted?"

Focus

This chapter lays out necessary components for setting the context of
contemporary Anglo-American and European theology. Note what specific
persons or ideas interest you. What does what you identify suggest about
what gifts and passions you have?

YEAR FOUR

Read

Peace, Rose, and Mobley, "Part II: Viewing Home Anew" and "Part III: Redrawing Our Maps"

Focus

After spending time in another culture and openly embracing the differences, a person returns home and sees what once seemed "normal" with new eyes. Cultural dissonance sets in that requires redrawing of familiar boundaries. What implications do you find in these accounts for mission, or a theology of mission? Think about how the stories in these two sections affect your sense of self. When have you experienced a different perspective that caused you to conceive "a new normal"? What resistance in yourself did you encounter? What helped you overcome that resistance?

ALL YEARS

Respond

Members of the theological team that worked with Paul Lakeland on the theme of "church" in *Constructive Theology* provide two short articles that flesh out the longer essay.[82] The following underscores the tensions around universalism and mission:

Mission and Christian Universalism[83]

Based on Christianity's own experience with universalism, Christians can discern both graces and problems that globalism entails. Throughout the ages, universalism has led many Christians to the insight that what deserves their ultimate loyalty is not any nation, ideology, race, culture, or other "local" affiliation, but only God's creation as a whole. Christian faith in a universal God has nurtured radical ideas of human dignity and equality; today, that same faith helps to define and defend human rights internationally. Christian

---

82. Serene Jones and Paul Lakeland, eds., *Constructive Theology* (Minneapolis: Fortress Press, 2005), 234–235. Amy Platiinga Pauw, the "Church" chapter editor, along with James. H. Evans, Mary McClintock Fulkerson, Roger Haight, Bradford E. Hinze, Leonard M. Hummel, Paul Lakeland, M. Douglas Meeks, Jamie T. Phelps, Kathleen M. Sands, Craig Stein, and Kathryn Tanner, collaborated around the theme (doctrine) of church. They augmented Lakeland's statement on mission (missiology) highlighting the effects of globalization.

83. Universalism is defined in the glossary contained in *Constructive Theology* as "the theological position that all people are saved by God." Jones and Lakeland, *Constructive Theology*, 304.

universalism can have salutary effects on the advancement of knowledge. If the truth of the gospel knows no limits, then the gospel can and must be reconciled with the best science and most profound thinking available.

Unfortunately, Christian universalism also has produced the opposite effects. Rather than a basis for equality, Christianity more often has built hierarchies of domination and submission. In relation to non-Christians, universalism has been a rationale for conquest and persecution. Confidence in the universality of the gospel too often has produced not open-mindedness but a lethal combination of ignorance about and arrogance toward knowledge that comes from other sources.

Universalism, then, can be emancipatory and redemptive. But it also can be destructive and imperialist. For Christian mission, both *ad intra* and *ad extra*, a great deal depends on telling the difference. If Christian mission is nothing more (or less) than the restoration of creation, criteria for discerning emancipatory universalism can be found in four features that the Bible ascribes to the world as God's creation: the world is good, free, historical, and participatory.

The goodness of creation implies, first and foremost, the material goodness of these bodies and this planet designed by God. Universalism can only be emancipatory if, first and foremost, it protects and promotes the physical well-being of humans, other life-forms, and the earth itself. An emancipatory globalization must create worldwide standards for wages, health care, and environmental protection. When globalization refuses these standards it shows the oppressive face of universalism.

The freedom of creation is the divine intention for each being and each community to be themselves. An emancipatory globalization can lead the peoples of the world to unprecedented levels of appreciation, encounter, and engagement with each other. But when globalization results in the homogenization or "Coca-colonization" of the world, this is cultural imperialism, not emancipatory universalism.

As a historical phenomenon, creation does not end "in the beginning." It continues through time, blending into the process of redemption. The process of redemption in history is not to be mistaken for the myth of progress, in which "developed" cultures are superior in every way to traditional cultures. A redemptive globalization will not impose the values of the modern West on other cultures but will emerge from multisided dialogue and sometimes struggle among the peoples of the world.

Finally, creation is participatory; all of humanity has both the right and the responsibility to be creatures who create. As globalization weaves information into a single web and economies into a single market, it can enable more and more people to take substantive part in the decisions that shape their lives. When globalization expands everyone's access to information and ideas, when it includes and empowers, then it is functioning as an emancipatory force. But when globalization takes decisions that ought be public and gives them over to the hands of private interests, then it becomes not a grace but a problem, a destructive expression of universalism.

What are the theological positions asserted in the short article?

Describe how your experience with Christians challenges or confirms the positions.

What support and challenge to the assertions do you find in your EfM reading throughout the year?

Use ABCD as you prepare what you will share in the seminar.

Practice

THEOLOGICAL REFLECTION BEGINNING WITH A MIND MAP

Identify a focus.

A mind map is a tool, similar to brainstorming and sometimes referred to as radiant thinking, that uses a graphical format to illustrate the connections between ideas and themes. The main idea is put in the center and secondary, tertiary, and so on, relationships are shown branching out from each level of connection.

More information about and illustrations of mind maps can be found at

http://www.mindmapping.com

http://www.mindtools.com/pages/article/newISS_01.htm

You may find other sources of information on this process.

Construct a mind map by making associations with a centering theme or word. Write associations around the theme, anything that comes to mind in association with that theme. A mind map usually has at least three main branches.

The mind-mapping technique can be used to start a theological reflection from a theme from Lakeland's essay, "universalism."

EXAMPLE:

After making several associations, study the entire map.

What images or metaphors express the nature of "universalism?"

Select one to explore.

Explore the world of the metaphor/image:

Identify a specific point from which to explore the chosen image.

For example, if an image is "open doors," identify a standpoint–from inside or from outside. Stay with just one standpoint during the reflection. Other standpoints can be the source of additional theological reflections.

What questions does the image raise for you? For example, what questions come up when considering an "open door" image from the standpoint of being outside the door?

Write down two or three questions and explore the image through those perspectives.

Connect with other areas of life.

Briefly state when you experienced the world depicted in the image/metaphor you are working with. Remember to work from the standpoint previously identified.

For example, in a "standing outside an open door" metaphor, someone would connect to times when they have "stood outside an open door."

Connect with other sources, such as contemporary culture and the Christian tradition. You may find that something from your reading over the past few weeks comes to mind. Essentially, consider how the culture in which you live or the Christian tradition you experience engages in an experience like your image.

Bring in your personal beliefs about "universalism." What do you believe? What do you hold to be true?

Apply

Notice how what you learn from the reflection applies to your life. For example, what light does this reflection shed on how you engage opportunities for ministry? What mission might your image be directing you towards?

Write a prayer about the learning or insight you have gained as a result of your reflection.

Note: There may be opportunity during the group's seminar time to explore the theological reflections of various group members, and/or to create a mind map to generate a reflection around a central theme of the group's choosing.

Week Thirty-three

YEAR ONE

Read

Daniel
1 and 2 Maccabees
Collins, Chapter 27, "Daniel, 1–2 Maccabees"

Focus

Terms and names to note: apocalypse; apocalyptic literature; Maccabee; pseudonymity as a literary device; martyrdom and militancy

What messages about personal identity, relationship with God, and mission do you find in Daniel and in the Maccabees books?

YEAR TWO

Read

1 John, 2 John, and 3 John
Powell, Chapter 28, "The Johannine Letters: 1 John, 2 John, 3 John"

Focus

Note how the Johannine letters make use of light vs. dark; children of God vs. children of the devil; truth vs. deceit; and good vs. evil. What are these letters saying about Christian identity?

Reflect on how the theme of "practicing love" relates to your theologies of vocation and mission.

YEAR THREE

Read

MacCulloch, Chapter 23, "To Make the World Protestant"

Focus

MacCulloch's chapter covers over two hundred years of history that is likely familiar. As the historian's work comes closer to the present, the line between history and journalism blurs. Identify a thread that runs through the chapter. In one or two sentences, describe it. Examine the thread using questions framed from the theological standpoints of human nature; creation, sin, judgment, repentance, and redemption; the way God is disclosed; and the kind of future desired. What connections can you find with concepts, images, or stories from current culture and society? Name what truths and beliefs you hold. Consider what you now see that you have not seen before. Describe ways this reflection may inspire to make a difference in your daily life as a Christian seeking to serve the world in Christ's name.

YEAR FOUR

Read

Peace, Rose, and Mobley, "Part IV: Unpacking Our Belongings" and "Part V: Stepping Across the Line"

Focus

Think back to any encounters you may have had with persons from other faith traditions than your own. What baggage did you need to unpack, what preconceptions did you find a need to let go of? If you have not had such an encounter, think of how non-Christians have been portrayed in the media you read or watch. When have you encountered a report that seemed contrary to your understanding or beliefs about persons of a faith not your own?

"Interfaith encounter forces its practitioners to assume responsibility for both the actual and perceived histories of their groups."[84] Reflect on the significance of what the authors in Parts IV and V deal with in such encounters and recall what you have experienced whenever you have encountered "the hospitality of your neighbor's faith."

ALL YEARS

Respond

What is the call to the church (or God's people) at the time described in your reading assignment this week? What would you say is the call to the church today?

Pay attention to signs on churches in your vicinity or visit their buildings and notice their bulletin boards or visit their web sites.

What can you identify about what the sense of mission might be in these churches?

Use ABCD as you prepare what you will share in the seminar.

Practice

Alan Jones, Episcopal priest, author, and spiritual director, offers a description of the spiritual journey as engagement with three great imperatives of the desert tradition: *Look! Weep! Live!* This mode offers still another way to guide and deepen theological reflection.

The first imperative is, *Look!* Looking means a contemplative willingness to see what is there in front of us without prematurely interpreting what we see. The

---

84. Peace, Rose, and Mobley, eds., *My Neighbor's Faith*, 125.

desert tradition claims that if we look long and accurately enough, the tears will begin to flow. Thus the second imperative is, *Weep!* The fruit of honest contemplation is "the gift of tears"; and the sure sign that our attentiveness has been focused and honest and the tears cleansing is joy. Joy is the fruit of desert patience. Thus, the third imperative, *Live!*

The pattern is simple. We look. We weep. We live. This pattern is repeated throughout the believer's life. It echoes and reverberates both in and out of the Christian tradition.[85]

When we Identify a focus from which to begin reflection and Explore that focus, we respond to the imperative to *Look!*, noticing how the world is. Exploring also takes us into the *Weep!* Imperative as a sense of what brings about separation from God and others begins to dawn. We enact the imperative to *Live!* as we explore that which restores wholeness and identify Insights and Implications that take us back into the action of life.

Practice reflecting with Jones's model on the various mission indicators you noted in the Respond section of this week's preparation. How does that sense of mission represent what the congregation appears to believe is "broken" in the world, and what represents their call to "*Live!*"?

Apply Jones's desert imperatives to your life as you have reflected on it during your experience in EfM. What have you looked at and seen as a result of EfM? What have you wept over? What have you lived in a new way?

Note: The preference is to work with actual evidence from local church statements—explicit or implicit—rather than just imagining what such statements or views might be. What are some ways that the seminar group might identify the sense of mission of churches in the area if there was not time for individuals to do this work before the seminar meeting?

---

85. Alan W. Jones, *Soul Making-The Desert Way of Spirituality* (San Francisco: Harper & Row, 1975), 22.

Week Thirty-four

YEAR ONE

Read

Ben Sira (Ecclesiasticus)
Wisdom of Solomon
Collins, Chapter 28, "The Deuterocanonical Wisdom Books"

Focus

The books of Ben Sira (Ecclesiasticus) and Wisdom of Solomon are not in all editions of the Bible. You will need a Bible that contains the Apocrypha, sometimes called deuteron-canonical books. An online edition of the Oxford Annotated Bible (NRSV) with the Apocrypha is available on the Oxford Biblical Studies Online website. Information about logging in to this site is at the front of this Guide, following the reading assignments chart.

Terms and names to note: Ecclesiastes; apocrypha; female personification of Wisdom; theodicy; Stoics; *cosmos*; the role of the Scribe; *beth midrash*; eschatology; Plato's *Republic*; Wisdom and the *Logos*; "natural theology"

YEAR TWO

Read

Jude
Powell, Chapter 29, "Jude"

Focus

What is a polemic? What examples of polemic do you find in your contemporary culture?

What is the mission of the church for Jude?

YEAR THREE

Read

MacCulloch, Chapter 24, "Not Peace but a Sword"

Focus

Terms and names to note: the major events for the Church from 1914–1960; key aspects leading to both World Wars; the four Christian emperors at the beginning of World War I; Bolshevik; Pius the IX and Christ the King feast day; Benedict XV; *Cristeros*; Bernardino Nogara; Charles Brent and Nathan Söderblom; Josiah Olulowo Ositelu

How does your view of change in the church connect with MacCulloch's?

YEAR FOUR

Read

Peace, Rose, and Mobley, "Part VI: Finding Fellow Travelers"

Focus

Terms and names to note: Howard Thurman; *ru'ah hakodesh*; William Sloane Coffin

Do you have a story about finding fellow travelers as your own call to ministry has developed?

ALL YEARS

Respond

A second short article from Jones and Lakeland adds the following thoughts on mission.

Post-colonial Critiques of Mission[86]

Although it is a call to spread good news, the "Great Commission" of Matthew's Gospel has done considerable damage. This is the judgment of post-colonial criticisms, which interrogate the effects of the past 500 years of Western expansion, in which Western values, including Christianity, were brought to every corner of the globe. Christian mission was woven into mercantile trading routes and imperial expansion from the very beginning. However, post-colonialists focus on the medium of Western colonialism, an economic and political relation between nations in which the sovereignty of one was dependent upon the power of the other "empire" nation. Emerging in the mercantile imperialism of the late 1400s to 1800s and accompanying missionary movements, colonialist forms of Western power were later enhanced through the force of monopoly capitalism in the late nineteenth through the mid-twentieth century.

Post-colonialist criticism reveals that missionary expansion has been inextricably complicit with forces of expanding power and the inevitable complexities of dominance and submission that attend them. Missionary literature of these centuries unabashedly brands the objects of mission as inferior in status. They were "the Heathen," according to a 1792 pamphlet. Africans were "savages" or "barbarians" practicing "primitive" religion. Even the "affirmation" in the 1537 papal announcement that Amerindians were human was rooted in an economy of Western superiority. Paradoxically founded in ostensibly well-intentioned desire to share good news, Christian

---

86. Jones and Lakeland, *Constructive Theology*, 236–237.

mission's imaginaries for the Other and the practices that accompanied them effectively obliterated the dignity and agency of many populations in colonized territories.

Although the "Colonial period" has passed, the "post" of post-colonial criticism is not a chronological indicator, signaling that Christianity and the world have moved beyond the problems of Western dominance. Even with the coming of political independence for most colonized nations and the end of official colonial relationships by mid-twentieth century, new forms of global economic, military, and cultural dominance associated with global capitalism have emerged, frequently termed neocolonialism. Coinage of such terms as coloniality to refer to the continued residual effects of colonialism also reminds us that grave problems persist.

Despite universal renunciation of the dehumanizing terms of the past, what is problematic in continuing forms of coloniality remains unresolved. Some would argue that the more egregious treatments of "natives" as barbarian or pagan are corrected by recognizing the legitimacy of indigenous cultures. The missionary task is to adapt the gospel to a local culture—a process known as indigenization for Protestants and inculturation for Roman Catholics. The problem of colonized consciousness is, for example, solved by a recovery of traditional African religion, or at least by empowering indigenous African theologians. Others, however, insist that not only is a search for pure origins impossible, but inculturation and its terms (for example, culture as "clothing" or "soil" for the gospel) are themselves a species of post-colonialist Western discourse. However it is understood, post-colonialist discourse about mission constitutes a formidable search for the power of gospel as God's justice and will be vital to ecclesiology in the new millennium.

Notice the emotions and thoughts that the article evokes in you. Identify what experiences you have had that impact your response.

How do you think other authors that you have read in EfM would respond to the article?

Use ABCD as you prepare what you will share in the seminar.

Practice

Use the outline to reflect theologically on the issue that you have identified. After completing the worksheet, reflect on the ways in which the theological reflection sheds light on your vocation and ministry.

Identify

Identify a focus.

For this Practice, work with the personal emotions, thoughts, and experiences you noted in the Respond section.

Explore the focus/***Look!***

As you think about your thoughts, feelings, and personal experience, what image or word might capture your sense of things?

Make some notes about the following:

Questions that arise for you as you consider the image or word.

What question(s) makes you ***Weep!***?

How does your image or word address separation from God or others?

How does your image or word relate to power/powerlessness/empowerment?

Connect

How do you answer those questions?
Where do you turn for the answers?
Whose "voice" speaks answers to you?

Apply/Live!

State any sense of restoration to wholeness you experience in the reflection and/or how you are going to foster such a restoration in your daily life.

Week Thirty-five

YEAR ONE

Read

Yee, Chapter 4, "Affirming and Contradicting Gender Stereotypes" by Judy Fentress-Williams and Melody D. Knowles
Collins, Chapter 29, "From Tradition to Canon"

Focus

Terms and names to note: boundary crossing as a blessing; *Megilloth*; genre; *hesed*; "otherness" of Ruth; transferring the child to Naomi; multiple identities in Esther; Esther's wisdom; good women vs. bad women in Ben Sira and Proverbs; skin color in Song of Songs; sexuality and allegory in Song of Songs; Wisdom in Proverbs and the Wisdom of Solomon; the virtuous woman in Proverbs; Job's wife; matrilineal; Sheerah

Collins notes that the Hebrew Bible contains stories from a community capable of lively internal debate and self-criticism. Thinking back over your readings this year, where have you encountered such stories?

Thinking back over your readings this year, where in the Hebrew Bible did you encounter positive portrayal of life in a multicultural world? Where did you encounter negative portrayal?

If you read this chapter at the beginning of the year, what is different for you now as you read it at the end of your study of the Hebrew Bible?

YEAR TWO

Read

The Revelation to John
Powell, Chapter 30, "Revelation"

Focus

State one new understanding and one thing that challenges you about the Revelation to John.

In what ways has the Revelation been appropriated in the culture of the United States? (Substitute your own nationality if you have encountered such appropriation.)

YEAR THREE

Read

MacCulloch, Chapter 25, "Cultural Wars"

Focus

Reflect on how MacCulloch's context as an Oxford-trained British citizen shapes his understanding of history. How does his understanding compare with yours and the context from which you read history?

YEAR FOUR

Read

Peace, Rose, and Mobley, "Part VII: Repairing Our Shared World"

Focus

Note any sense of call you are experiencing as you read this final section.

ALL YEARS

Respond

This unit brings attention to one's vocation as hearing and responding to God's call. State your deepest sense at this moment of what God is calling you to do to contribute to the restoration of wholeness in the world.

Use ABCD as you prepare what you will share in the seminar.

Practice

Describe how you experience something as a call from God.

What practices best help you attend to God and be available to experience a call?

What would hold you back from that practice?

Either in employment or a volunteer capacity, what activity most engages you in a sense of God's call to you?

What wholeness does that work contribute to?

What brokenness does it address?

How are you transformed in doing that work?

Describe your understanding of ministry for yourself.

Week Thirty-six: Closing the Year

The mentor and group will decide how they want to incorporate this work and its sharing into any celebration of the year they might want to create.

ALL YEARS

Read

We sustain each other in the constant interplay between absence and presence. A sustaining ministry asks ministers to be not only creatively present but creatively absent. A creative absence challenges ministers to develop an ever growing intimacy with God in prayer and to make that the source of their entire ministry.[87] —*Henri Nouwen*

Closure is a time to acknowledge what has been, to celebrate what now is, and to anticipate what will come. The time given to this depends on the length of time the group has been together and the personal styles of group members and the mentor. EfM provides an opportunity to form a close and supportive community that cannot be easily replaced. It is important for participants to acknowledge the blessing of the group's time together, while also helping each other shift to new forms of emotional, spiritual, and intellectual support for their ministry.

Closure includes telling stories about significant events in the life of the group and the ways the group has affected each person. Name any regrets or frustrations people have, look ahead to what steps seem to be in view, and help one another plan for alternative forms of support for future life and ministry. The following work combines closure with a focus on ministry going forward.

Focus

The *Guide* invited us this year to use theological reflection perspectives of restoration and wholeness and perspectives of power, powerlessness, and empowerment, in addition to other familiar perspectives of the world, sin, judgment, repentance, and redemption. We also were invited to develop a personal Rule of Life.

Review the theological perspectives of Bishop Tutu's cycle of Wholeness-Restoration.

---

87. Henri Nouwen, *Bread for the Journey: A Daybook of Wisdom and Faith* (San Francisco: Harper San Francisco, 1977), 77.

- **Wholeness/goodness**
  What is revealed about wholeness or goodness of creation?

- **Brokenness/separation from God**
  What constitutes threats to wholeness or goodness or as brokenness or separation from God?

- **Recognition**
  What is a threat to goodness or to a relationship to God? How would you recognize such a threat?

- **Reorientation**
  What reveals a reorientation to relationship with God, if any? What would such a reorientation cost? What would it promise?

- **Restoration to wholeness**
  Where is there a possibility of restoration to wholeness?

Review theological perspectives based on Eric Law's Cycle of Gospel Living: being powerful, loss or yielding up of power, and empowerment.

- **Give up power: choose the cross**
  This is a point of entry for the powerful. Who has power? What has to be yielded?

- **Cross: death, powerlessness**
  This is a point of entry for the powerless. What sacrifice(s) might be called for? What are the temptations of the cross, of powerlessness? To whom or what is power yielded?

- **Empowerment: endurance**
  How is power transmitted to the powerless party? What is required in order to enter the cycle that leads to empowerment? What builds endurance?

- **Empty tomb: resurrection, power**
  What is left behind? How does resurrection occur? What is the hope of the power received?

A Rule can reflect decisions about prayer, study, and action related to these categories.

- Listening

- Commitment

- Time

- Hospitality

- Reflection

Review notes you made during the year, material you studied, reflections and discussions and celebrations with the group, and your spiritual autobiography.

Respond

This year's theme is "Living Faithfully in a Multicultural World." With that theme in mind and your review of your EfM work, respond to the following.

Experience in EfM has helped me:

- let go of . . .

- adopt . . .

- affirm . . .

- focus on . . .

Practice

Read the following before you begin so you can have a sense of the process.

Set a timer for whatever period you wish to remain in silence. You may want to use your journal to note your responses to the questions below.

Begin with prayer.

Still yourself. Allow yourself to become present to the Spirit of God. When the timer alerts you, continue with the following.

What feelings did you experience?

Write about anything that came to your awareness in the silence.

Read through what you wrote to consider:

- what movement(s) of the Spirit carried you during your silence with God;

- where the movement(s) took you;

- what images arose;

- who came to mind;

- what possibilities stretch before you;

- what you sensed about God.

Complete the following:

Directions I sense for my ministry as I practice living faithfully in my world are:

- for the next three months . . .

- for the next year . . .

The spiritual practices that sustain me at this time are . . .

Go forth in peace to love and serve the Lord.

Plan with your seminar group a way to celebrate your time together as a community this year. As a way of acknowledging the sending out of those who will not be part of the group next year, whether graduating or for another reason, you may wish to incorporate this litany as part of your closing of the year together.

A Litany of Farewell

Fellow Christian ministers, let us pray for the saving presence of our living God.

>**In this world:**
>*Christ is risen.*
>**In this community:**
>*Christ is risen.*
>**In this gathering:**
>*Christ is risen.*
>**In the hearts of all faithful people:**
>*Christ is risen.*

We pray and give thanks now for [name(s)], leaving our community.

>**For expectations not met:**
>*Lord have mercy.*
>**For grievances not resolved:**
>*Lord have mercy.*
>**For wounds not healed:**
>*Lord have mercy.*
>**For anger not dissolved:**
>*Lord have mercy.*
>**For gifts not given:**
>*Lord have mercy.*
>**For promises not kept:**
>*Lord have mercy.*

>**For this portion of our lifelong pilgrimages which we have shared in this place:**
>*Thanks be to God.*
>**For friendships made, celebrations enjoyed, and for moments of nurture:**
>*Thanks be to God.*
>**For wounds healed, expectations met, gifts given, promises kept:**
>*Thanks be to God.*
>**For trust and confidence shared; times of good humor and moments of gentle leadership:**
>*Thanks be to God.*
>**For bread and wine, body and blood:**
>*Thanks be to God.*

And so, to continue your ministry with other members of the family of Christ:

Go in peace.

To continue to live faithfully with new companions and new adventures, new gifts to give and receive:

Go in peace.

To offer wisdom and experience, competence and compassion, in the ministry to which you are called:

Go in peace.

With whatever fears, whatever sadness, whatever excitement may be yours:

Go in peace.

With our faith in you, our hope for you, our love of you:

Go in peace.

[Offer intercessions, petitions, and thanksgivings, closing with this prayer said together.]

Now, we pray, be with those who leave and with those who stay; and grant that all of us, by drawing ever nearer to you, may always be close to each other in the communion of your saints. All this we ask for the sake of Jesus Christ, our Savior. Amen.

PART II

Resources

Supplemental Readings in the Christian Tradition

Week Three, Reading Assignment for Year Four

On Being Theologically Literate[74]

I. On Being Literate

At its simplest, to be literate is to be able to read and write. But there is a stronger sense to the word. To be literate is to be well read in, or at least familiar with the literature of a particular subject. It is this sense that interests us: that is, with being literate in the field of Christian theology; of having a grasp of the tradition through its written deposit.

This could suggest merely an attempt to provide an annotated select bibliography, or a Cook's tour of key theological debates. Such an enterprise would, indeed, have its value. However, the intention is to explore a more fundamental implication. It is important to ask, what is the purpose of being literate? How fundamental is it to Christian believing? But to be literate has also meant to be a member of the literati, an aficionado, a member of an elite. Are we merely trying to boost the standing of the specialists in theology, professional or amateur, who play an esoteric game, far apart from ordinary discipleship? Or is it relevant to a core Christian concern that affects us all?

The basis of my argument is that Christianity sees itself as historical in a unique sense and that therefore tradition is an essential part of living in and with that historical reality. Of course Christianity shares the basic human experience of finding identity in historical continuity embedded in story and culture. There are also, as with many other religions, foundational events which are normative for its existence. But Christianity, taking further its Jewish heritage, has classically affirmed that revelation and salvation were uniquely embodied (incarnate) in these particular events. Thus the historical is not merely the stage for religious discovery or the medium for a religious idea but essential to the substance of Christian faith. The human experience, therefore, of being historical is of the heart of Christian existence and that tradition, in all its ambiguity, is necessary to Christian self-identity, part of being caught up in the drama of salvation. Therefore, to have a sense of the past is a key element in Christian awareness; and being literate is very much bound up with that. There are bound to be wide variations among Chris-

---

74. Paul H. Ballard, "On Being Theologically Literate," *Modern Believing* 38 (3), July 1997, 34–42. When this article was written Ballard was head of the department of Religious and Theological Studies at the University of Wales, Cardiff, where he taught practical theology.

tians as to how this is experienced and expressed. There are different callings and concerns: for some it is at the centre of their ministry as theologians but for most literacy is a backcloth to their particular Christian obedience; some will have grown up on the stories of the past heroes and heroines, but others will have only just begun to explore their new found faith. There is no 'national curriculum' that everyone must meet, but all can begin to recognize and draw on the spiritual, intellectual and artistic resources to which all in fact are indebted.

2. The Issue Today

The idea of theological literacy only becomes an issue when it appears to be under threat. Otherwise it is taken for granted. I am continually alerted to this year by year as I have to recognize that it is less and less possible to assume a basic cultural background as the starting point for teaching. The present generation seems to have lost the western (British) classical tradition which included some debt to Greece and Rome as well as to Shakespeare, the Prayer Book and the Bible. There may be a new tradition emerging but a hiatus, a complete break, will cut future generations off from their heritage.

Our society has, in the last quarter of the twentieth century, been going through a significant cultural sea change. Thomas Kuhn has taught us to use the phrase 'paradigm shift' to describe the transition from one world view, with its fundamental cultural patterns and assumptions, to another that will express itself in new habits, customs and intellectual norms. It has been widely argued that we are going through such a Copernican revolution, watching the end of the Enlightenment of the Modern era and the emergence of Postmodernism, some kind of New Age.[75]

It is never possible, however, from the midst of events to see precisely where history is leading. We cannot be sure whether what we are experiencing is a total 'paradigm shift', like the emergence of the modern world out of the middle ages, or merely a further out-working of the process of modernization. At the same time it is important to ask how total any historical change can be. There are always elements of continuity as well as discontinuity. Perhaps we are only going through a period where the latter, discontinuity, is temporarily dominant and the continuities will again reassert themselves.

Nevertheless the last decades have been a period of far-reaching social change which are significant for this and subsequent generations. In a number of ways basic attitudes have changed. This is, of course, significant for Christianity, for the Church, too, is inevitably caught up in the process. And this poses a problem for, to paraphrase the words of Reinhold Niebuhr,

---

75. Thomas S. Kuhn, *The Structure of Scientific Revolution* (Chicago: Chicago University Press, 1970). See also theological explorations of this idea in Hans Kung and David Tracy (eds) *Paradigm Change in Theology, a Symposium for the Future* (Edinburgh: T & T Clark, 1989) and David J. Bosch, *Transforming Mission* (Mary Knoll: Orbis, 1991).

it is necessary to distinguish between what cannot be changed and has to be accepted, indeed affirmed, and what has to be resisted and possibly changed, and that always carries risk and courage.[76]

3. Significant Trends in Contemporary Culture

What then are some of the characteristic features of the present that are significant for our theme? These may or may not be mutually compatible, which is not surprising in the maelstrom of history.

3.1. We live in an increasingly pragmatic society

Francis Bacon recognized that knowledge is power. In our generation the experiential growth of scientific understanding of the mechanisms of the universe suggest that we can unlock the key to existence. However, there has been a change in the relationship between science and technology. Science is increasingly harnessed to technology. Knowledge is valued in relation to its uses. This can be seen in the emphasis at all levels of education on learning for economic and social purposes. The question thus becomes 'What can we do?' and moral truth is dependent on being able to do what we want. Kant's 'I ought therefore I can' can be so easily inverted into 'I can therefore I ought'. All problems that might arise are susceptible to solution by further applications of technology whether by producing new techniques and more sophisticated tools or by social management. The computer is the model of life. Appeals to past wisdom or alternative lines of argument are regarded as outdated and retrograde.

3.2. Paradoxically, there is a new emphasis on holism

The analytical methodology of classical enlightenment thinking has led, it is argued, to mechanistic fragmentation. It is necessary to recover the inter-relatedness of all things. This ranges, on the one hand, from the physicist's interest in cosmology to the biologist working on the ecological structures of habitat, including our own. On the other hand it has also stimulated a quest for more religious and mystical ways of looking at existence, a feature that frequently rejects Christianity because that has been too closely bound with the destructive tendencies of Western science. Instead there is attraction to the unities of the Indian religions or the nature mysticism of traditional tribal religion. There is, thus, an increasing desire to search for inclusive ways of thinking about our world that will give a framework for the resolution of the confrontational attitudes that seem endemic to the modern world.

3.3. There is a new romanticism

The rationalism of modernism has, from time to time, been challenged by forms of romanticism. Romanticism emphasizes the intuitive and emotion-

---

76. This reflects the well known prayer used by Alcoholics Anonymous.

al. There is a sense of the immediacy of knowledge whose truth is grasped through inward conviction. The creative freedom of the human spirit has to be given free rein. The artist is the priest of humanity, the channel for expressing the power of the human spirit. Tradition and the past are often seen as inhibiting, quenching the flames of human potential.

Since the late 1960s there has been a resurgence of romanticism. There has been a flowering of religion, mainly of a mystical kind, frequently rejecting the apparent formalisms of Christianity for the esoteric possibilities of the East and elsewhere. This has been heralded as a new era, the Age of Aquarius or the New Age or the Age of the Spirit. Within Christianity itself there has been a renewed emphasis on these elements in the tradition that look to immediacy and religious experience. Most clearly this has been found in the Charismatic movement, which has its exaggerated and sometimes dangerous side; but it can be found in more Catholic forms and in the interest in the search for spirituality in non-Western traditions such as Orthodoxy or Celtic Christianity.

3.4. We live in an increasingly pluralistic and relativistic society

The pluralism is most clearly seen in the ethnic and cultural mix found in our inner cities. But pluralism is much more pervasive. The cohesions of our common history are more and more tenuous as religions and ideological traditions disintegrate. There is an increasing fragmentation which begins, in places, to threaten social cohesion. People are being forced to find security and identity through belonging to different, often embattled, associations.

This fragmentation has been boosted by the advocacy of personal rights and the consumer society. Diversity and choice are seen as the supreme social good. In the competitive market of the enterprise culture, everything is up for grabs. Marketing has taken over, even in the area of values and faith, seeking to catch the attention of the passing customer who may be more attracted to the wares next door.

3.5. There is a belief in the future at the expense of the past

Part of the mind set of the modern person is the explanatory value of history. Something can be understood when seen in its historical context. But there is a conflict here. The emphasis can be on the importance of origins or of destiny. Today our eyes are on the future. This has been true of technology which promises a brighter tomorrow and of policies that, especially in Marxism but also in Capitalism, hold up the possibilities of a renewed society. It has also become a marked feature of contemporary theology, especially political and liberation theology: the promise of the Kingdom of God already present in the resurrection of Jesus and the life of the Spirit. But such a drive can downgrade the past, relegate it to an irrelevant curiosity. History or tradition has today to justify itself as having a positive contribution to make to human welfare.

Alvin Toffler and others warned about 'future shock'.[77] It may appear that some of their expectations were exaggerated. Many of the old traditional perspectives persist, and the future is never entirely predictable. Yet a lot of what they foresaw has come about. And we are just on the threshold of the electronic revolution. The new world would seem to be markedly different from the old.

As has been indicated from time to time, this cultural shift has affected religion along with the rest of society. Religion is not dead but is a many-headed hydra which grows two heads where one is cut off. As Madeleine Bunting in the Guardian expressed it, 'it's DIY; forget tradition, just find a few friends and make it up as you go along'.[78] This is confirmed by Rosalie Osmond in her study of contemporary religion, i.e. Christianity. She detects a sharp separation between tradition and faith. The former is embodied in the burdens of old dead intellectualism, ritual, buildings and social trappings. The new faith is immediate, personal, experiential, God in the unusual and exciting. It is all rather simple and naive.[79]

4. The Importance of Literacy

For Christianity there is an obvious and crucial dilemma. The Gospel has indeed to be proclaimed in ways that connect with and are accessible to the new cultural context. Indeed the present time has seen a great flowering of new forms of worship and presentation—even if some go well over the top! But it cannot be at the expense of forgetting the tradition, for that threatens to reduce faith to mere sentimentality.

The importance of being literate is precisely because it addresses this fundamental relation between the present and the past. By definition a literature is the cumulative deposit of the tradition. And Christianity, as an incarnational religion, is essentially rooted in history. There is a focal point in past time—the life, death and resurrection of Jesus Christ—to which the Christian community is anchored. There is also a commitment to being part of a community that has forged its self-awareness and identity in the course of a pilgrimage of faith—a cumulative storehouse of wisdom that cannot be cast aside. The present can only be understood in the light of the past and, normatively, knows itself to be Christian by its loyalty to its origins. That is, history is part of the existence of faith.

But this is not to advocate mere traditionalism. Tradition can be a dead weight, an unadventurous reproduction of a received pattern of faith. To talk about all this in terms of literacy, however, also insists on the hermeneutic imperative; the need to be critically aware of the past in a discerning and open way so that there is a creative and liberating dialogue with tradition.

---

77. Alvin Toffler, *Future Shock* (London: Bantam, 1984).
78. *The Guardian*, 24th December 1995.
79. Rosalie Osmond, *Changing Perspectives* (London: Darton, Longman and Todd, 1993).

Past and present are knit together in a living obedience to the faith that has fed and nurtured the saints.

4.1. Being literate makes one aware of one's roots

Arthur Hayley's book and television series *Roots* highlighted for so many what it meant to search for origins and to understand the tradition.[80] This is a basic human motivation. In a cosmopolitan and often hostile world it helps to provide an identity. So for the Christian, it is important to secure identity with the household of faith, not only in the Bible but subsequently, as part of world history and the history of nations.

4.2. Being literate also gives a sense of belonging

To begin to know the story is to discover that one is a member of the household of God, enfolded in the communion of saints, both down history and across the globe. It is indeed a motley crew, with skeletons in the cupboard and episodes of which properly to be ashamed. But it also includes great heroes and heroines of the faith, martyrs, confessors, doctors, evangelists and countless ordinary people who, like ourselves, just get on with being obedient. From them can be drawn inspiration and wisdom, challenge and vision.

4.3. Being literate widens our horizons

Even in an age of mobility and television, we remain parochial in Christian experience. But there is a whole world out there of spirituality, service and witness that can fill out and challenge our limited perspective. Like the householder in the Gospel it is possible to bring out treasures old and new. We will, thus, begin to understand our own tradition, appreciate its positive strengths, set it in a wider context and review it in the light of the wider tradition. It was precisely out of such exposure in such bodies as the Student Christian Movement that the ecumenical quest arose. Sometimes it may be necessary to take a stand but each affirmation can also be the loss of another truth by denial. We need each other. One of the saddest trends of recent years has been the diminution of the ecumenical imperative, a theme that needs to be re-woven into the counterpoint of Christian living.

4. 4. Being literate brings new resources in our search for Christian understanding

Other cultures, past or present, often see things very differently from the way we do. Their experience is not ours; their ways of thinking can be strange to us. But this sets up a dialogue between us, for their seeming oddity may hide wisdom that illuminates and challenges our assumptions in surprising ways. Especially at a time when so much of our inherited wisdom seems to be running into the sand, it is valuable to explore alternatives that may open up new possibilities. For example, the Orthodox tradition of the East is meeting the quest for a greater mystical emphasis; Evangelicals are

---

80. Arthur Hayley, *Roots.*

rediscovering their spiritual and radical roots, not least by looking at the early and medieval Church; or Christians in Korea are exploring traditional spiritualities to understand better the communion of saints.

4.5. Being literate helps us recognize that our problems are not unique

Others have been there before and may help us in our situation. Of course circumstances are never the same but there is no need to reinvent the wheel. A good example is the issue of cultural pluralism. For us, after so long a period of Western hegemony, it comes as a shock but this was precisely the situation of the early Church. They had to ask what to make of the traditional paganism, the mystery religions and minority faiths. They also had to discover how to enter into dialogue with the dominant philosophical traditions of their day as we do with the rationalist and postmodern culture of our own. It is also the situation of Christian minority groups in the ancient cultures of the far east—India, China, Japan. The surprising thing is that these are seldom cited in our debates, yet they have experience of struggling to find their identity in a culture that is both theirs and yet not theirs.

4.6. Being literate means that we can faithfully reappraise the past

The hermeneutic dialogue also allows us to question the past on the basis of our own situation. The striking example of this is the concern for the status of women in the Church which has traditionally, within the social conventions, been male dominated. But once the question is asked, then it is possible to look afresh at the tradition and to discover that there is a hidden strand waiting to be discovered of women's spirituality; a strand which itself interacts with the contemporary dialogue.

5. How to be Literate

To be literate, therefore, enables us to relate to the tradition with a freedom and creativity that both strengthens faith and, through a critical solidarity, opens up a creative dialogue, exploring new avenues of believing and obedience. But how do we become literate?

5.1. A word of caution

Modernization has eroded the possibility of living in a tradition based society. From time immemorial a tradition was handed down through the normal social structures of family, communal customs, rites of passage, peer group activity, education, religion, folk arts. Ideas, vocabulary, etiquette, expected roles and customs were picked up accidentally and absorbed subliminally. Now it has to be a conscious effort. Faith has to be kept alive, traditions deliberately sustained. The Church is in the business of creating and sustaining a counter culture. But absorbing a tradition takes time. There is no quick fix. To become literate is a time consuming, deliberate, demanding effort. It is not possible to rely on it happening naturally anymore.

5.2. To become literate means, therefore, entering into a journey

Christian initiation is admission into the community of faith, including its tradition. This, as part of the journey of faith, is a life-long process. At its heart is a participation in the drama of salvation, focused in the scripture and the communion. But it is also to seek to be steeped in the traditions of the Church. Hymns and prayers and other means put before us the resources of the past. Preaching and teaching draw on the wisdom of others. The Prayer Book, missal and hymn book are treasure stores from which we can each, variously, learn. Beyond this there are the other activities of prayer and study, of reading and shared witness and service that give shape to Christian discipleship both locally and in the wider Church. It is important, therefore, to pay attention to the routine of daily life in the Church for it is this that will create the images of Christian commitment and mould the lives of those that participate.

5.3. There are indeed classics

For Christians this is, first and foremost, the Bible. But we live in a generation for whom the Bible is a closed book, no longer the basic literature of education and culture. The plethora of new translations may not have been helpful. Even for practising Christians the selected readings heard weekly hardly begin to offer any real insights. We have to find our modern equivalent of systematic daily reading through the scriptures. Moreover it has to be done in the light of two hundred years of critical historical scholarship. The Bible has to become both a living scripture and an historical resource in the religious quest of humanity.

There are also other Christian classics that have traditionally been used for devotional reading, a source of inspiration and wisdom: Augustine's *Confessions*, Julian's *Shewings*, Thomas a Kempis' *Imitation of Christ*, Bunyan's *Pilgrim's Progress*, Bonhoeffer's *Cost of Discipleship*, Henri Nouwen's *The Wounded Healer*, and many others.[81] There are convenient anthologies that open up wide selections very quickly, and many modern writers not only draw on them but offer introductions and commentary. Indeed this age is producing its own literature, some of which will themselves become classic.

Theological literacy is not primarily a matter of erudition—though the Church needs its theological high flyers. It is first and foremost about having an open and inquisitive spirit that is glad to become engaged with the Christian story because that is the family to which we belong. Besides there is a great sense of reward and it is often real fun. James Stewart, in his classic on preaching admonishes his readers.

---

81. Augustine, *Confessions* (Oxford: Oxford University Press, 1992); Julian of Norwich, *Shewings* (New York: Paulist Press, 1978); Thomas a Kempis, *The Imitation of Christ* (Harmondsworth: Penguin, 1956); John Bunyan, *Pilgrim's Progress* (Edinburgh: Banner of Truth, 1989); D. Bonhoeffer, *The Cost of Discipleship* (London: SCM Press, 1959); Henri Nouwen, *The Wounded Healer* (New York: Doubleday, 1972).

There is another resource which will come powerfully to your aid . . . your fellowship with the great minds of the centuries. . . . Keep alert to what theology is saying. Refresh your soul with the living waters of the spiritual classics—all these and many more are your rightful heritage: and who could dwell there and not be 'strengthened in the inner man' . . . Such intercourse will impart new qualities of breadth, insight, dignity and precision to all your work. Therefore, in the words of the Apostolic injunction, 'give heed to reading'.[82]

Stewart may have had the preacher in mind, but the preacher is enabling the congregations to enter into its heritage. This is a promise for the whole people of God.

5.4. There is a growing and continuing need to stimulate Christian reading and learning

It is encouraging to recall how many are engaged in various forms of theological education from evening classes and public lectures to degrees and research. It is also interesting that the present demand seems to be precisely to obtain familiarity with the foundational elements—Bible study, doctrine and spirituality. It seems that there is an instinctive awareness of a need to rediscover the tradition and to dig new foundations in a strange and changing world. And there is an increasing volume of good literature and other aids on the market; though there is also a ready supply of doubtful rubbish. Perhaps the greatest need is at the level of the local congregation where more could be done to introduce a sense of critical yet challenging exploration.

All this, however, cannot be left as a form of antiquarianism, of curiosity about their past. Our society is very good at creating theme parks and calling it heritage. Rather it is an engagement with the Gospel in the realities of the world. To be Christianly literate, like all theological activity, is an act of prayerful obedience, an offering of ourselves to God that we may be guided and used by his Spirit in the place where we have been set. Maybe something of what has been attempted here is summed up in the versicle and response from the 1662 Book of Common Prayer, itself a quote from scripture:

O Lord, save thy people and bless thy heritage.
O Lord, Govern them and lift them up forever.

---

82. James S. Stewart, *Heralds of God* (London: Hodder and Stoughton, 1946), p. 197.

Week Five, Reading Assignment for Year One

The Priestly Creation Story[83]

The Priestly creation story in Genesis 1–2:4a is one of the shortest and yet most tightly packed theological statements in the Bible. In its present form it dates from the time of the Restoration in the fifth century BCE. It had developed, however, over a much longer period and had been polished smooth by the time P gave it its final working. We must study it line by line in order to unpack the many levels of meaning in it.

Let us go over the main points.

First read **Genesis 1–2:4a**.

Then read again the biblical reference for each point in conjunction with the discussion.

1. God alone is the creator of all, with no divine helpers. The world is not simply shaped by God. (1:1)

2. God creates by speaking; God simply says, "Let there be . . . ," and what is spoken comes to be. (1:3, 6, 9, etc.)

3. God creates light; it is not the gift of the sun, which shines only with the light God has given it. (1:3)

4. God keeps the waters of chaos in their place by calling for a firm dome to keep out the waters that are above and by gathering the waters below into the seas so that the dry land appears. (1:6–10)

5. The heavenly bodies–sun, moon, planets, and stars–which were thought to be gods by many cultures in the ancient Near East, are only creatures of God. (1:14–18)

6. The earth shares in the task of creation, though only at God's command: the earth brings forth vegetation. The waters also bring forth sea creatures and the earth, animal life, but not in the same way as the earth brings forth vegetation. God creates the higher forms of life. (1:11, 20–21, 24–25)

7. God creates humankind in God's own image and gives it dominion over all the creation. (1:26)

8. God creates humankind male and female, and this fact is connected closely with humankind's creation in the divine image. (1:27)

---

83. *Education for Ministry–Year One: Old Testament,* 4th edition, ed. Patricia Bays (Sewanee, Tennessee: The University of the South, 2006), 29–46.

9. God blesses humankind with sexuality and the gift of children. (1:28)

10. The final work of creation is God's rest on the seventh day. (2:2)

The First Words

Even from this brief outline we can see some of the things that were on the mind of the author. First, one important aspect of this story cannot be seen in most English translations. Grammatically, the Hebrew begins in the middle of a sentence. What could this mean? Is it a mistake? Was the first corner of a manuscript lost? No, there is a theological meaning. Beginning a sentence in the middle is a way of saying, "We do not know what God was doing before our world came into being. Our knowledge cannot pry before the beginning of our world; God's beginning is unknowable to us."

God and Creation

Next, it is important to say, above all else, that God is completely different from everything else. Other religions may have said that there were all sorts of divine beings: animal monsters, heavenly bodies, the seas, storms—anything that seemed powerful or mysterious. For the P writer, nothing in the world is divine. Rather, the whole universe is God's creation. Some religions may have thought of at least part of the universe as being made out of the substance of the divine, flowing forth out of the god. For P, nothing of God flows into the universe; God is God, and all else that exists is not God and is not divine.

Third, there is no need to look to lesser gods for the fertility of the earth. Vegetable crops and animals are included in God's design for the world, and the earth brings forth her increase at God's command. The worship of Baals (fertility gods), with all the gross practices that went with it, is not necessary; indeed to worship them would be to deny the power of the one Creator.

Fourth, the whole creation leads up to the creation of humanity. Life has not been created in order to provide playthings for the gods nor to act as slave-servants to the gods. Humanity, man and woman, is created to be God's representative in governing creation. It is a position of great dignity and worth.

Israel, the Chosen People

Each of these points was important in the life of Israel. She had been chosen to be God's people; God had made a covenant with her and had promised that, through Israel, all the nations of the earth would be blessed. The covenant was the basis for all of Israel's religious faith. After the Israelites had settled in Canaan, they were tempted and led away from God to the worship of the Baals and the *astral deities*—the sun, moon, planets, and stars—which the other nations worshiped. The prophets constantly tried to overcome the worship of these false gods so that Israel would be faithful to the covenant. When the northern kingdom was destroyed and the leaders of Judah (the southern kingdom) were carried into exile, the warnings of the prophets were shown to have been correct. Thus we can see the P writer—in the circumstance of exile—expressing in this story the true dignity of humankind and the complete sovereignty of God as these facts had been learned in Israel's life and taught by the prophets. All of what Israel stood for was expressed by the covenant. This was how Israel knew God; God was the God who had made the covenant with Abraham, Isaac, and Jacob and who had sealed it at Sinai through Moses. This God, and this God alone, had created the nation of Israel, and this God alone had created the heavens and the earth and all things.

The creation story expresses the faith of Israel learned by her experience as the people of God's covenant. Just as God had made Israel God's people at Sinai, so also God had made all of humanity in God's own image at creation. Both the covenant story and the creation story say the same thing: God has given humanity dignity and worth and dominion; therefore, the creation story reaches its climax in the creation of humankind.

The Sabbath

The P author does not end the story with the creation of humanity. The final day of creation is not the sixth, on which human beings are created, but the seventh, on which God rests. This rest does not mean only a mere recuperation from the exhaustion of creation. Rather it is a cessation of regular work in order to enjoy the fruits of that labor. God rests in order to enjoy creation. The P author, with special interest in the *cult*—the practices of worship—leads us to the practice of the Sabbath. This is not, however, a contradiction of what we have just said about the creation of humanity as the climax. The covenant, the basis of Israel's faith in the dignity of all people, is what the Sabbath is all about. The Sabbath is the celebration of the covenant. Therefore, the story leads to two ends, both of which refer to the same central point of Israel's faith: (1) God's gift of life and authority—a people under God—and (2) the Sabbath, which is the celebration of this people under God through the covenant.

You are not expected at this point in your studies to be able to feel all that is involved in the covenant. The point you should be able to grasp at this stage is that the P creation story sums up the experience of Israel and is not a simple childish story. You will come back to this story again and again, and the more you become familiar with the rest of the Old Testament, the more you will feel the power of it. Now look back again to the beginning of the story, and we will go over it more closely.

The Priestly Creation Story

This verse, which looks so simple in the English translation, is very strange in the Hebrew because it begins mid-sentence. The text can be translated, carrying it on through verse three, in several ways. (1) "In the beginning God created the heavens and the earth. The earth was without form and void, and darkness. . . ." (2) "When God began to create the heavens and the earth, the earth was without form and void, and darkness. . . ." (3) "In the beginning of God's creating of the heavens and the earth–(when) the earth was without form and void, and darkness was upon the face of the deep, and the wind of God was moving over the face of the waters–God said, 'Let there be. . . .'" None of these translations really fits the text as we have it, but each one is possible. Somewhat closer might be to start with an ellipsis ". . . " and then use the wording of option 3 above.

What difference would it make which translation we pick? Some people have argued that if we use the first one, there is nothing before God creates. God creates the heavens and the earth, and they are formless and empty until God then shapes and fills them. While it is fine theology to believe God created from nothing–*ex nihilo* is the Latin phrase that is used–Genesis 1 does not make such a claim. If we take the second or third translation, there is already a formless empty abyss and God begins to create; God shapes and fills a chaos that already existed.

Dualism

Later theology, especially Christian theology, has insisted that God created out of nothing not simply as a way of choosing one of these translations over the other. Theologians have been trying to oppose a point of view which was very common in the world of the first few centuries of the Christian era and is still very much with us. This point of view is called *dualism*. It says that there are two aspects of the world: the material and the nonmaterial, sometimes called the "spiritual." The material is usually regarded as less good, sometimes evil. Theologians have not wanted to say that there was something, anything, already existing when God began creation, because this already existing something, chaos, could be used by the dualists to refer to matter, the material stuff, which God shaped. They could then say that this matter is the source of evil. So the theologians said that God created *ex nihilo,* out of nothing; anything and everything that is, matter included, is created by God and is good. You can begin to see here that many beliefs, many truths, are not stated explicitly by every biblical passage on a similar theme.

Dualism had a great effect on the thinking of the early church. It came from eastern roots. In Persia the religion of Zoroastrianism taught that there were two gods, one evil and one good. The good god was the god of light; the evil god, the god of darkness. (The name of the god of light, Mazda, is known to many people although they may not know where it originated.)

A man named Mani, who was greatly influenced by Zoroastrianism, developed a religion, dualistic in nature, that prescribed ways of combating the power of the material world and escaping into the world of spirit and light. His religion, usually called *Manichaeism*, flourished in the third and fourth centuries, especially in North Africa, and influenced many Christians. St. Augustine, one of the greatest theologians of the church, was a Manichee before he converted to Christianity.

Plato

The teachings of the great pre-Christian philosopher Plato have also led to dualistic conclusions. Plato taught that, although individual things in this world come and go—they are born and they die, they come into being and they decay—there lie behind the individual things the *ideas* of them. There are many individual trees, each different to some degree from the others and each destined to die and decay, but each is a partial representation of the idea Tree. The idea contains all that it is possible for a tree to be; it is complete and single, not needing many separate examples of itself to express its completeness; it lasts forever, eternally existing while the individual representations of it come and go. Why Plato said this, what problems he was trying to understand, we shall look at later. The fact that he said it, however, allowed people of a later time—during the third through the fifth centuries CE—to develop a religion that was dualistic in a much more subtle and sophisticated way than was Manichaeism. The *Neo-Platonists* taught that the ultimate *One* lies beyond all things, and it is impossible to speak of that One at all. The *via negativa* is all that is possible. From the One all the rest of the universe emanates as light emanates, flows, or shines from a light bulb or a candle. The farther away from the source, the less like the One a thing becomes, until finally, at the farthest remove, there is matter. A human being, according to Neo-Platonism, is really spirit, akin to the One, but the spirit is trapped in a material body. Below humanity there is no spirit; all is merely material. Only by mystical exercises can humankind rise above the material body and reach union with the One. This point of view has influenced much of Christian piety. Augustine was also a Neo-Platonist before becoming a Christian.

Whatever the correct translation of this verse may be, theologians were right in thinking that the Old Testament opposed dualism. The Hebrews did *not* make a distinction between matter and "spirit." As we shall see in the JE (Yahwist-Elohist) creation story, the first human being is made from the dust of the earth and has life breathed into him so that he becomes "a living being." The entire creature, without division into body and spirit, is a living being. When the Christian church said that Jesus is the word of God made flesh, it also spoke against any kind of dualism.

This is why many theologians prefer the reading of verse one that says, "In the beginning God created the heavens and the earth." But there is no way to decide on the basis of the text itself. The P writer has other ways of dealing with the problem of dualism.

Genesis 1:2

Whichever way you translate the first verse, when the earth appears it is without form and void—that is, it is chaotic, empty of all form, design, or meaning—and darkness is upon the face of "the deep." "The deep" is a translation of the Hebrew word *tehom*. Behind this word there lies a whole mythic tradition. In the ancient world of the Mesopotamian basin there existed a story of the creation of the world by means of a great battle between a warrior god and a dragon, a sea-monster, who represented watery *chaos*. To many peoples who lived in desert lands far from the sea, the sea was fearsome. Its great storms were powerful and destroyed ships and houses built close to the shores. Stories of sea monsters were told by returning sailors. So "the deep," the waters of the sea with its monsters, was a symbol of chaos to the ancient people.

The Babylonian creation myth is a long story about the birth of various gods and about the eventual conflict between the god Marduk and the goddess Tiamat. In the course of the conflict, Tiamat is slain, and it is from her body that the firmament, the great dome of heaven, is made. It is worth noting here that the name Tiamat is closely related linguistically to *tehom*. By slaying Tiamat, the chaos monster, the monster of the deep, Marduk makes it possible for order to reign.

Much has been made of the common background out of which the Babylonian and the Hebrew creation stories come. The differences between the stories are more important—and more instructive—than their similarities. The Babylonian myth is an involved story of the birth of the gods and of the struggles among them for supremacy. Human beings are created almost as an afterthought, to serve as slaves for the gods, tending the earth so that the gods might have leisure. In the P story, the reference to "the deep" is virtually the sole remnant of this older myth. There is no birth of God; God is there before the story begins. Only by taking a broad meaning of myth as we have done can the P story be called a myth at all. P has stripped the narrative of all features of a "story about the gods" and has reduced it to a statement of doctrine, using the older myth as a framework only. By using an older framework with which people were familiar, the writer is also able to "start where they are" and show them greater truth.

The capriciousness of the gods and the denigration of humanity in the Babylonian myth stand in complete contrast to the picture of the sovereign and loving God of the Hebrew story. Nothing is told of God except God's acts toward the world he is creating. No questions of God's origins are raised; no relationship to any other god is assumed (until we get to the plural pronouns in verse 26); and the dignity of humankind toward which the whole story moves is a contradiction of the Babylonian estimate of human worth.

Still, the symbol of chaos, tehom, the deep, like Tiamat—the monster of the deep—is important. Chaos, or the threat of chaos, is always present in life. We know that we are insecure in the world we live in. We feel the threat of destruction. The world itself is not secure. The ancients felt this, too, in the dark, a storm at sea, a tornado, wild forces of any kind. As the P story of creation unfolds, by bringing order to chaos, God takes possession of it and subdues it. In Hebrew thought, it is God alone who keeps chaos under control. In the story of Jonah, a man who refuses to obey the word of God finds himself thrown back into chaos where he is swallowed up by the very monster of the deep herself. Jonah returns to dry land when he promises to obey God.

There is an additional level of meaning in the use of tehom/Tiamat. Since the Priestly account comes to us through the experience of exile, using the term may be a subtle way for the Israelites to remember that ultimately the Lord and not the Babylonian gods is the source of all creation. (We see another example of this with the creation of the sun and moon.)

The wind or storm of God was moving over the chaos. The word that the English Bible translates "spirit" is *ruach* (pronounced ROO-ahk). This word can mean "spirit," but also means "wind, breath, or storm." In this verse, the picture is that of the great divine wind blowing storm-like over the sea, or "hovering" over the deep like a great bird about to light on its nest, especially one incubating its eggs. The "spirit" of God here should not be thought of as acting to create; it is simply there, a storm, almost part of the chaos itself in wildness, yet showing forth the presence of God about to create, to bring order into the chaos. The image of the "hovering" of the spirit is one of almost-life, of the care and tending immediately before birth.

Genesis 1:3

Light is created. It is not some god-like stuff that flows from God into the darkness. Some religions have thought of light itself as a god. With the fear of darkness that most people have, it is understandable that light should be thought of as divine, as saving in some way and giving safety. In Genesis light is from God. God alone is the source of the safety that light brings. Notice also that light is created before the sun, stars, and moon. Light does not come from them, according to this story, but directly from God.

The form of words in verse 3 is important: "God said . . . ." God creates by his word. In the P account God creates by speech alone. This shows God separated from his creation and speaking to it. It portrays God with such immense power that it takes only a word for there to be a creative response. Later philosophers and theologians speak of both the transcendence of God and immanence of God. Transcendence refers to the separateness of God from God's creation; immanence refers to God's nearness. The creation-by-speech here in Genesis 1 shows God's transcendence. In Genesis 2 the immanence of God is evident in the manner of creation, for God shapes the clay.

Thought about God swings between these two poles. On the one hand, if God is not transcendent, God tends to become confused with the rest of the world. Pantheism is a form of religion that overemphasizes the immanence of God at the expense of transcendence. The term means literally "all is God." Stoicism is an ancient religion, prominent in the world of the first few centuries of the Christian era, which is pantheistic. Much modern thought tends also toward pantheism, confusing nature with God. Unless God is not the world, God loses the dimension of divinity.

On the other hand, if God is not immanent, near to us, then God is irrelevant. A merely transcendent god who was not accessible to his people could not even be known, let alone worshiped. In the eighteenth century, when people were supremely confident in the power of human reason to know and understand all things, a view of the world developed that did not allow God to have any significant relationships with the world. The universe was thought to be like a huge machine, operating according to the laws inherent in it. A theological school of thought called deism pictured God as a clockmaker. God designed the universe and made it as a clockmaker makes a clock, in such a way that it could continue to run on its own. Then God withdrew from it, allowing it to run in accordance with its inherent laws, never intervening again. This is a doctrine of God that overemphasizes the divine transcendence. If it be true, there is no point in praying to God or expecting any relationship with God other than adoration for the work that the almighty has done in time long past.

By saying that God creates both by the word and by handling the stuff of creation, the biblical writers express both the transcendence and the immanence of God. God is the one who stands over against us, completely different from us, and speaks the divine word to us; God is also the one who is immersed deeply in the world with the stuff of it clinging to God's hands. God is not the world, but God is deeply involved in it.

There is one further point that P wants to make: the world is "good." It is like a refrain in a song. Here, God declares the light to be good. This does not simply mean that it is pleasant or beautiful. God also creates the great sea monsters and creeping things and calls them good. When God calls them all good, the meaning is that they fit in with the great overall purpose of creation. They have their place in the grand design. The goodness of creation is based on God's purpose, not on our sense of beauty.

Genesis 1:4–5

Notice that although God creates the light, darkness is not created. God separates the light from the darkness, but darkness continues. Primitive people, like many of us moderns, feared the darkness, especially when there was no moon or when it was cloudy so that there were no stars. Evil spirits—and evil people—can work their wills in the darkness.

Notice also that, even though God does not create darkness, God calls the light "day" and the darkness "night." In naming the darkness God takes possession of it. Throughout our study of the Old Testament we become aware of the power that ancient people ascribed to the act of naming. If you were able to name something, you had power over it. Even today we see something of this. A parent gives a newborn child her or his name; the child has nothing to say about it. When children grow up, they can legally change their names, but while they are children, it is the parents who decide what they shall be called. It may be that the custom that teenage children have of taking a nickname by which their friends know them is an unconscious attempt to break loose from the bonds of parental control. A remnant of this control-by-naming can also be seen in the care with which some people try to ensure that coworkers never discover that childhood nickname. To know someone's embarrassing nickname would be tantamount to having a certain degree of control over the person.

In the Old Testament we see events in which God changes a person's name: Abram is changed to Abraham, Jacob to Israel. The meaning of the name is not as important as the fact that God has changed it and has thereby claimed the person. When God names the darkness "night," God claims it, takes possession of it, and thereby restrains it by his power. We said earlier, in discussing the first verse, that P had ways of combating dualism: This is one of them. The possibility of chaos taking control of God's creation is overcome because God takes possession of darkness and is Lord of the night as well as of the day.

The final sentence in verse 5 shows the Hebrew system for counting the days: A day goes from evening to evening, not from morning to morning as ours does. In Jewish custom this is still so; the Sabbath, for example, does not begin on Saturday morning, but on Friday evening at sundown. In the Christian church holy days are first celebrated on the evening before. Christmas eve and Hallowe'en (which is "All Hallows' Eve," the eve of All Saints' Day) are well-known examples, but the rule applies in all cases. Worship services held on such "eves" characteristically contain prayers and scripture readings concerned with the theme of the holy day itself.

Genesis 1:6–8

The word translated "firmament" means a hammered metal bowl; the firmament is like a great upside-down metal bowl that separates the waters. In this imagery we have the ancient view of a three-tiered universe, which was held, with modifications, until the sixteenth century CE when Copernicus put forth his theory of the motion of the planets around the sun. In the Genesis picture, the earth is a disk with waters beneath it and the firmament above it holding back the waters. So the three tiers are the waters under the earth, the earth, and the waters above the firmament. We see this cosmology (picture of the earth) again in the second of the Ten Commandments, when we read, "You shall not make for yourself an idol, whether in anything that is in heaven above, or that is on the earth beneath, or that is in the water under the earth. . . ." The reason for this commandment is that all the things in this three-tiered universe are creatures, not God.

Notice that heaven is not the sacred dwelling-place of God; it is simply the firmament. God dwells above heaven. The important point about this is not that it tells us where God is, but that it says God is not to be localized in any point within creation.

The creation of the firmament to keep the waters in their proper place reflects the ancient fear of water in large quantities; a deluge of water symbolizes chaos. Once again, the P writer deals with chaos and dualism. Chaos is held in check by the firmament, which God has made. Humankind is dependent only on the good God for safety. In the P account of the story of Noah and the flood, God opens the windows of heaven and the springs of the deep and releases the waters of chaos to destroy a large part of creation. As we see when we study that story, God makes a covenant with Noah promising never to do that again—God's creation shall stand and the watery chaos be held back forever.

Genesis 1:9–10

Again we see the fear of water, and God sets the proper limits of the seas so that the dry land appears. This is a different form of the creative act of God of withholding the power of chaos.

By having God name the dry land "Earth" and the waters that were gathered together "seas," the P writer is using the names of powerful gods in ancient religions. Because God both creates and names these, we are to see that they are merely creatures, not gods. The P writer thus combats the influence of polytheism (belief in many gods). Once again comes the refrain: "And God saw that it was good."

Notice that the refrain did not occur at the end of the second day when the firmament was constructed. This formula of approbation does not reappear until the seas and the dry land are created. This is because the creation of the firmament is only part of the complex work of creating the world of cosmos within which the rest of creation will take place. The formula of approbation designates the completion of an act. On the second day a creative act is left incomplete, and on the third day two acts occur. The fact that two days are spanned shows that P is using older traditional material, fitting it, sometimes awkwardly, into a seven-day scheme. The liturgical interest of P, the concern that the whole story leads up to the Sabbath, compels the use of a seven-day scheme and the fitting of material into that scheme as neatly as possible.

Genesis 1:11–13

In the ancient world, wherever the growing of crops took the place of hunting or herding as the chief means of life and livelihood, people became concerned about the fertility of the earth. Without the proper mixture of good soil, water, and sunlight, the crops would not grow. Almost all agricultural societies have religions that try to bring about the fertility of the earth. In the ancient Near East these religions often tried to do this by practicing sacred prostitution. By having sexual relations with a temple prostitute, one guaranteed that the land would be fertile. In these verses the P writer combats this kind of religion.

Plant life is created by God. But notice how this happens. Previously, God has created by his word. Here God speaks to the earth, commanding it to "put forth" vegetation. P does not try to deny the obvious fertility of the earth. The wonder of the seasonal rebirth of green things from the earth is too clear to be denied. But P has the earth act at God's command. The earth's fertility is God's gift.

The reference to "plants yielding seed and fruit trees of every kind on earth that bear fruit in it" is to grasses and herbs that yield seed directly, and those plants and trees that have their seed inside a fruit or nut. That is, all kinds of plants have within them the means of reproduction. The earth is fertile and plants have the power to reproduce, due to the command of the word of God. The self-contained powers of nature to bring forth life are not nature's own; nature is a creature. And it is good.

Agricultural fertility cults frequently have in their mythology a dying and rising god. When scholars of the history of religion noticed this, and especially when they saw the forms it took in the Near East, many of them suggested that this accounted for the Christian belief in the death and resurrection of Jesus. This, they thought, was simply a variant on the dying and rising god of the agricultural fertility cults. In fact there is much of the symbolism of the rebirth of nature in the proper celebrations of Easter. The lily, the rabbits, Easter eggs, all speak of the rebirth of natural life. (But for those of us who live in the northern hemisphere, it is too easy to drift into a belief that Jesus' resurrection was somehow part of the natural order, rather than a gracious act of a loving God.)

The ancient Hebrews were surrounded by these kinds of religions, particularly in the myths surrounding Baal, the Canaanite god of fertility, and Anath, his sister. The myth tells of the death of Baal. The god of death, Mot, holds Baal in the prison of death. Anath goes to Mot, slays him and cuts up his body, casting it about over the land, and Baal comes back to life. The prophets of Israel constantly fought against Baal worship. Israel had been created as a nation by God and must remain faithful to him. Still, the need for successful agriculture was obvious. In the P creation story the author maintains that the God of the deliverance from Egypt is also the one who gives fertility to the earth. Faithfulness to the covenant will suffice to ensure the fertility of the land.

The figure of Jesus comes out of this kind of background. There can be no possibility of adequately describing his death and resurrection in the terms of the fertility cults. His death was a once-for-all event and his resurrection has its meaning only in connection with the promises God made to Israel in the covenant. It speaks not of life coming naturally out of death, but of God being faithful to God's promises.

Genesis 1:14–19

On the fourth day the heavenly bodies are created. Worship of the astral deities—the sun, moon, stars, and planets—was widespread in the ancient world. Indeed, almost anywhere you go around the world you will find evidence of such worship. The stars and planets are one feature of nature that is there for all to see. Hunting tribes may not be concerned with growing crops; different animals that have been worshiped may not be known in places far from where they live; oceans may be unknown to inland dwellers, and deserts with their sandstorms may be unfamiliar to people who live along the coasts. But the lights of the heavens can be seen anywhere in the world.

One of the things about the stars that impresses people who pay close attention is that they move with such regularity. We are sometimes amazed that our astronomers can predict with accuracy where a particular planet will be at a specific time, but the ancient astronomers could do this, too. Ancient people were impressed with the fact that, although much in life was uncertain, the movement of the stars was always the same.

Because of the regularity of the heavenly bodies, many believed that the stars controlled everything else and determined what was to happen on earth. Even today astrology, the study of the stars to see what they tell of life, is popular. Some people really believe what their horoscopes say. Others may view astrology as mere superstition, but in ancient times it was a serious matter. All of life was thought to be governed by the astral deities. Men and women, in this view, simply live out lives that have already been determined at the time of their birth. They have no freedom and nothing much matters, since all is determined in advance.

For Israel, however, this could not be so. God had called the people Israel and made a covenant with them. God would be their God and bless them, and they were to keep God's commandments. Israel could be faithful to God or unfaithful. Israel was free—to obey or disobey. Therefore, Israel was responsible for what she did. To believe in the astral deities and their control over life was a denial both of the lordship of God and of human responsibility.

The P editor says that God created the lights in the firmament—they are not gods. Although P used the names of the gods Earth and Sea, "Sun" and "Moon" are not used. By using the clumsy expressions "greater light" and "lesser light," P makes it plain that these, too, are creatures of God. We may have here another example of the exiled Israelites being able to find a "safe" way to jeer at their captors. "You worship 'big light' and 'little light,'" they are saying, "while we worship the creator of all that is."

The heavenly bodies are creatures of God, and they have quite simple jobs to do. They do not control the lives of people: they are the means by which to tell time! They divide the day from the night and they mark off the seasons and the years. They also give light on the earth, but it is not their own light, but the light that God created first of all creatures. This, too, is good; another act of creation is completed. With this, the cosmos (the universe itself) is finished.

Genesis 1:20–23

On the fifth day living beings are created, beginning with those that are least like humans and moving, on the sixth day, to humankind, which is created in the image and likeness of God. Living creatures are treated in a special way in this story. The plants, which were brought forth from the earth, are not thought to be forms of life. They have their seed and reproduce, but they are not called living creatures. When we look at this first creation story, we see that humans were allowed to eat vegetables but not meat. The life given to God's creatures is sacred and is not to be taken away by any other creature.

There is a Hebrew word used in this chapter that is not translated into English in every instance. When used of human beings, the word *nephesh* is usually translated "soul." But when used of other members of the animal world, it is often left out. This is unfortunate, for the P writer's use of nephesh makes some important theological points. There is no simple English word or phrase to cover the two aspects of nephesh. It refers to the life force that separates animals from rocks, for instance, or stars, and also from plants. Nephesh also refers to the individuality of each creature. We are accustomed to recognizing each human being as unique; the P writer believes every animal—even the "creepy crawlies"—is unique to God.

Of the living creatures, first the sea monsters are created, then the rest of the sea creatures and the birds. The seas have been separated from the dry land and held in their place—chaos has been controlled. Now even the fearsome monsters of chaos are discovered to be creatures of God and are called good; they are nothing to fear. These living creatures are then given the gift of procreation as a blessing. Even for living creatures, fertility is not simply a power contained within them but is a special gift from God. Only God is the source of creativity.

Verse 21 uses the verb *bara*: create. This is a different verb from those used before, except in verse 1 when bara is used for the whole process of creation. This verb never has anyone or anything except God as subject. Both God and people can "make," "shape," "form," and so on; only God is said to bara.

Genesis 1:24–25

On the sixth day the earth brings forth living creatures: domestic animals (cattle), wild animals (beasts), and creeping things—all the forms of life on dry land. All are connected very closely with the earth, which acts as mediator of God's creation. There is no blessing or command to be fruitful; apparently, as with the plants, this is part of their nature. Perhaps the blessing was necessary for the creatures which came from the sea because the sea was not given the ability to give power to reproduce. This is the suggestion that Gerhard von Rad makes in his book on Genesis. He says, The absence here of divine blessing is intentional. Only indirectly do the animals receive the power of procreation from God; they receive it directly from the earth, the creative potency of which is acknowledged throughout. Water, by creation, stands lower in rank than the earth; it could not be summoned by God to creative participation. (p. 57)

Yet in verse 20 it seems that the same command is given to the waters as was given to the earth: "Let the waters bring forth. . . ." This is a case in which the English translation is somewhat misleading. In the Hebrew three different verbs are used in those places where the English reads "bring forth." In verse 11 the verb is *dasha*, "to yield tender grass," and it is in the causative form—"cause to yield tender grass." In verse 12, the verb is *yatsa*, "to go out," again in the causative—"cause to go out." Thus in the case of the earth's "bringing forth" vegetation, the verb is in the causative: the earth causes the grass to come forth. In verse 2 also the verb is yatsa in the causative, so the earth causes the living creatures to come forth. In verse 20, however, the verb is *sharats*, "to swarm," and it is in the simple form not indicating causation. Verse 20, therefore, means, "Let the waters swarm with living creatures. . . ." God created them directly, without the mediation of the waters, and gave them the power to reproduce.

The real significant contrast seems to be not so much between the creatures of the water, the birds of the air, and the animals of the dry land, but between the animals and human beings. The animals are closely tied to the earth, whereas humans are more intimately related to their creator.

Genesis 1:26–28

This is the climax of the story. In all the other acts of creation the form of words is very direct: "Let there be . . ."; "Let the earth put forth . . . ." Here, God takes counsel with God's self for a more deliberate and important act: "Let us make man in our image, after our likeness." This is a very strange expression. The name for God in this story is Elohim. When we discussed this before, noting that it is the name which the E writer uses and also the P writer at this point in the story, we mentioned that the word is in the plural: the gods. We also said that there was no doubt that both E and P believed in only one God. All through this story of creation the word Elohim has been translated "God," but now, in verse 26, the plural is used: "Let us . . . in our. . . ."

In the ancient world the idea of a heavenly court was common. The main god was surrounded by other heavenly beings the way a king or queen is attended by the members of an earthly court. In most of the old religions the court was made up of lesser gods. In the Old Testament there was only one God, but God was frequently pictured as being served by a court. In some present-day eucharistic liturgies this same imagery occurs: "Therefore with Angels and Archangels, and with all the company of heaven. . . ."

God is submerging God's self in the heavenly court. "Man" is made in God's image. "Man" is like God, but is also quite distinct from God. The P writer in this whole section seems to be saying these two things about humankind. On the one hand P uses the words "image" and "likeness":

An "image" is a copy of the original, like a statue, and a "likeness" is an outline or silhouette. This would indicate a very close likeness to God, even in a physical sense. On the other hand, God is submerged into the heavenly court, so the likeness to God must be somewhat blurred.

In addition, the Hebrew word for man used here is 'adam (the same word that later will be used as a proper name, Adam). This word is closely related to the word for earth, 'adamah. Thus P also shows that though humankind differs from the animals, it remains tied to the earth and therefore to the animals and indeed the rest of creation.

The result of this very subtle use of words is to give a picture of humankind ("man," male and female: see below) as a being who is very much a creature, not to be confused with God, but one who stands in a very special relationship to God and is very much like God. It would seem that the point here is not so much to say that humanity, as the image of God, can give us an idea of what God is like, as it is to say that humanity is to act like God in the world: God gives human beings dominion over all the living things in the world. Their purpose is not to rule, but to act as God's agent or steward.

It was a common practice in the ancient world for statues of a king to be set up throughout his realm. These were not regarded simply as carved statues, but as the king's representatives, looking out for his interests in those places where the king himself could not always be. This seems to be the idea expressed here: Humankind is God's representative, looking after God's interests in the world. This authority, dominion over God's creation, is given in the creation.

'Adam is not a sexually specific word. There is another word for a male person: 'ish. In spite of the male domination of ancient society, P means both "man" and "woman" when he uses 'adam. (Notice the change of pronouns in v. 27: "In the image of God he created them, male and female he created them.") In the P account, sexuality, male and female together making up 'adam, is a direct creation by God from the outset. (The JE story has woman made after man.) God blesses and commands humankind to procreate: "Be fruitful and multiply, and fill the earth and subdue it." Sexuality, then, is a gift of creation, a blessing, and a command.

Genesis 1:29–31

Notice that there is a limit to human dominion: Only vegetables may be eaten. Both humans and beasts are given vegetables for their food, though to humans both herbs and fruit are allowed while the animals have only herbs (green plants). The shedding of blood is not part of the divine plan for creation. In the Old Testament it is a basic belief that "in the blood is the life." God alone gives life, and it is not to be taken. Those who spill blood put an end to what cannot be revived. Later visions of the perfect time that will come when God brings in the kingdom show animals and humans living without shedding blood. The P writer, of course, knows that both animals and humans eat flesh, but a complete respect for life leads the writer to say that this is not part of God's plan. We shall see that P has God give animals to humans for food at the time of Noah. Even then the blood is not to be eaten. It is to be poured out to God as giver of life.

The final refrain is emphatic: ". . . indeed, it was very good." The world as it comes from the hand of God is perfect. This is the basic faith expressed in the Old Testament: whatever evil there is now in the world is not due to God. As God created the world there was no evil in it, and no dualistic power of evil. As the JE account will go on to show, evil comes when human beings overreach their assigned role. Not content to be God's representatives in the world, humans aspire to be as gods themselves.

Genesis 2:1–3

We would expect the P writer to say that creation ended on the sixth day, but this does not happen. God finished the work by resting on the seventh day. Rest is part of creation. To us rest sounds like doing nothing. To those who have to work until they are exhausted, to fight for the very possibility of life, leaving the old to die by themselves because there is no time to tend to them and still carry on the struggle for life, rest is an activity of sheer bliss. This is the kind of life that was usual for the ancient people, and is still true for most of the earth's people now. Rest, for them, is a necessary activity of life; without it, life is ground down into death. Thus the seventh day is not a day apart from creation, but the time of the creation of the act of rest. The Sabbath, in the Israelite calendar, is not a day of inactivity, but a day when work is not done so that rest may be done. As a celebration of the covenant, the Sabbath was especially seen as the day of recreation, of being restored to the very basis of life. God has hallowed, set apart, this day for this use. Verse 4a says that all this is a genealogy, the generations of the heavens and the earth. P usually puts this kind of verse first as a title. Here, since the creation story has its own introduction, it had to be put at the end.

Summary

1) *Dualism is rejected.* Light is created and comes from God. Though light is good and necessary, it is not to be worshiped. Darkness, though it is fearsome because it conceals evil action and makes it easier to commit evil, is not in itself to be feared; God claimed it and is Lord of it when God named it "night." The waters of chaos are set within their proper limits by God: the waters above are held out by the firmament and the other waters are gathered together as the seas and kept in their place by God's command. The monsters of the deep are like playthings to God, who created them and gave them the seas in which to roam. All this may sound very far from our way of thinking, but its message to us is clear. Biblical faith does not allow us to call anything that God has made evil or unclean, nor does it support our fears of the unknown. God is behind all that is, and we need fear nothing but God's absence.

2) *God is both transcendent and immanent.* God is the absolute Lord over creation. Nothing else is to be mistaken for God and worshiped. This means that we need not bow down before anything in the world! But God is also very near to everything in the world. God is involved in creation, so that we cannot treat anything that God has made as though it did not matter. The immanent side of God is presented more explicitly in the creation account of Genesis 2.

3) *There is freedom in the world.* Nature acts as God has created it to act, but it does so in respect to God's command to it. Human beings are given a role to play in God's design, but they must respond from their own freedom. The sun, moon, and stars do not control the things that happen. Nothing is decreed beforehand and sealed in fate. The astral bodies measure time, but they do not control it.

4) *Creation is fertile by the gift of God.* Ancient people thought that the powers of nature that gave or withheld fertility had to be worshiped. P says that fertility is from God, and God alone is to be worshiped. This belief, by assuring us that nature is not sacred, has allowed us to subdue it and bring it under our control. Much mischief has been done under the auspices of this word "subdue." The notion is one of responsible stewardship, not at all one of exploitation. We need now to remember that it belongs to God and brings its resources to us as a gift; ours to control, it is not ours to plunder.

5) *Humanity is in the image of God.* Humankind is shaped after the pattern of the elohim. This strange imagery both expresses the dignity of humankind and sets its limits. "Man," male and female, is like God, but is not to be confused with God.

6) *"Man" includes woman.* Sexuality is not simply a sign of our kinship with the animals and therefore a lower bestial function to be concealed and denied as unworthy of us. Humankind, 'adam, is not complete as male or female; neither is humankind originally a complete being, solitary and alone, who later "falls" into sexuality. From the outset God created humankind so that both sexes were needed for completeness. The modern notion of the self-sufficient individual is ruled out by this, as is the idea of male superiority. (This is quite remarkable since the place of women in ancient society, Hebrew included, was definitely lower than that of men. We can see this, and how it was made somewhat better, when we turn to the JE creation story.)

7) *Human beings are God's representatives.* Although the blessing of reproduction is given to humankind and animals alike, only human beings are commanded to fill the earth and subdue it. This has sometimes been taken to mean that we are given complete ownership of the world, but this is not the case. Humanity is God's steward. It is to fill the earth so that God may be

represented everywhere and to subdue the earth for the purposes of God. In spite of being made in God's image and being given the dominion, 'adam is still connected to 'adamah: that is, 'adam is of the earth and thus has limits set.

In these terms the P writer sees a perfection in humanity's original relationship to God and to the world. There is no downgrading of humanity as a mere puppet or slave to a tyrannical God; "man" (male and female) has great dignity and value. The terms of human dignity are clearly spelled out. The P writer was well aware of the fact that humankind had sunk to a level lower than that of the beasts, that we had denied our own dignity and taken it away from others, that we were such as to be worthy of complete condemnation before the righteousness of God. This merely points up the rightness of the terms of human life which humankind has violated. All, even the downfall of humankind, is set within the order which God has created.

Week Thirteen, Reading Assignment for Year Four

God as Trinity: An Approach through Prayer[84]

I. Why The Neglect Of The Doctrine Of The Trinity Today?

Christians confronted with the claims of other religions may be aware that their faith can be distinguished from other brands of theism by its particular kind of trinitarian structure. It is neither bald, undifferentiated monotheism, nor is it polytheism. Yet the majority of Christians in the West today, it must be admitted, would be hard pressed even to give an account, let alone a defense, of the developed doctrine of the Trinity as expressed in Christianity's historic creeds and the documents of its Councils. Most professing Christians know how to use the language of Father, Son and Spirit in the varied and unsystematic way that we find in the New Testament. There are 'rules' for this language that are generally acknowledged in the Church. Christians know that there is something wholly inappropriate, for instance, in saying that 'God the Father died on the cross', even if they cannot give a coherent explanation of the reason. The way Luke unfolds the story of God's salvation is the dominant influence here in controlling our use of the language of Father, Son and Spirit: at the historical level there was first the Father God of the Old Testament, then the Son, then, at the Son's 'departure', the Spirit.

What many perhaps do not realise is that efficiency in operating the 'rules' of this New Testament language is still a very far cry from acknowledgement of God as Trinity. Even Paul's familiar grace in 2 Cor. 13.14 is not trinitarian in this stricter sense: 'the grace of the Lord Jesus Christ and the love of God and the fellowship of the Holy Spirit' clearly indicates that 'God' here means the Father alone, despite the close (but theologically unclarified) juxtaposition of Son and Spirit.

The developed doctrine of the Trinity, then, is another matter. This was enunciated by the end of the fourth century, and is implied by the Nicene creed, the creed used today in most celebrations of the eucharist. Here God is seen as eternally triune, which means that in the Godhead there are united three 'persons' ('hypostases'), who are distinguishable only by number and relation to one another, and inseparable in their activity. It is this latter understanding of the doctrine of the Trinity with which this chapter

---

84. Sarah Coakley, God as Trinity: An Approach through Prayer in Doctrine Commission of the Church of England, *We Believe in God* (London, Church House Publishing, 1987), 104–121. Written while Sarah Coakley was a lecturer in Religious Studies in the University of Lancaster.

is concerned; and it is this that seems to have lost its allure for the majority of contemporary Western Christians, so that Karl Rahner has justly marked that 'Christians, for all their orthodox profession of faith in the Trinity, are virtually just "monotheist" in their actual religious existence' (*Theological Investigations* IV. 79). Many, that is, if asked to describe 'God', would give a description of the Father only.

Why is this? Many factors have contributed to this quiet anti-trinitarian tendency in Western Christianity, and cumulatively they are certainly powerful. As far back as the medieval period, scholastic theology made philosophical discussion of God as *one* a prior and preliminary task to discussion of his revelation as three-in-one; and this in itself, it has been argued, implicitly promoted an undifferentiated monotheism at the expense of trinitarianism. But even more significantly, people today are now heirs of the Enlightenment. They are not afraid of a critical approach. Many are less prone to believe a doctrine simply because it is taught or because it is part of our tradition. 'The wise man apportions his belief to the evidence', wrote David Hume. Free enquiry must take place, and if it does not lead to orthodoxy, then this is part of the liberty that must be granted to the human mind. 'Whosoever will be saved . . . (must) . . . worship one God in Trinity' is not the kind of constraint which Christians of this generation are likely to heed.

In modern theology, too, there is a good deal to militate against belief in the doctrine of an eternally triune God. As we have seen, it appears at first sight to have been built up from the inherited belief in the Father God of Israel as the one supreme God, through the growing awareness of Christ as God, and of the Holy Spirit as co-equal with the Father and the Son in his divinity. To explain how all three could be God and yet affirm belief in the one God without 'confounding the persons' or 'dividing the substance' was the task of the leaders of the early Church. But today it is nothing like so clear that the evidence provided by the New Testament and related sources demands this belief in the divinity of Christ and the distinctness and divinity of the Holy Spirit in the way it was understood in the early Church. Historical-critical study of the New Testament has here been the major force for criticism and change; and the portrait of Jesus of Nazareth which emerges from nearly two centuries of enquiry has for many become far more alluring than the seemingly alien formulas of fifth-century Chalcedonian orthodoxy.

Furthermore (in the Western Church in particular) the doctrine of the Holy Spirit has received limited attention. For centuries orthodox trinitarianism led to the inclusion of the Holy Spirit with the Father and the Son in doxologies, prayers, ascriptions and most artistic representations. But in speaking of the Spirit of God at work in the cosmos, were Christians perhaps really just meaning God the Father at work in a particular way? Is there any need to apportion a separate 'hypostasis' to the Holy Spirit? Is this not basically a question of imagery and language? Even in the most charismatic circles today the experience of the Spirit is the experience of God with us.

Do we then really need 'another Paraclete?' Or is John making this distinction simply to account for the difference between the historical experience of Jesus among his disciples and the continuing presence of the risen Christ in the church?

There is therefore a good deal in modern Western theology to dispose people towards the undifferentiated monotheism which has been detected in twentieth-century Christians. Some would argue that the experience of dialogue with other faiths makes abandonment of traditional trinitarianism an even more compelling possibility. A further consideration, highly significant for an age intent on authentication by direct experience, was put classically by Schleiermacher (*The Christian Faith* II 738): 'The Trinity is not an immediate utterance concerning the Christian self-consciousness.' That is, or so Schleiermacher claimed, the doctrine of the Trinity is not apparently verifiable through religious experience. But this is an assertion which calls for careful enquiry.

II. Rediscovery Of The Triune God: An Approach Through Prayer

Most Christians would probably say that their experience of God is not obviously or immediately perceived as trinitarian in structure. But does a deepening relationship to God in prayer, especially prayer of a relatively non-discursive or wordless kind, allow one to remain satisfied with a simple undifferentiated monotheism? Naturally there are all sorts of tricky philosophical difficulties about this line of approach. The phenomenon of prayer is varied, and certainly not easy to describe with exactitude. Further, its interpretation is inevitably affected by certain cherished concepts (e.g., biblical ideas, tradition and liturgy), so that there is some circularity in the attempt to capture in terms of doctrine what may be happening. Moreover, competing interpretations abound for so-called 'contemplative' experiences (including the Buddhist way of eliminating the concept of God altogether). But this does not mean that it is impossible to find in the activity of Christian prayer some telling experiential basis for trinitarian reflection.

What is it that Christians who attend silently to God discover? We are not talking of some 'contemplative' elite, but of anyone who regularly spends even a very short time in a quiet waiting upon God. Often, it must be admitted, what will be encountered is darkness, obscurity and distraction. It is no wonder that the experience has such a strange lack of obvious content, for the relationship is one unlike any other, one that relates those who pray to that without which they would not be in being at all. It is (and here Schleiermacher was surely right) a relationship of 'absolute dependence'. Yet perhaps, amid the obscurity, a little more may be said. Usually it dawns bit by bit on the person praying that this activity, which at first seems all one's own doing, is actually the activity of another. It is the experience of being 'prayed in', the discovery that 'we do not know how to pray as we ought' (Rom. 8.26), but are graciously caught up in a divine conversation, passing back and forth in and through the one who prays, 'the Spirit himself bearing witness with our spirit' (Rom. 8.16). We come to prayer empty-handed, aware of weakness, inarticulacy and even of a certain hollow 'fear and trembling', yet it is precisely in these conditions (cf 1 Cor. 2.3–4) that divine dialogue flows. Here then is a way of beginning to understand what it might be to talk of the distinctiveness of the Spirit. It is not that the Spirit is being construed as a divine centre of consciousness entirely separate from the Father, as if two quite different people were having a conversation. Nor, again, is the Spirit conceived as the relationship between two entities that one can assume to be fixed (the Father and the person praying), a relationship which is then perhaps somewhat arbitrarily personified. Rather, and more mysteriously, the Spirit is here seen as that current of divine response to divine self-gift in which the one who prays is caught up and thereby transformed (see again Rom. 8.9–27, 1 Cor. 2.9–16).

Now if this is so, then, logically speaking, what the one who prays comes first to apprehend is the Spirit in its distinctive identity, and only from there do they move on to appreciate the true mystery and *richesse* of the Son. This too is of course a Pauline insight (1 Cor. 12.3: 'No one can say Jesus is Lord except by the Holy Spirit'), but needs spelling out further. For the apprehensions to be made in the light of prayer about the second person of the Trinity are varied, and only indirectly lead one back to the human career of Jesus of Nazareth, although they do indeed lead there.

First, and most fundamentally, when Christians pray like this, their experience of participation in a divine dialogue is an experience of a God who actively and always wills to be amongst us, God Emmanuel. This being so the very structure of prayer is already 'incarnational' (in one sense of that admittedly ambiguous word), and thus immediately focuses attention on the second person in the Godhead.

But second, and more specifically, in allowing the divine activity of prayer to happen, the one who prays begins to glimpse what it might be to be 'in Christ' or to 'have the mind of Christ' (1 Cor. 2.16), or to be 'fellow heirs with Christ' (Rom. 8.18). It is to allow oneself to be shaped by the mutual interaction of Father and Spirit; and in praying the prayer of Christ, in letting the Spirit cry 'Abba, Father' (Rom. 8.15, Gal. 4.6) to make the transition from regarding Christ merely as an external model for imitation to entering into his divine life itself. Paul does not idly say, 'It is no longer I who live, but Christ who lives in me' (Gal. 2.20). To discover this posture of prayer is to be remodelled by the activity of God in the redeemed life of 'sonship' (Rom. 8. 15). It is to become nothing less than 'other Christs' in the particularity of our lives, not by any active merit of our own, but simply by willing that which already holds us in existence to reshape us in the likeness of his Son.

But thirdly (and here the reference to the historical life of Jesus of Nazareth again becomes vital), the God whom Christians meet in this prayer is also one who appears, sometimes for very long periods, to desert us; or worse still (as in St John of the Cross's 'Night of the Spirit') to press upon us with apparently negative pressure, causing disturbance, deep uneasiness, the highlighting of sin and even the fear of insanity. Such are the death-throes of the domineering ego. But only in the light thrown on the activity of the Trinity by the story of Christ is this endurable. If we are being 'conformed to the image of (the) Son' (Rom. 8.29), it is precisely aridity and disturbance that we should expect. Only through suffering comes glorification (Rom. 8.17). If we take our cue from the agony in the garden, or from the dereliction of the cross, then the authentic cry of 'Abba' (Mark 14.33–6) indicates that the most powerful and active presence of God is mysteriously compatible with the all too human experiences of anxiety and desolation. Only afterwards do we come to see that what we had thought to be divine absence was in actuality the grace of divine hiddenness. Fidelity to prayer in times such as these, though not always perhaps very consciously Christ-centred, is the measure of our Christ-shaped love.

Fourth, and equally significant in its 'incarnational' implications, is the disconcerting discovery in this kind of prayer that the God who acts thus in us wants us whole conscious and unconscious, soul and body. 'We await redemption of our mortal bodies' (Rom. 8. 11, 23), for the test of the authentic activity of the Spirit is the apprehension that Jesus Christ has 'come in the flesh' (1 John 4.2). Though Christian tradition is notoriously littered with those who have evaded these implications, it is truly an effect of this prayer that we are gradually forced to accept and integrate those dark and repressed strands of the unconscious that we would rather not acknowledge, and along with these, all aspects of our sexuality, both bodily and emotional.

But it is also true, fifthly, that to find ourselves 'in Christ' is gradually to break through the limitations of the individualism and introspection that often characterise prayer in its earliest stages. The Pauline language about being 'in Christ' describes a mode of being or a status rather than an experience. But because it is corporately shared, it calls in question the supposed absoluteness of the self as an individual or self-contained entity. For all prayer has its corporate dimension; and to pray 'in Christ' is to intuit the mysterious interpenetration of individuals one with another, and thus to question our usual assumptions about the boundaries of the self. It is to discover that central aspect of Pauline christology, the notion of the mutual interdependence of the members of the 'body of Christ' (1 Cor. 12); it is to perceive the flow of trinitarian love coursing out to encompass the whole of humanity.

Sixthly and lastly, the whole creation, inanimate as well as animate, is taken up in this trinitarian flow. To make such a claim could be reckless. Yet it has often been the perception of the mystics to see creation anticipatorily in the light of its true glory, even while it is yet in 'bondage to decay' and 'groaning in travail' (Rom. 8.21–22). Although concern with prayer experience may at first sight reflect a peculiarly modern obsession with direct personal authentication (and indeed carry with it dangers of a kind of narcissistic introversion), nonetheless sustained prayer leads rather to the building up of community than to its dissolution, to intensification rather than atrophy of concern for the life of the world.

The attempt has been to indicate an experience of prayer from which pressure towards trinitarian thinking might arise. As such it is simply a starting point, and no more. But it is clear that we do not here begin with two perfect and supposedly fixed points, Father and Son, external to ourselves and wholly transcendent, with the Spirit then perhaps (rather unconvincingly) characterised as that which relates them. (That, of course, is a caricature of the 'Western' doctrine of the Trinity, but it is a prevalent one.) Rather, we start with the recognition of a vital, though mysterious, divine dialogue within us, through which the meaning and implications of being 'in Christ' become gradually more vivid and extensive. Thus the Trinity ceases to appear as something abstract or merely propositional. It is not solely to do with the internal life of God, but has also to do with us. The flow of trinitarian life is seen as extending into every aspect of our being, personal and social, and beyond that to the bounds of creation.

This approach has strong roots in the thought of Paul. Despite this fact, reflection on prayer is often thought not to have constituted a significant resource for trinitarian discussion during the tortured years of controversy which led to a normative statement of the doctrine at the end of the fourth century. But was this really so? To this question we now turn.

III. Roots In The Tradition

Many accounts of the development of the doctrine of the Trinity pay limited attention to the personal encounter with God through prayer. A good deal of the material available for a study of this development was provoked by challenge and controversy, and it is understandable that historians of the doctrine should focus their attention on the proceedings of Church Councils and the writings of theologians attacking or defending particular positions, as well as emphasising the political considerations that often became entangled in the debates.

Yet the resulting account of how the church came to profess first the faith of Nicaea in 325, when the Son was declared to be 'of one substance' with the Father, and then that of Constantinople in 381, by which time the doctrine of the Trinity was given normative expression, is sometimes tidier than it deserves to be. The New Testament, after all, presents varied traditions of early Christian belief about the person of Christ and of the Holy Spirit. It is all too easy to take, for example, the Luke-Acts sequence of the revelation of the God of Israel through the story of Jesus to the day of Pentecost, and to see the pre-Nicene church first establishing Christ's identity with, yet distinction from, God the Father, and then in the wake of Nicaea doing the same for the Holy Spirit. Considerations as to whether the Spirit is in fact regarded by the New Testament authors as a separate Person tend to be brushed over in the light of the strong emphasis on his full acceptance as such in the late fourth century. The tendencies of the second-century defenders of Christianity to think in terms of only two divine Persons, the Father and the Son, are seen as a fumbling after truth. Whatever happened *en route*, the faith of Nicaea is assumed to be at least embryonic in the earliest traditions of the primitive church.

The study of controversy however, is not without its purpose. Councils concerned with faith in the Trinity were not periodic bureaucratic reviews of a continuing theoretical problem, but were urgently called to meet passionate demands. What was the source of this passion? Why did it manifest itself only rarely in academic circles but all too frequently at congregational level, in the gossip of the court, or in banter over the shop counter? Were all the Lord's people theologians? Or was their argument about their own experience of God as Trinity, and the variety of the interpretations of this experience?

It is important in the first place not to underestimate the degree to which Christians of the first three centuries at least were committed to the regular practice of prayer and worship. People in the ancient world would never have called themselves Christian simply because they believed themselves to be clean-living citizens who dropped into church on family or civic occasions. Baptism marked a clean break with the past. Preparation for baptism lasted two and sometimes three years, and a strict watch was kept over the candidates by their sponsors. The end of the course demanded daily attendance at church; and throughout they were directed to pray at least twice a day (morning and evening, and in some places also at the third, sixth, and ninth hours of the day), and were urged to attend the assemblies of the church in the mornings (Hippolytus), where they would be assured that angels and saints prayed with them (Origen). In other words Christians of this period tended to spend a good deal longer in prayer and reflection than many of their twentieth-century counterparts, and the idea of 'the spiritual life' as something only seriously practiced by a special group of professionals was wholly alien to the outlook of the period.

Second, the public prayer of the church allowed considerable opportunity to the congregation for being receptive, for listening and for being 'prayed in'. Congregations at the liturgy for the first four centuries were for the most part silent. There were some responses, but very few. Responsorial psalms were introduced, hymns were composed, but the tendency to leave all the music to the choir increased as the years went by; and, with the increasing gap between the language of the liturgy and the vernacular, people no longer 'followed the service' in detail but simply allowed themselves to be caught up in the flow of the eucharistic action, which was felt by them to unite heaven and earth and to bring them through Christ by the Holy Spirit to the Father. If we were to say then that the understanding of God as Trinity grew in the early centuries through the Christian's experience of God in prayer, then the opportunity for this was not inconsiderable, and we must now look at this experience in more detail.

1. *The public prayer of the church.* Two examples may be given to illustrate the intrinsic connection between eucharistic prayer and trinitarian reflection, and thus to indicate how liturgical usage was operative in fostering and guarding some sort of trinitarian notion of God.

(a) The introductory dialogue to the eucharistic prayer in the Western liturgy begins with the words 'The Lord be with you'. Recent scholarship has suggested that this phrase is either a statement or a prayer, meaning probably 'The Spirit of the Lord is with you' or 'May the Spirit of the Lord be with you'. The reply from the congregation is 'And with thy spirit' ('and also with you'), praying that the celebrant may be given the Spirit of God in order that he may properly celebrate the eucharist. For a long period the eucharistic prayer was prayed extempore (Justin, I *Apol.* 65 ff), and presidents of the eucharist were chosen (among other reasons) for their recognised gift of offering prayer of this kind. Hence the importance of invoking the Spirit of God as Trinity, since 'we know not how to pray as we ought' (Rom. 8.26). In another example, this time from the Byzantine liturgy, before the eucharistic prayer begins there is a dialogue between priest and deacon in the course of which the priest prays, 'May the Holy Spirit come upon you and the Power of the Most High overshadow you' (as at the Annunciation), to which the deacon replies, 'May the same Holy Spirit celebrate with us all the days of our lives'. This echoes the same theology, even though by this time the central prayer of the eucharist is no longer extemporised. The experience attested by St Paul therefore (1 Cor. 2, Rom. 8) is here highlighted in the liturgy. We do not presume to come to the Lord's table by our own efforts. We are brought to the presence of God through Christ by the Holy Spirit.

(b) It would of course be equally true to say not only that the celebrant of the eucharist is conscious of being prayed in by the Holy Spirit, but that the prayer which he offers is not his but the prayer of Christ—in other words, Christ prays in him. This, however, needs to be understood carefully. We could say that the celebrant of the eucharist in Justin Martyr's time was conscious that the eucharistic gift of the body and blood of Christ was given in virtue of 'the prayer of the Word who is from him' [*sc.* God the Father] (I *Apol.* 66.3) (and not by any mystical incantation of the celebrant as the emperor might have heard about the mysteries of Mithras). In this case the response is to the prayer of Christ who prays through his mystical body, the church. In this connection, Origen also notes that this too is the experience of Christians who prepare themselves by obedience and devotion for prayer, who will then 'participate in the prayer of the Word of God who stands in the midst even of those who know him not, and never fails the prayer of anyone, but prays to the Father along with him whose mediator he is' (*De Oratione* 10.2). Thus Christ himself in this instance does the praying, and Christians who pray (cf, ibid. 22.4) become like Christ through their prayer: like him they are sons, like him they cry 'Abba, Father', and all this by the indwelling of the Holy Spirit. So that Christians being 'the image of an image', i.e. being like Christ, who is the 'image' of God (*De Orat.* 22.4), pray *as* Christ and pray Christ's prayer. 'Now you became Christs', writes Cyril of Jerusalem, 'by receiving the . . . Holy Spirit; everything has been wrought in you because you are the likenesses (i.e., images) of Christ.'

2. *Prayer in general.* If in liturgical prayer it is possible to discern the pattern of a trinitarian experience of God, of being brought to the Father through incorporation into the Son by the power of the Holy Spirit, then we should expect the same to be true of accounts of prayer in general. This is certainly the case in some authors. Origen's treatise on prayer belongs to the latter part of his life and was written at Caesarea. We have already given some indication of his understanding of the dynamic of prayer, and it is significant that the introductory chapter is given to an exploration of the themes of 1 Cor. 1.30–2.11 and Rom. 8.26 ff. It has already become clear that, for Origen, it is the Spirit who initiates prayer, who makes us Christ-like, and so brings us to the Father. Origen is also insistent that 'we may never pray to anything generated— not even to Christ—but only to God and the Father of all, to whom even Our Saviour himself prayed as we have already said, and teaches us to pray.' Christ for Origen is always High Priest, always intercessor, always Son as we become sons, so we never pray to him but only through him. Origen's teaching on prayer here is clearly linked with his trinitarian theology, in which the Son is not truly co-equal with the Father, and for which he was later censured. It cannot therefore be claimed that those who pray aright end up inexorably in trinitarian orthodoxy. But it can at least be said that any genuine experience of Christian prayer involves an encounter with God perceived as in some sense triune.

Basil the Great's treatise *On the Holy Spirit*, on the other hand, recounts a similar experience with a modified conclusion in the direction of a more traditional orthodoxy. On first reading it is a keenly dogmatic work written in the heat of controversy, with a good deal of invective against the poor logic of the heretics. Well known (and often greatly disliked) for his defence of Nicene orthodoxy, Basil appears here as a staunch defender of tradition, not least of the baptismal formulas of the church, with the result that one could read him as a person with 'party' interests and a merely intellectual grasp of the position he feels bound to defend. From what we know of his life, this is clearly to underestimate him. Given to the monastic life from an early period, and never as archbishop abandoning his ascetic practices of prayer and self-discipline, it is not surprising that something of personal experience emerges in the course of his defence. The following passage reflects his personal discipline as well as his vision of truth:

The Spirit comes to us when we withdraw ourselves from evil passions, which have crept into the soul through its friendship with the flesh, alienating us from a close relationship with God . . . Then, like the sun, he will show you in himself the image of the invisible [*sc.* the Son], and with purified eyes you will see in this blessed image the unspeakable beauty of its prototype [*sc.* the Father] . . . From this comes knowledge of the future, understanding of mysteries . . . a place in the choir of angels, endless joy in the presence of God, becoming like God, and, the highest of all desires, becoming God (*On The Holy Spirit*, 9.23).

The significant feature here is that through this direct encounter of the individual's spirit (or soul) with the Spirit of God (cf. 1 Cor. 2, the spiritual with the Spiritual) we are enabled first to see Christ and through this perfect Image to behold the Father, and secondly, as a consequence of our inner illumination, to become spiritual ourselves through God's gracious act of deification. The entire experience, in other words, is trinitarian; and Basil here is setting out a distinct logic and progression in the roles of each divine 'person' in assimilating the Christian to God. Hence, although all three 'persons' do indeed act together, it is important to note that Spirit and Son cannot be seen as mere alternatives.

IV. Conclusions

What then, may be concluded from the analysis of these Pauline passages and their spiritual and trinitarian significance for the early Greek fathers? We have seen that the development of the doctrine of the Trinity in the early church, though so often and necessarily described in terms of theological controversy and the activity of Councils, has its roots firmly in Christian experiences of God through liturgy and personal prayer. The technical trinitarian formularies that were eventually agreed in the fourth and fifth centuries grew in part out of that experience. Nevertheless they were primarily intended as defences against theological alternatives that were deemed misleading, and in themselves rarely conveyed much to inspire and reveal the true nature of the Godhead. Nor indeed did their original exponents propose them as descriptions of their trinitarian God. Rather, they provided the best available means of protecting from erroneous interpretation something that was to a large degree intellectually overwhelming. Only two centuries after the Council of Constantinople, Maximus the Confessor could express his profound dissatisfaction with the use of the term *ousia* ('substance') about the Godhead at all. His objection was spiritually motivated: the reality of God must of necessity transcend all attempts to capture it, even in these hallowed conceptual terms.

If then it is the experience of prayer, both personal and corporate, which is our primary access to God as Trinity, several important conclusions accrue for today. First, we become aware that prayer must have priority, and that no amount of sheer intellectual effort on the one hand, or authoritarian bludgeoning on the other, will effect a lively belief in a trinitarian God. One may undergo the regular discipline of reciting the Athanasian creed; but to no avail if 'the one thing needful' is lacking.

Secondly, the experience of being mysteriously caught up by divine dialogue into the likeness of Christ, while indicating the necessity for thinking in some sort of trinitarian terms, will never in itself yield hard-edged conceptual certainty. The actual business of prayer is itself so varied that the fact that there are differences between various conceptual models for the Trinity should not so greatly surprise us, nor should the constant impression, especially when examining the mystics of the church, that their experience continually chafes at the limits of the traditional and authoritative formularies. This is not to say that it is impossible to establish workable and agreed criteria for distinguishing good from bad doctrinal accounts, or even for effecting some rapprochement between Eastern and Western traditions. But it does mean that any desire for crude and absolute certainty is likely to go disappointed.

If this is so, then, thirdly, light may also be thrown on the pressing contemporary issue from which this chapter started: that of Christianity's relation to other world religions. For here we confront a paradox. On the one hand, the approach to the Trinity through prayer does indeed point up differences between Christianity and other forms of faith. Not only does the Christian who prays, if the account given here is sound, come to discover some felt need for a particular sort of threefold differentiation in the Godhead, a feature unique to Christian theism; but there are also the further ramifications of the 'incarnational' characteristics of prayer—the positive attitude to the body and to the material world on the one hand, and, even more significantly, the haunting image of a God exposed in Christ crucified, of divine presence mediated precisely through weakness and dereliction. These, surely, are the central distinguishing features of Christian theism. Yet from the same experience of prayer emerges the other side of the paradox. For the obscurity, the darkness, the sheer defencelessness of wordless prayer usually lead rather to a greater openness to other traditions than to an assured sense of superiority; and the experience of God thus dimly perceived brings about a curious intuitional recognition of the activity of 'contemplation' in others, whether or not the concept of God to which they adhere is congruous with the Christian one. This latter factor we can surely ill afford to ignore, however difficult it is to incorporate it into a convincing intellectual solution to the problem of vying religious truth claims.

Fourthly, an approach to the Trinity through prayer has implications for the currently vexed issue of masculine and feminine language as applied to God. This is neither a digression, nor a purely contemporary fad, as any comprehensive survey of trinitarian thought would quickly make plain. It has again and again been the insight of those given to prayer that description of the triune God which is not fatally inadequate must somehow encompass, as a matter of balance, what we are conditioned to call feminine characteristics—patience, compassion, endurance, forgiveness, warmth, sustenance and so on—no less than the strength, power, activity, initiative, wrath and suchlike that our society has tended to regard as peculiarly masculine. Sometimes in the Christian tradition this insight has led to a somewhat curious compensating for the assumed masculine stereotyping of the Father by the use of feminine language to refer to one of the other Persons—Spirit or Son. (In the early Syriac theology and in the pseudo-Macarian homilies, for instance, the Spirit is feminine and motherly; in Julian of Norwich, as is better known, Christ is described as 'Our Mother'.) At other times, and perhaps more convincingly, there has been a primary insistence on the ultimate unknowability of God, transcending all categories of gender, combined with a secondary realisation that Prayer also forces us to recognise, at the level of anthropomorphic description, the need for a balance of so-called masculine and feminine characteristics in the undivided activity of all three 'Persons'. (Gregory of Nyssa at times approaches this position.)

Just as it is a not uncommon experience among those who give themselves seriously to the practice of prayer that sooner or later they have to face their own need of an integrated sexuality, and of an inward personal balance between activity and receptivity, initiative and response, so too prayer may bring us to a deeper, more comprehensive and more satisfying doctrine of the triune God. Through prayer God can be recognised both as the creative power on whom all depend for their existence, and also as the one who in the dereliction of Christ's cross is disclosed as enduring in patient weakness, and coming perilously close to defeat. The Spirit who prays in us and is known in prayer is indeed Lord and Lifegiver, but also one who cries 'Abba, Father' with us in doubt and darkness and in the sharing of Christ's sufferings. Both man and woman are 'in the image of God', and God is the fullness of the Trinity. The 'masculine' and 'feminine' qualities (as we call them) which we all share in varying admixture are both of them for us clues and glimpses of the wholeness of divine life and love.

Week Twenty, Reading Assignment for Year One

Micah[85]

This section on Micah is extracted from John J. Collins's longer text, *Introduction to the Hebrew Bible*, because Micah is not addressed in the *Shorter Introduction to the Hebrew Bible*, our current text for Year One.

Roughly contemporary with Isaiah was Micah of Moresheth, a small town about twenty-three miles southwest of Jerusalem. According to the superscription of the book, he prophesied in the days of Jotham, Ahaz, and Hezekiah, and his oracles concerned both Samaria and Jerusalem. In contrast to Isaiah, Micah was a rural prophet and not so closely engaged with the Davidic dynasty. As in the case of all the prophetic books, however, we must reckon with a process of edition and supplementation that may have gone on for centuries. A clear example of this is found in Mic 4:10, where Zion is told to writhe like a woman in labor, "for now you shall go forth from the city and camp in the open country; you shall go to Babylon. There you shall be rescued, there the Lord will redeem you from the hands of your enemies." The initial prophecy that the city would be undone, and that its inhabitants would have to camp in the open country, may well have been uttered by Micah. It is quite compatible with the critique of the ruling powers by the rural prophet. The extension of the prophecy to include the Babylonian exile and the subsequent restoration must have been added by a postexilic scribe, who felt impelled to update the oracle in the light of subsequent history.

The actual extent of the supplementation of the oracles of Micah is a matter of controversy. One scholarly tradition, developed in Germany in the late nineteenth century and still widely influential, attributes only material in chapters 1–3 to the eighth-century prophet, and that with minor exceptions, most notably the prophecy of restoration in 2:12–13. These chapters consist primarily of judgment oracles. The more hopeful oracles in chapters 4–5 are usually dated to the early postexilic period. Chapters 6–7 are also regarded as later additions. At least the conclusion in 7:8–20 was added to adapt the collection to liturgical use. This kind of analysis may go too far in denying the prophet any hope for the future. At least a few passages in chapters 4–7 are likely to come from the eighth century. In contrast to this approach, some recent commentaries have tried to defend the essential unity

---

85. John J. Collins, *Introduction to the Hebrew Bible* (Minneapolis: Augsburg Fortress, 2004), 321–324. Used by permission.

of the book (Hillers, Andersen and Freedman). There can be little doubt, however, that the oracles underwent a process of transmission and that the book, like those of the other pre-exilic prophets, was given its present form after the Babylonian exile.

The Social Critique

The opening oracle invokes an old tradition of the theophany of the divine warrior. In Judges 5 the imagery of storm and earthquake were used to express the terror caused by YHWH going to help his people in battle. In Micah they describe the terror of YHWH coming to judge his people. The wrath is directed against both Samaria and Jerusalem. The focus on the capital cities is significant. The offenses are primarily charged to the ruling class. Jerusalem is derisively called a "high place." Micah makes no distinction between the guilt of the two kingdoms. In 1:6 he prophesies that Samaria will be made a heap. In 3:12 he predicts that "Zion shall be plowed as a field; Jerusalem shall become a heap of ruins." The latter prophecy is cited in Jer 26:18, where its nonfulfillment is explained by the fact that Hezekiah repented. Micah says that he will go naked and barefoot as Isaiah did, but where Isaiah symbolized the captivity of Egyptians and Ethiopians, Micah's action is a gesture of mourning for the destruction of Judah. The statement that "it has reached the gate of my people" recalls the invasion of Sennacherib (cf. Isaiah 1), but it more likely refers to the Syro-Ephraimite war, in view of the date ascribed to Micah and his concern for Samaria as well as Jerusalem.

The initial charge against Samaria and Jerusalem is idolatry. Jerusalem is compared to a high place; Samaria is accused of prostitution (cf. Hosea). More typical of Micah, however, is the accusation of injustice. The statement that "they covet fields, and seize them; houses and take them away," refers to the same phenomenon noted in Isa 5:8, which is addressed to those who add house to house and field to field. The punishment will fit the crime. Their own houses and fields will be seized by the invaders. Micah's condemnation of the exploitation of the poor is more biting even than that of Amos. The rich "tear the skin off my people and the flesh off their bones; eat the flesh of my people . . . chop them up like meat in a kettle" (3:2–3). The punishment to come will be a response of YHWH to the cry of the poor. Like Amos, Micah disassociates himself from the professional prophets (nebî'îm, 3:5–12). These people, we are told, give oracles for money (3:11; rulers and priests are similarly venal). They cry "peace" when they have enough to eat, and mislead the people by saying "surely, the Lord is with us" (3:11). If Isaiah saw this Davidic slogan as ambiguous, Micah sees it as a misleading illusion. We have no narrative of the call of Micah as we have of Amos. It seems safe to assume that he did not consider himself to be a nābî'. Like Amos, his preaching encountered opposition and some people tried to suppress it (2:6). It has been noted that the formula "thus says the Lord" occurs only once in chapters 1–3, and that Micah sometimes speaks in his own name (3:1). Nonetheless, he also speaks in the name of the Lord (e.g., 1:6: "I will make Samaria a heap"), and he claims to be filled with power, with the spirit of the Lord, to denounce the sin of Israel (3:8).

The critique of the cult in chapter 6 is also in line with what we have seen in the other eighth-century prophets and is plausibly attributed to Micah. This passage is cast in the form of a rib, or legal disputation, and can be viewed as a covenant lawsuit. God reminds his people Israel that he brought them up from the land of Egypt and redeemed them from slavery. There is a clear implication that Israel should have responded by serving the Lord with justice and has failed to do so, but the offenses and consequent punishment are not spelled out. While the exodus played no part in the preaching of Isaiah of Jerusalem, it figured prominently in the oracles of Amos and Hosea, even though Amos, like Micah, came from the southern kingdom. Micah too addressed Israel as well as Judah. Many scholars assume that the appeal to the exodus here is the work of a Deuteronomistic editor, but this is not necessarily so.

Micah 6:6–8 considers the misguided reasoning of an Israelite, or Judean, worshiper. The assumption is that God will be impressed by the cost of the sacrifice. Even human sacrifice is contemplated. As we have seen in connection with Genesis 22, human sacrifice was practiced in ancient Israel and Judah. King Manasseh of Judah, son of Hezekiah, was said to have made his son "pass through fire," which is to say that he sacrificed him as a burnt offering (2 Kgs 21:6). Human sacrifice, however, is much less likely to have been an option in the postexilic period. Micah's critique of sacrifice is essentially the same as that of the other prophets we have considered. It indicates a misunderstanding of what YHWH wants, which is "to do justice, and to love kindness, and to walk humbly with your God" (6:8). Most of the positive oracles in chapters 4–5 are likely to have been added by postexilic editors, when the time of judgment had passed and the need was for consolation and hope. Micah 4:1–5 repeats an oracle found in Isaiah 2:1–5, with a variation in the concluding verse. The imagery of tôrāh going forth from Jerusalem and the peoples streaming thereto fits better with the aspirations of Second Temple Judaism than with what we know of the eighth century. The oracle probably circulated anonymously. That it is associated with two eighth-century prophets is striking, but probably coincidental. A more difficult case is presented by Micah 5:2–5, which predicts the advent of a ruler from Bethlehem of Judah, the ancestral home of David. Many scholars take this as a postexilic prediction of a restoration of the Davidic line, and the obscure statement in v. 3, "the rest of his kindred shall return," can be read as supporting this interpretation. But the focus on Bethlehem, as opposed to Zion, may be significant. Micah of Moresheth may have felt that the Davidic monarchy could be redeemed if it returned to the humble roots symbolized by the ancestral village. The prediction of a ruler from Bethlehem would then be a rejection of the ruling king and the Jerusalem court, but not of the Davidic line. The oracle would still have been read in a messianic sense in the postexilic period. In the later context Assyria would be understood as the archetypical enemy. The fantasy of a final defeat of invading nations appears frequently in the later prophetic and apocalyptic books (e.g., the prophecy of Gog in Ezekiel 38–39).

Resources
for Listening
and Spiritual
Autobiography

Spiritual Autobiographies: Some Guidelines

A spiritual autobiography is your life story—the telling of your journey told with the purpose of discerning and proclaiming how your experience has shaped your relationship with God. Each year in the program you are asked to recall your life story. Later, you are given an opportunity to share what you think is appropriate with your seminar group. A different structure is provided for your use for each of the four years of the program. These structured methods allow you to look at the whole sweep of your life. Constructing your autobiography provides a firm foundation for the continuing work of integrating the content of your year's study with the events of your life. Your experience is a primary resource for your theological education; the yearly review of your life story enables you to hear how the timbre and direction of that story has changed in the last twelve months. Your call, discernment, vocation, and ministry are imbedded in your spiritual journey. This process of telling and retelling your story helps those themes come more clearly into your consciousness.

A spiritual autobiography may contain both religious material—significant people or times within the religious community—and everyday material like people and times in your life that have influenced who you are now and how you understand God's presence or absence in your life.

The work you do on your spiritual autobiography is private, "for your eyes only." This allows you to be free, without concern about how others will interpret either the context or expression.

Preparing a spiritual autobiography each year provides a way to deepen your understanding of both the Christian life and ministry. By virtue of your baptism you were called to ministry, guided and pushed by personal gifts, passions, skills, experiences, and interests.

Once you prepare your spiritual autobiography, you need to decide what you want to share with your seminar group. Martin Buber, a twentieth-century philosopher and Jewish theologian, is reputed to have said that he could never hold a significant conversation with another person until he had heard the other's life story. The purpose of sharing autobiographies is to build trust and understanding within the group and to begin to make connections within your own story. We need the experience of hearing other life stories to know that we are not alone in God's world. By sharing appropriate stories of our lives we form learning communities that can challenge and support us throughout our lives.

Your mentor will relate her or his own story and help the group structure the time for sharing of autobiographies. Most groups give each member **around ten minutes** to tell his or her story, followed by time for the rest of the group to respond. Spiritual autobiographies are the focus of most of the seminar time for the first few meetings of the year. This is a special time for your group. This component of your group's life will carry you to the next phase of your year together. This may be the first time to tell your story in this way. It may seem a bit daunting at first. Remember that you should offer what you feel comfortable sharing in the group. This is not an opportunity for "group therapy" or psychologizing, so the group should not engage in raising questions about motives or probe for information beyond what you share. Feel free to say "no" or to say that you do not wish to explore questions that others may raise out of curiosity or concern.

Sharing your "spiritual autobiography" is a way to say, "Here I am," and to join your EfM group as a full participant. Over the years in EfM you will probably find that your spiritual autobiography changes. You may find yourself free to talk about things which were previously guarded. You also may find that your freedom to "be yourself" will grow as your personal story, the life of the group, and the story of God's people relate to each other.

Listening Skills

Listening is one of the greatest gifts we can give one another and a key component of a functioning group. Often we primarily focus on what we plan to say next rather than really listening to what others say.

For effective listening, make eye contact without staring at the other person. When you listen to the other person, listen to four things:

- What the person describes (what facts, events, situations, or information the person is trying to convey);

- How the person feels (what emotions accompany the information);

- Where the person places emphasis and shows energy;

- What the person's body is saying (sometimes one is unaware of the mixture of reactions and important information the body gives).

Effective listening is undermined by the following:

- *Answering emotions with logic.* When someone is excited about something, he or she does not want the first response to be a critical analysis. The speaker wants the other person to share some of their excitement.

- *Bringing in old issues.* When people want to discuss a problem, they do not want to be told that they always have similar problems or that they failed to do something about the problem three months ago.

- *Using sarcasm or cynicism,* or not taking the other person's issues seriously.

Types of Listening

Types	Purpose	Examples
Clarifying	• To get additional facts • To help explore all sides of a problem	• "Can you clarify this?" • "Do you mean this . . . ?" • "Is this the problem as you see it now?"
Restatement	• To check out meaning and interpretation with someone else • To show you are listening and that you understand what he is saying • To encourage someone to analyze other aspects of matter being considered and to discuss it with you	• "As I understand it then your point is . . . ?" • "This is what you have decided to do and the reasons are . . . ?"
Neutral	• To convey that you are interested and listening • To encourage person to continue talking	• To convey that you are interested and listening • To encourage person to continue talking
Reflective	• To show that you understand how he feels about what he is saying • To help persons to evaluate and temper their own feelings as expressed by someone else	• "You feel that. . . ." • "It was a shocking thing as you saw it." • "You felt you didn't get a fair shake."
Summarizing	• To bring all the discussion into focus in terms of a summary • To serve as a spring board for future discussion on a particular problem.	• "These are the key ideas you have expressed. . . ." • "If I understand how you feel about the situation. . . ."

Practice for Developing Effective Listening Skills

1. Ways Not to Listen
PURPOSE: To demonstrate how non-listening techniques reduce the sense of individual participation, detract from group cohesiveness, and contribute to conflict.

Divide your group into smaller groups of four. Each person will share something good and exciting that has happened to him or her in the past few months. The others in the group will demonstrate the following non-listening methods:

a. *Passive listening:* not concentrating on what the person is saying. One person in the group shares for two minutes while the others demonstrate passive listening—no eye contact, no responses, etc. After the two minutes discuss what speaker and listeners felt about passive listening.

b. *Happy hooking:* constantly changing the subject to center the conversation on you and not on the speaker. Many times people become very competitive and try to devise a topic that is similar but more exciting than the speaker's. After the two minutes discuss what speaker and listeners felt about happy hooking.

c. *Mind reading:* completing the other person's sentences, acting as if you understand what they are saying, giving advice before you have heard them through. After the two minutes discuss what speaker and listeners felt about mind reading.

d. *Inappropriate body language:* jiggling your foot, clicking a pen, staring at the person, touching them without being sensitive to whether they want to be touched, saying you are interested while showing the opposite with your body, showing aggression and impatience with your body while saying you are concerned. After the two minutes discuss what speaker and listeners felt about inappropriate body language.

2. Improve Your Listening Skills
PURPOSE: To provide an opportunity for people to practice listening skills.

Each person pairs off with one other person. Each of the two has ten minutes to share while the other person practices listening. The topic for sharing is a childhood event that was important or enjoyable.

At the end of each ten-minute sharing period the listener in the pair tells the speaker:

a. A synopsis of the sharing;

b. What he or she heard as the speaker's feelings about the event and about sharing the event;

c. Words, images, and metaphors that stood out;

d. What one thought the speaker was saying with his or her body.

The speaker confirms or corrects the listener's perception. Then the speaker tells the listener what he or she liked and what he or she wished were different about the other's listening style. The speaker's comments should emphasize:

a. How the listener asked questions;

b. How the listener's body posture encouraged sharing;

c. What other listener responses helped the speaker feel understood and helped the speaker clarify what he or she was saying.

After analyzing how each spoke and listened, the speaker becomes the listener. The same process of sharing and analyzing is repeated.

The Art of Framing Questions

Ministry begins in relationship. Relationship begins in sharing our own stories and listening to the stories of others. You can learn to frame questions that invite others to open up and share themselves more deeply. You may find it useful to differentiate between three levels of such questions.

"Who, What, Where and When" are foundational or Level 1 interrogatives. Ask questions framed with these interrogatory pronouns first to encourage the narrative to begin. However, if these questions are probing at delicate areas, there may be obfuscation, evasion, or avoidance. These questions may describe an action: What happened? Two cars collided, one was red and one was blue. They may be emotive: What did you feel when two cars collided? I was frightened. They may be intellectual: What did you think when two cars collided? I thought the blue one was driving too fast.

Level 2 questions, which begin with the interrogative "How," seek to analyze the information in a narrative. If such questions are asked too early, they may put the teller on the defensive. When we ask the question, "How did that happen?" we may communicate an accusatory tone that shuts down any possibility of openness.

Why did you do that? Level 3 questions beginning with "Why" invite explanations and defensive responses because they aim at our motives. Motives for our actions tend to be mixed. Sometimes we may not even know them. Some motives may be acceptable, and others are very difficult to admit because we are ashamed of them. When the invitation to share a story begins by asking questions about motives, using the interrogative "why," we may be perceived as asking for an apology, a defense, or an explanation. While this may be useful in certain circumstances, it is best to avoid questions aimed at motivations. The question may be better phrased in terms of "what," such as: "What led you to make that conclusion?"

Helpful Questions

1. Build trust: "Can you give some examples so that we can understand your idea better?"

2. Open varied data: "Has anyone an example he or she can tell us about?"

3. Give possibility of creativity: "Who can play a musical instrument of some kind?" "Anyone for getting up some games on the lawn this afternoon?"

4. Give an opportunity for a self-revelation of the answerer: "Would some of you like to share your ideas of what you would do?"

5. Lead to data of possible common interest: "What high schools are represented in our class?"

6. Raise morale or interest level: "Shall we brainstorm for some program ideas?"

7. Move the group toward decisions: "What can we draw from the discussion?"

8. Elicit helpful feedback: "What did I do that caused your head to hit the dashboard?"

9. Help the group establish its norms: "What things would you like to schedule for the weekend?"

10. Help leader learn what the group and individual standards are: "What are some dating standards you feel some kids agree on?"

11. Facilitate drawing learning from within group: "How might we plan for next time so that everyone can get more out of it?"

12. Help to free the silent member: "Would you like to tell us your feelings on this, Mary?"

Unhelpful Questions

1. Threaten: "What do you mean by that?"

2. Limit area of response: "What does the scripture say?"

3. Predetermine the response: "Can anyone play the piano?" "Tennis anyone?"

4. Allow only for structured or content responses: "What ought to happen in a case like that?"

5. Start sub-group conversations: "How many of you go to Broughton?"

6. Encourage pessimism or disinterest: "What can we talk about this year?"

7. Block movement of group: "Is this getting us anywhere?"

8. Bring only reinforcement of unhelpful behavior: "I haven't been very helpful, have I?"

9. Force norms without consensus: "How many times will we go to church?"

10. Imply standards that may not be accepted: "Shouldn't we list some rules for the party?"

11. Predetermine learning by implications: "Doesn't all of this indicate that sex is a no-no?"

12. Drive the silent member farther out: "Why so quiet, Mary?"

Resources
for Reflecting
Theologically

Primary Aspects of Theological Reflection[86]

How did the process of theological reflection evolve? We all from time to time have conversations that are memorable. When these conversations lead to satisfying insights, result in life-altering decisions, and leave participants feeling and thinking that the Spirit of God has been among them, then something special has happened. The EfM seminar is designed to be a focus for such conversations.

When we reviewed these conversations, we began to ask questions. Why did they proceed so well rather than degenerate into gossip, arguments, or unproductive prattle? We tried to identify the significant interventions and then replicate the experience in a new way. Three things emerged from our efforts: a four-source model, the recognition that certain elements were necessary to the conversation, and the knowledge of how to replicate the process.

The Four-source Model has become central to the EfM method of theological reflection.

The four sources are:

- Our actions, our personal lives, the things we do every day—We are part of the text of Christian experience.

- Our personal beliefs—What each of us holds or affirms as the way we think and what we think motivates our behavior.

- The culture—The world in which we live in all its complexity of languages, ethnic groups, and secular diversity.

- The tradition of the church—The Holy Bible, the liturgies, the imagery, and the historical tradition of the church as it has come to us through custom, texts, and monuments.

The elements necessary to make the discussion flow are:

- The personal engagement of the participants (the conversation cannot remain abstract);

- A love of the subject under scrutiny (in this case, all that comprises theological studies);

- A method to abstract and image the crucial aspects under scrutiny (metaphors, images, and issues);

- An examination of the matter at hand using theological categories (i.e., creation, sin, judgment, and redemption);

---

86. This and other material in this section adapted from *Common Lessons and Supporting Materials* (2006), previously published by Education for Ministry.

- The ability to compare and contrast the various voices (our own lives, our religious tradition, the culture, and our personal beliefs or positions);

- A time to draw insights and reach conclusions that lead to implications, first on a personal basis, and then for our community and the world we inhabit;

- An opportunity to draw all this together within a supportive atmosphere of trust and support, rooted in a full life of prayer.

To sustain our learning activities the seminars normally contain three aspects:

1. The community is maintained through sharing our lives and prayer, both expected to be a regular part of the life of the group.

2. There is an opportunity to reflect on what we learn in the texts as we read about Christian Tradition. This is a time to raise questions, perhaps argue with the text, and look for themes that connect the past to itself and to us so that our stories may become woven as one with the story of God and the people of God.

3. There is opportunity for reflective activity that may encompass our spiritual autobiographies, as we engage in theological reflection, deepen our spiritual connections, or examine the meaning of the ministry we all share by virtue of our baptism.

The EfM Four-source Model

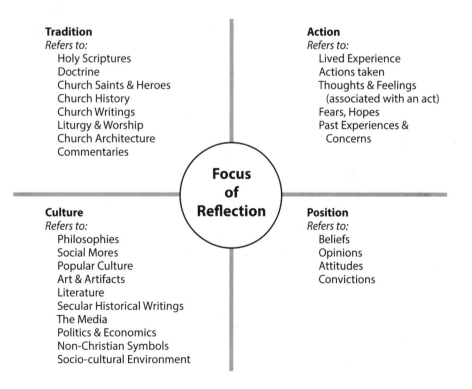

Tradition
Refers to:
    Holy Scriptures
    Doctrine
    Church Saints & Heroes
    Church History
    Church Writings
    Liturgy & Worship
    Church Architecture
    Commentaries

Action
Refers to:
    Lived Experience
    Actions taken
    Thoughts & Feelings
      (associated with an act)
    Fears, Hopes
    Past Experiences &
      Concerns

Focus of Reflection

Culture
Refers to:
    Philosophies
    Social Mores
    Popular Culture
    Art & Artifacts
    Literature
    Secular Historical Writings
    The Media
    Politics & Economics
    Non-Christian Symbols
    Socio-cultural Environment

Position
Refers to:
    Beliefs
    Opinions
    Attitudes
    Convictions

Theological Reflection in EfM

A theological reflection in EfM begins in one of the four sources: personal experience/**Action**, the **Tradition** of the faith, personal beliefs/**Position**, or **Culture**/society.

The movement of theological reflection is: **Identify** a focus, **Explore** the focus, **Connect** the focus to other areas/sources, and **Apply** learning.

A reflection takes on theological strength by viewing the image/picture, issue, or matter through some theological lenses, asking questions concerning the nature of the world, the relationship of God to the world, the nature of repentance and forgiveness, the nature of human community, or the quality of redemption and restoration of relationship. These are also known as **theological perspectives**, sometimes identified by the traditional systematic terms of Creation, Sin, Judgment, Repentance, and Redemption/Resurrection. Theological perspectives may also be framed in everyday language that carries the themes of the traditional terms, such as wholeness, brokenness, recognition of brokenness, reorientation, and restoration.

Theological reflection remains only an interesting exercise if learning is not embodied in ministry. It is important to ask what can be carried forward from the reflection.

In the following pages you will find several different ways of explaining and depicting the way EfM does theological reflection in four movements, drawing from four sources. Some may be more helpful to you than others; we all have different learning styles. The best advice is to use the approaches that are helpful, and don't agonize over the ones that aren't.

Select Bibliography for Theological Reflection

Killen, Patricia O'Connell and John DeBeer, *The Art of Theological Reflection*, New York: Crossroad, 1994.

Paver, John E. *Theological Reflection and Education for Ministry: The Search for Integration in Theology*. Ebook. Aldershot, England: Ashgate Publishing, 2006.

Thompson, Judith, Stephen Pattison, and Ross Thomason. Ebook. *SCM Studyguide to Theological Reflection*. London: SCM Press, 2008.

The Basic Structure of EfM Theological Reflection in Four Movements

IDENTIFY A FOCUS *This is the most crucial step of all. A good focus propels the reflection.*	Identify the beginning point on which to reflect. Is it something from a Personal Experience, from the Christian Tradition, from the Culture, or from a Personal Position? If the beginning is in a personal experience, identify a specific moment in the experience and the thoughts and feelings at that moment. If from a Bible passage, what is the main idea or image? If from something in Culture, what is the main focus? A Personal Position statement is itself the focus. Create a focus as either an image or a concise statement that captures the main energy of the beginning point and decide the specific standpoint from which the focus image or statement is viewed.
EXPLORE THE FOCUS IMAGE/STATEMENT *Asking the theological perspective questions is what turns general reflection into theological reflection.*	Investigate the focus by posing two or three theological questions around the focus image or statement. Exploration grows out of examining the breadth and depth of the identified focus. What's the story in the image? What kind of world is this? What could be destructive in this world? What could change things? What would make things work out? Those are questions that deal with classic systematic theology's perspective categories of creation, sin, judgment, and redemption. Another way of expressing theological perspectives is the language of wholeness, brokenness, recognition, reorientation, and restoration. What statement can be made about God, human nature, or grace as a result of your exploration of the image? How does the image relate to the theological affirmations of humanity being created in the image and likeness of God?
CONNECT OTHER SOURCES TO THE REFLECTION *This is the heart of reflection that helps us connect our lives and our faith.*	Exploring the focus image or statement theologically generally prompts natural connections to occur—Bible stories may be recalled that relate to the focus, or events in the Culture come to mind, or Personal Beliefs rise up. Theological reflection deliberately attends to those sources. If a theological reflection begins in Personal Experience, consider how our Christian Tradition, our Culture, and our Positions/Beliefs can guide us when life is like the image or statement that provides a focus for the reflection.
APPLY LEARNING AND INSIGHT TO MINISTRY *A reflection that does not end with implications for our own lives as ministers in the world is incomplete.*	Insights lead to implications that are applicable to one's ministry in daily life. Decide how the theological reflection calls us into actions of ministry in our daily life. Implications may take the form of a reframed question, a commitment to a specific action, or a new attitude.

Theological Reflection Process Chart[87]

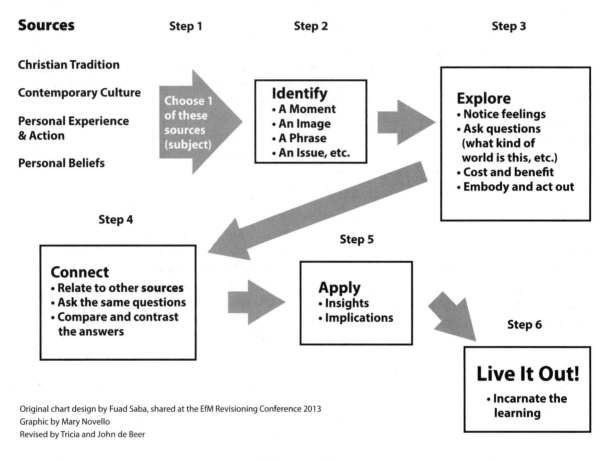

Sources

Christian Tradition

Contemporary Culture

Personal Experience
& Action

Personal Beliefs

Step 1

Choose 1
of these
sources
(subject)

Step 2

Identify
- A Moment
- An Image
- A Phrase
- An Issue, etc.

Step 3

Explore
- Notice feelings
- Ask questions
  (what kind of
  world is this, etc.)
- Cost and benefit
- Embody and act out

Step 4

Connect
- Relate to other sources
- Ask the same questions
- Compare and contrast
  the answers

Step 5

Apply
- Insights
- Implications

Step 6

Live It Out!
- Incarnate the
  learning

Original chart design by Fuad Saba, shared at the EfM Revisioning Conference 2013
Graphic by Mary Novello
Revised by Tricia and John de Beer

TR Process Chart

87. Like many of the resources in the EfM program, this one is the product of a collaborative effort. The original process design was developed by EfM mentor Fuad Saba and shared at the Re-visioning EfM conference in Sewanee in July 2013. The graphic presentation was designed by Mary Novello, EfM Coordinator for the Diocese of Western Michigan. Tricia and John deBeer, EfM trainers, further refined the language.

Four Phases of Movement
in Theological Reflection

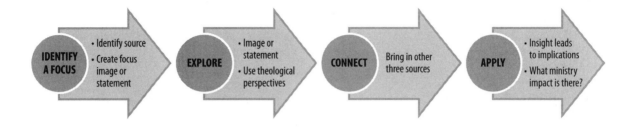

Framework for Theological Reflections[88]

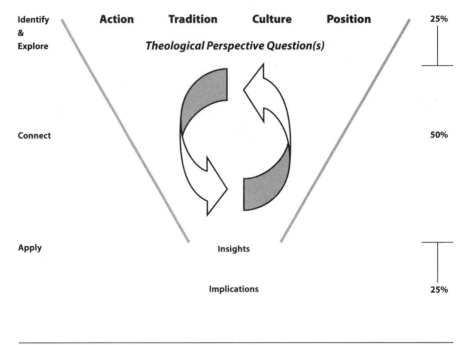

	Internal	External
Group	Tradition	Culture
Personal	Position	Action

Personal Experience/Action—Behavior and activity define this source; what actually happened that can be communicated using neutral words (RRG-B, p. 47). Actions are behaviors that can be seen by those external to ourselves. A video camera has to be able to view them.

Personal Belief/Position—Opinions, beliefs, viewpoints, and convictions held by a person constitute the position pole of the four-source model (RRG-B, p. 47). The important opinions are those that directly influence our behavior.

Faith Tradition—Whenever the language, concepts, terms, or images in a conversation come from the Bible or some other document or story that is part of the Christian lore, then one is drawing from the Christian Tradition source (RRG-B, p. 46).

Culture/Society—This source of the four-source model refers to a very large body of material. Literature, music, paintings, and other artifacts are part of the Culture Source (RRG-B, p. 46). Other parts are movies, television shows, and books. Focus on the aspects that influence your Positions and Actions.

---

88. Created by Joshua D. Booher.

Unpacking the Framework for Theological Reflections[89]

When two words are placed together, for example "theological reflection," the second word is the primary or focal word. In this case, we are engaging in a reflection. A reflection indicates there are two things. The first is the item (our lives) to be reflected and the second is the item the first item reflects off of. For it to be a "theological" reflection, one of the two items has to originate from our Tradition source.

There are four sources from which you can begin a theological reflection (TR). To help my own understanding, I have them in a two-by-two grid (see chart). The rows are us as individuals (Personal) and us in a group (Group). The columns are things that only we can know (Internal) and things that can be seen from the outside (External). In this grid, things about us that can be seen from the outside are our behaviors or Actions. The things about ourselves that only we can know are our Positions. Things about a group that a person outside a group can see is the Culture of the group. Things about a group that are primarily known only to people inside a group are the Tradition of the group. Though not perfect, this grid helps to show that the influences on our behaviors come from us or a group we are in and/or from inside or outside ourselves. This helps to explain why these four sources help us work our way through a TR. They cover all the influences in our lives.

Though you can start a TR from any of the four sources, for it to be a theological reflection one of the first two sources has to be Tradition. For this example our point of origin will be a personal action.

After identifying the story from your life that you want to reflect on (Action), you need to ask a theological perspective question to explore the story. This question helps to align the mirrors to get a more accurate and meaningful reflection. These questions can take on many forms, from creation/sin/judgment/repentance/redemption to love, grace, salvation, transubstantiation, and transfiguration. Often a good theological perspective question that can be used will arise during the text reflection portion of the seminar.

To be a "theological" reflection, after exploring the Action source from the theological perspective question, the group needs to explore the Tradition source. This allows the Tradition source to "reflect" and inform the Action source. Once a piece from the Tradition source has been identified, ask the EXACT SAME theological perspective question of it.

---

89. This framework was designed as a training tool to help mentors understand the overall map of the TR process and as a supplement to the four-source model so that when a TR is not proceeding well or there is confusion the mentor has a mental framework to help participants get back into the process and to assess what else needs covered to complete the TR process. EfM participants may also find the tool helpful as they work with individual reflections in the Reading and Reflection Guide and group reflection in their seminar.

Asking the EXACT same theological perspective question is the best way to ensure that you align your two mirrors correctly. For instance, asking, "What is your age?" and, "What year were you born?" get to related information, but do not line up exactly. To get from one to the other you have to execute mental arithmetic. The same would be the case if you ask of the Action source, "What was the world like in this story?" and of the Tradition source, "What was Creation like in this story?" As the mentor you might mean the same thing by these two questions, but the participants are likely answering different questions.

Once the group has explored the Tradition source with the exact same theological perspective question, you are ready to move on.

To have a reflection, you only need two things: the item to be reflected and the item doing the reflecting. So, at this point, we have set that stage. Our life story (Action) is being viewed against the mirror of our Tradition. The mirror was aligned by asking the exact same theological perspective question of both sources. At this point, the actual reflection begins. Everything before this point has been setting up the reflection by exploring the Action source and the Tradition source.

Now, the group will sift through the material that has arisen in the two explorations and see where there are points of similarity (Compare) and differences (Contrast). Begin discussing the similarities and differences.

After the Compare/Contrast discussion, you can move directly to the Insights/Implications. You have done everything required of a theological reflection. You have examined the point of origin (Action), the point of reflection (Tradition), and how they reflect upon each other. However, to have a richer reflection, bring in the other two sources. You do this by seeing how the sources resonate with the discussion through the lens of the theological perspective question. Don't go sequentially through the sources, though. Allow the sources to speak to each other as resonates arise.

Then, as time and/or energy start to wane, ask the group what insights and implications have arisen for them in this discussion.

Other Comments on Framework Application

This framework matches the RRG's four step model of Identify/Explore/Connect/Apply. In the Identify step, you are choosing the point of origin. You Explore the point of origin by way of the theological perspective question. You then Connect to the Tradition source. You also Connect to the other sources as time and energy allow. Finally, you Apply your learnings by way of Insights and Implications.

In addition, TRs have limited time in which to be completed and you want to make sure to give each section enough time. Through my experience, this is done by allowing 25 percent of your time to get through the Tradition theological perspective question discussion. At the 25 percent mark, you should be starting the compare/contrast of the two Explorations. (This covers Identify/Explore and the beginning of Connect.) At the 75 percent mark, you should stop wherever you are and go to Insights/Implications. (This is Apply.) Going to Insights/Implications at the 75 percent mark allows time to go into some detail in identifying learnings and applications from the discussion. This leaves the middle 50 percent (25 percent to 75 percent) for having a good, rich, flowing discussion. In my experience, this middle 50 percent is the heart of the TR. It is where the strongest energy is and where the learnings and insights occur. So, you tighten up the beginning 25 percent to allow more time for the heart of the TR. This is done by being more directive and not overanalyzing the first few steps. Then, when you reach the Compare/Contrast point, you step back and let the conversation flow more freely.

Questions tend to stop the flow of a conversation as participants have to reorient to what is being asked, think about the question, and restart the conversation. One way to avoid this problem is to make statements. Statements allow the participants to either follow the statement or stay where they were. If they are ready, they will move on by following the statement's content. If they are not ready, they will stay with the content they were previously discussing. For instance, if the group is discussing comparisons and contrasts and you think it is time to add content from the Culture source, you could make a comment relating the Culture source to the discussion. If other participants are ready they will follow your lead. Otherwise, they will continue discussing comparisons and contrasts.

All of the sources are very broad. It is good to find a way to narrow them to a more manageable size. The key is to focus on what aspects of the source influence your behavior. For example, in the Culture source, there are a lot of areas that don't influence my behavior. However, what I learned from my parents, my favorite books, and school does influence my behavior. So, when discussing the Culture, those are the areas I will focus on. Phrased another way, the way I look at sources is through the lens of "What from *Source* influences the way I think about *Theological Perspective Question*?"

Theological Reflection in a Group

During the first phase of reflection the subject is identified. This may be something that has happened to the group member, a particular belief the member holds, something from our Christian tradition, or an aspect of contemporary culture. Before we can begin, we need to name the subject. What exactly are we going to talk about? Where does it begin? Where does it end? How are we involved?

Identify

The more sharply defined the focus of the reflection, the more likely it is that the reflection will shape the understanding and the actions of the participants. Using the "theology of the Psalms" as a starting point for reflection is likely to lead to a very general discussion. However, using the first two verses of Psalm 37, for example, provides much finer focus:

> **Fret not yourself because of the wicked, be not envious of wrongdoers! For they will soon fade like the grass, and wither like the green herb.**

Dealing with a particular passage makes it more likely that our partner in conversation will be the tradition itself and not merely our opinions about the tradition. Similarly, when the starting point for reflection is an experience from our life, it is important to describe that experience with specificity and clarity in order to avoid merely rehashing previously held positions. The focus that is chosen for reflection should not only be clearly identified, but it should also matter to the participants. Whether the reflection begins with Action, Tradition, Culture, or Position, the focus should engage the interest and attention of the group members. Unless this happens, the reflection is likely to lack energy.

Explore

The second phase explores the subject that has been identified. What is it like? What language best describes it? What do we discover as we examine it from different vantage points? If the subject has been raised by some life event, what does this event say to us about our world? If we are reflecting on some belief that we hold, to what does this belief apply? What assumptions and values are implicit in the belief? If our starting point is a text from the Christian tradition or from another text, what does the text say to us on its own terms?

As we explore the subject of our reflection, we will often find it useful to use the language of metaphor. Using an image or metaphor deliberately encourages the evocative, intuitive quality of exploration.

Connect

The third phase makes connections between what has been discovered so far and the wider sources of meaning and truth. A reflection becomes theological by making deliberate connections between the Christian tradition and our own experience. Christian theological reflection links the Christian heritage with the personal and cultural dimensions of our lives. In this phase we are interested in the following general categories of questions:

- How does our exploration of this particular subject fit with our beliefs, with the scriptures, and with the creeds of the church?

- Does our exploration test out in everyday life? What would others in our family or at our work say about this?

The questions above are too broad to be of much practical help. More sharply defined questions help us connect and compare one source with another. A particularly helpful question is one that moves us right inside the subject of our exploration so that we can see what things look like from this perspective. We refer to questions like these as perspective questions. An example follows:

> *What kind of world* is depicted in the first two verses of Psalm 37? It is a world in which there are wrongdoers, and the wrongdoers sometimes flourish, but not for long. The question "*What kind of world?*" gives us a structure for developing a conversation with other sources of meaning. For example, we can think back to our own experiences with wrongdoers. Have they in fact "faded away like the grass"? What kind of world do we seem to inhabit when we look at what happens to us and at how we actually behave?
>
> Then we can move from questioning the Action source in this way to questioning the Culture source. What is the wisdom about wrongdoers in the magazines we read? What kind of world do our newspapers' editorial pages assume, and what of our own Position? What do we really believe about the place of wrongdoers in the world we inhabit?

This example illustrates *"What kind of world?"* as a question that allows us to explore the perspective of a particular source and then structure a conversation with elements from other sources by asking the same question of those sources. A question focuses our attention on a particular aspect of a given source.

In the EfM program we frequently use perspective questions designed to investigate the doctrinal themes of Creation, Sin, Judgment, and Redemption. *"What kind of world?"* is a question that opens up our perspective on the doctrine of Creation.

Apply

The final phase of theological reflection deals with the insights gleaned from conversation among the sources and with the implications for action decided by each individual on the basis of these insights. A desired outcome of theological reflection is a renewed understanding of what it means to be one of God's ministers in the world. To this end group members take their insights and learning from the reflection and apply them to their lives and ministries. Sometimes this involves a clear direction for action. More often the resulting application clarifies their questions, thereby preparing them to explore further their study of the Christian tradition. During this phase of reflection, questions fall into the following general categories:

• How can I apply my learning and questions?

• What am I being called to do differently?

• What do I want to take into our time of prayer?

The more specific each participant can be about the next small step necessary to apply the insights, the more likely it is that the reflection will be of lasting value.

Theological Reflection in Motion[90]

Reflection in an EfM group tends to be a "sitting" activity—lots of action in the head and heart, but not much going on for those who like to move around some while they think and learn. The topics discussed may indeed describe action-filled experiences replete with dramatic moments, but we tend to reflect in a sedentary way.

Reflection in Motion (RiM) began as an experiment exploring the possible use of physical movement as a way to "enhance" theological reflection. The experiment succeeded and people began to experience and "see" the way their thoughts—and the thoughts of others—move. The flow of the thinking process became visible as people literally moved among the four sources: Action, Tradition, Culture, and Position. People learned new things about theological reflection: how much thinking people do even when they are quiet; how meaning often comes as a mixture of sources; how the four sources operate in someone's thinking as one comes to insight and implications; and how movement can contribute to bringing head and heart, body and mind, together.

Reflection in Motion may not be a method to be used every week. Its strength lies in its ability to help people clarify how theological reflection happens. Once people physically see and experience how a reflection moves among and draws from the sources, they can turn to other TR methods with a new appreciation. People have reported learning how some thoughts evolve as a commingling of two or more sources. For example, a deeply held position such as "God is love" can come from **Tradition** (1 John 4:9) as well as from experiencing God's love directly. In addition, people can "track" their movement from one pole to another, perhaps noticing a familiar pattern. One person might move from the **Action** to the **Culture** poles and back to **Action** before connecting with **Tradition**. Another might follow a different pattern and prefer to move from **Action** to **Tradition** to **Position**. Reflection in Motion is a method that permits people to move (literally) from source to source according to how they think, rather than according to prescribed steps.

People have reported that reflection in motion helps them to:

- understand theological reflection because they are kinetic learners and movement aids their learning;

- discover individual styles of reflection (i.e., how a person characteristically moves around the sources);

---

90. Designed by Richard E. Brewer and Angela K. Hock, Oaces Inc. Tulsa, OK. Adapted from *Common Lessons and Supporting Materials* (2006), 2-6-1–2-6-4.

- realize that everyone in the group is thinking during reflection—even the very quiet people;
- sort out the source of their thoughts by standing between two poles;
- move reflection more deeply inside themselves where they can more clearly identify insights and consider implications for action.

To prepare for a theological reflection in motion:

1. Make four signs for the sources: Tradition (T), Culture (C), Action (A), Position (P).

2. With tape, place each sign on walls, backs of chairs, or wherever you can put them, placing each sign on a separate wall or other support (if possible) to form a square, leaving some room to move from one location to another and making each sign visible to everyone:

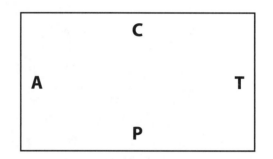

3. Set up the room—try to clear space for ease of movement. Leave the center of the reflection space open to allow movement.

Although the example below begins with personal experience, thus in the Action Source, this method frees a group to begin anywhere in the Four-source Model. A group may take a metaphor as its beginning point, explore that world, then scatter to the four sources. The focus of reflection may be identified from a wide-angle lens or from a dilemma. The work can be done with intermittent conversation and silent thought.

Identify

The mentor and presenter stand at the **Action** location while the presenter tells the incident. The rest of the group remains seated and listens carefully. Try to notice any metaphors the presenter uses in telling the incident and where the energy seems highest for the presenter. After hearing the incident, the group helps select a moment that seems to be the "heart of the matter," i.e., where the incident really seems to be centered.

All can help the presenter name the thoughts and feelings present at the central moment. Someone records those on newsprint or a whiteboard if that's helpful. Work very hard to name two or three really strong "feelings"; do the same with "thoughts"; this helps everyone to connect more clearly with their own lives.

Everyone takes a little time to come up with an occasion in their own lives when they experienced the described thoughts and feelings. As each person makes a connection to his or her life, they physically move to the **Action** pole. Once everyone is at that pole, take a few minutes for some to briefly tell about their connection; it isn't necessary for everyone to relate the moment aloud. Just be sure that everyone can identify with the named thoughts and feelings.

Everyone can either continue to stand at the **Action** pole, or sit if desired, to brainstorm for metaphors, images, phrases, and the like that seem to best represent what it is like in moments with those thoughts and feelings. If any metaphors were named during the incident, do they suggest others? Is there another image or phrase that everyone can work with better? Try for an image or phrase that is active, rather than passive, for example, "It's like running up a slippery slope" rather than "It's like being caught in an avalanche." Get playful. Help people get in touch with the physical reality of those thoughts and feelings—ask where they feel that moment in their body—that can suggest metaphors.

Watch and listen for a metaphor or phrase or term that seems to provide interest for everyone.

Since reflection moves from and through the metaphor, draw the metaphor or write the phrase on one large sheet of paper and, if possible, place that in the center of the reflection space.

Explore

Seated if desired, explore the world of the metaphor or phrase with one or more of the following theological perspective questions:

- What kind of world does the metaphor represent (or what is life like, or what is creative)?

- What makes things go off track in this world (or tempts us, or is destructive or negative—of what might we need to repent in this world)?

- What questions come up in this world?

- What questions might we ask God—or might God ask us?

- What judgments do we have to make in this world?

- What makes us realize that we have a choice about destruction or redemption?

- What makes us realize that we might need to repent? What is a cause of celebration in this world?

- What can we recognize as redemption?

Write the responses where everyone can see them, or remain present only in the conversation and reflective responses—whichever seems most helpful and does not get in the way of the reflection.

Connect

Take a minute or so of quiet time. Ask everyone to notice what connections they are making to any of the other poles or sources of **Culture, Position,** or **Tradition**.

In silence, everyone moves to the source with which he or she is connecting.

Each briefly speaks about the connection she or he made. The mentor helps conversation and responses to occur by paying attention to who has talked and who has not and by encouraging responses.

Let people move again if they notice other connections. Encourage them to speak the connection as they walk from one source to another. The mentor helps them notice when perhaps they actually need to stop between two poles because both are stimulated. For example, someone may be connecting to both **Culture** and **Position** at the same time. They can stand between the two sources and talk about the dual connections.

Apply

Everyone sits back down and considers insights that may be arising. What concerns seem to be surfacing? What positions are we stating? What contradictions and confirmations are present? What part does grace or God or the Holy Spirit or faith play in where we might go from this reflection?

Consider the implications for ministry in daily life. Each person identifies what he or she would pray for or act on now and what help they need, from others in the group, from the greater community, or from some other source.

Examples of Theological Reflection

Examples from the four volumes of the Reading And Reflection Guide follow, arranged by the source in which the reflection begins.

Please note that these are *not* different methods of theological reflection. All theological reflcetion in EfM follows the same process.

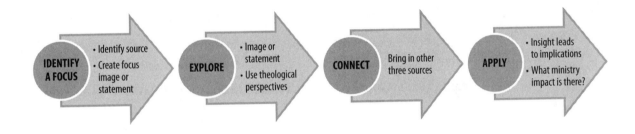

The Action Source

Theological Reflections beginning with a personal experience or dilemma

Theological Reflection Beginning with a Personal Experience (1)

Identify a focus.

In writing, describe the conflict you recalled in the Respond section. This places you in the Action/Experience source of your life; you recall something you've experienced or done.

Narrow the narrative by looking for a point in the conflict that had high energy.

Name your thoughts and feelings at that point of energy.

Draw a picture of a metaphor that illustrates what it was like when you had those thoughts and feelings. Think about color, sensation, heat/cold, location in your body of energy or tension. When you have/had those thoughts and feelings, it's as if. . . .

Explore the focus with theological perspectives.

Continue the reflection using your picture and considering these questions.

In the picture you created, what kind of interaction do you see?

How is that interaction revealing goodness or brokenness?

What kind of relationship does God have with those in that world?

What kind of relationships exist in that picture?

What crises are suggested in that picture?

What would persons in that kind of picture-world hope for?

Connect to other sources.

What personal beliefs (Position source) come to mind as you reflect on the picture and the world it captured?

Who or what in the Christian story (Tradition) or the world around you (Culture) helps you make sense of the world in the picture? In those sources, who are the wisdom figures or groups to help or guide you in a moment like you pictured?

Apply learning.

What prayer would you offer to God as a result of your reflection?

Name two areas in which you have the opportunity to minister in your life.

How will this reflection make any difference as you live in those areas?

How has your EfM study given you a way to view the circumstances of your life?

Theological Reflection Beginning with a Personal Experience (2)

Identify a reflection focus.

Recall a time in your life when you believe you experienced the Presence of God.

Make some notes about the experience.

Locate the central moment of the experience, when your awareness of God's Presence was most vivid.

Name two to three attendant thoughts and feelings in that moment.

"It was like_____." Draw a picture that represents that moment's thoughts and feelings or make a brief statement of six to nine words.

Explore the focus image or statement.

Bring theological perspectives to the reflection.

Study the image or statement in silence. Let the "voice" of the image or statement become present.

What questions about the image/statement surface for you? List those and your responses.

Identify the type of theological questions those are. That is, are the questions about the nature of the world, the nature of God, the relationship of God to the world, the nature of mercy, of grace, of hope, and so forth?

Connect to other sources of meaning in your life.

When life is like that image/statement for you, how do you make sense of the experience?

What wisdom do you draw on for understanding? Who or what have you studied in the Christian tradition or the world around you that can "speak" to you or teach you about a moment like that?

What do you deeply believe about the experience you had? What doubts and hopes are present for you? Where do those feelings originate?

Apply insight/learning.

Sit quietly with the image, exploration, and connections, perhaps lighting a candle as you reside with the reflection.

What prayer begins praying in you? Try to write that down.

How does the theological reflection support or challenge one commitment in your life?

Theological Reflection Beginning with a Personal Experience (3)

This variation of theological reflection has sometimes been referred to as the "microscope method" because it describes the refining process that helps focus intently on a beginning point for theological reflection. Typically, the method begins in someone's experience and systematically focuses the circumstance to one fleeting moment in which to open the self or group to the eternal. In this form of theological reflection, we move into the particular to discover the eternal.

Identify a focus from which to reflect:

Recall and recount a time when you were confronted with a barrier of some sort. Describe the circumstance in as much detail as possible.

Notice when there were significant shifts in energy in the event and identify the one moment of greatest energy for you. Let all else fall away and mentally stand just in that discrete instant.

List two or three primary feelings and two or three key thoughts you had *at that tiny moment*. Decline any internal mental invitation to explain, justify, or interpret. Just let yourself accept your key thoughts and feelings of the moment.

Let yourself feel the feelings and notice where in your body they are. What is that like? Do they create a sensation of heat or cold? What color do they have? Settle into those thoughts and feelings and create a picture of what it's like for you when you experience that combination. For instance, is it like a tea kettle whistling because pressure has built up, or like walking barefoot on rocks, or like hanging from a limb high off the ground?

Write or draw a picture of what it's like when those feelings and thoughts are present. From this point forward, the reflection is on the image or picture-world that represents your thoughts and feelings, not on the original incident.

Theologically explore the world represented in your picture.

Stay inside the picture-world for this exploration. How does that world reveal something about wholeness or goodness, or about brokenness?

What does someone in that picture-world have to recognize in order to know there is brokenness? What would that person have to change in order to move towards wholeness?

What would it take to restore wholeness?

Connect by letting your mind freely move through and around the image.

What does your image-world call to mind for you? Are there events in the world around you that relate to the image and help you make sense of those kinds of moments?

If you've been thinking of some scripture passages or a hymn or prayer, stop and look those up. This is a very important part of theological reflection. How do any of those connections help make sense of this kind of moment?

What do you believe about living in a world such as the image captured? What helped to form that belief? Do you sense any other possible beliefs?

Apply to daily life. Theological reflection provides support for living a life of maturity in faith and action.

In what ways might this reflection inform your behavior when you again have an experience that raises these thoughts and feelings? Make notes about how reflecting theologically on this moment helps you integrate belief and behavior and raises any kind of possibilities for you in ministry and maturity.

There may be opportunity during the group's seminar time to explore the theological reflections of various group members. There may be time to do a group reflection around a central theme of the group's choosing. If so, what do you notice about the difference(s) between reflecting alone and reflecting in a group?

Theological Reflection Beginning with a Personal Experience (4)

Identify a focus:

Recall several times when you were the object of destructive behavior. It may be something like a practical joke, or being the subject of a playful trick. Or it may be something more physically dangerous like being mugged or robbed.

Make a list of the experiences for your eyes only.

Look for threads that run through that list. Do several of the experiences relate to the same person, or do some share a similar aspect? List all the threads you can identify. Pick one as the focus on which you would like to reflect further.

Explore the focus:

Reflection on the focusing thread may produce an image (picture) or metaphor ("It's like this when I experienced the violence . . . .") or an issue. Write or draw an issue or image suggested by the thread you selected. Whatever form it takes can be explored using theological perspective questions:

Develop questions to explore the world of the thread. For example, what kind of world does the image or issue assume?

What destroys in that world?

How is God revealed (or not) in that world?

Consider the view of humanity assumed or actively present in the world of the image.

Examine what unexpected influences are present in that world.

Connect to other sources of meaning:

Culture: Record literary works, scenes from movies, or song lyrics that come to mind.

What pieces from the Christian tradition feed the conversation? Especially look at Psalms, liturgies and prayers (A resource may be The Book of Common Prayer), hymns, etc.

Ask, "What seems to be the truth about this reality?" Allow yourself to think deeply and write one or more of your own beliefs concerning the ideas and images you surface in the reflection.

Apply learning to daily life and ministry:

Sometimes a good reflection leads to better questions. What questions arise for you in light of this reflection?

How might your participation in prayer and worship be impacted?

Close with a collect:

O God who _is everpresent in our._

I pray ~~that we are~~ _spiritual eyes to_

So that _____

In Christ's name. Amen.

P.

Theological Reflection Beginning with a Personal Experience (5)

This reflection begins in an individual's personal experience and systematically focuses to one moment in which to open an individual or a group to the Eternal.

Identify a focus in an experience:

Recall and recount a time when your ethical standards were challenged. Describe the circumstance in as much detail as possible.

Notice where there were significant shifts in energy in the event and identify the one moment of greatest energy for you. Let all else fall away and mentally stand just in that discrete instant. Stay with any discomfort that you recall.

List two or three primary feelings and two or three key thoughts you had *at that tiny moment.* Decline any internal mental invitation to explain, justify, or interpret. Just let yourself accept your key thoughts and feelings of the moment.

Feel the feelings and notice where they are in your body. What is that like? Do they create a sensation of heat or cold? What color do they have?

Settle into those thoughts and feelings and create a picture of what it's like for you when you experience that combination. Maybe it was like a vise tightening in your chest, or a fire erupting in your head, or a dark cold tunnel before you, or another image.

Write or draw a picture of what it's like when those feelings and thoughts are present.

Theologically explore the world represented in your picture. Stay inside the picture-world for this exploration.

What is whole or good about that world?

What separation does the image represent?

What does someone in that picture-world have to recognize in order to know there is separation? What would that person have to change in order to move back towards wholeness?

What do conversion and transfiguration look like for those in the image world?

How would God's glory be manifest in such a world?

Connect to our other sources:

What seems to be the heart of the matter in the focus metaphor or statement? What is this theological reflection about?

Since this reflection begins in personal experience (Action source), draw in the Culture, Tradition, and Position sources.

What about your own beliefs (Position)? Considering the heart of the metaphor and the issue it represents, state your position. How did you form that position—from something you learned in church (Tradition) or by experience (Action) or in a book you read (Culture)?

Think about (and write if you have time and inclination) how that mix of sources speaks to the metaphor's heart. What wisdom can you gain from the reflection?

Apply to daily life. Theological reflection guides us to living a life of maturity in faith and action.

Make notes about how reflecting theologically on this moment helps you integrate belief and behavior and raises any possibilities for you in ministry.

Theological Reflection Beginning with a Dilemma (Action Source) (1)

First, read through this method and then apply it to a dilemma in your life.

Identify a focus: The focus goal is to create a universal statement of the dilemma. This kind of reflection especially requires that the personal experience be something that is over and done with, no decisions remain to be made.

Describe something that happened in your life that posed a dilemma; you wanted two things that could not both happen at the same time. *For example, you want the promotion and transfer you have been offered and you want to remain in the same location where you are.*

Find the central moment of your incident by noting where or when in the event the tension was greatest. Write what you thought and felt at that moment.

To create a dilemma statement, list what you wanted at the moment you felt the tension. You will likely have several "I wanted" statements. Keep this list in the form of "I wanted" rather than "I did not want." Note: The dilemma is between two goods, but a choice has to be made. *Example: I wanted to advance in the company. I wanted to try my wings. I wanted to see a new location. I wanted to stay where I know what I am doing. I wanted to keep my life and friends.*

From your list, select the pair of statements that best represents the central dilemma. Record the dilemma statement as "I wanted _____ **and** I wanted _____." The challenge is to get an "I wanted" statement rather than "I wanted but I didn't want. . . ."

Turn the dilemma pair into a universal statement. What is this dilemma actually about? A universal statement of the example dilemma could be "This is a dilemma over the challenge of expanding one's horizons and hanging onto the familiar." Or, "This is a dilemma over not knowing whether a step is one that I'm ready for." There are other possible dilemma statements for the example, so do not get hung up on the "correct" one.

Universalizing is especially necessary when reflecting in a group in order to avoid advice-giving and problem-solving. If this were a group reflection, each person would identify a moment when they, too, experienced the same universal dilemma. In a group, this is another way in which a tendency to continue to focus on the presenter can be redirected.

Explore your universal dilemma either through the lens of Cost/Promise (Risk/Hope) *or* Theological Perspectives.

Cost and Promise names costs (risks) and promises (hopes) of the dilemma.

Theological Perspective Questions can be used in the universal dilemma by considering what that dilemma reveals about wholeness, brokenness, recognition, reorientation, or restoration.

Connect to other sources in which this dilemma has occurred—Christian Tradition, Culture, and Positions. Remember, these connections come in any order. This is not a rote exercise, but a reflection. Consider such questions as:

Tradition: Identify some stories from scripture or church history that relate to the dilemma. In the stories of the people of God, who has been in the same dilemma? Or perhaps some prayers or hymns come to mind that relate to this reflection. Look up what you recall and spend time with the story or account or prayer or hymn. How does the connection help or challenge you in this dilemma?

Compare Tradition and Dilemma: Compare and contrast what our Christian Tradition and the initial experience have to say about that dilemma. What choices would the Tradition support? Not support? Why?

Culture: Have there been news stories about this kind of dilemma? Have you read a book or seen a movie that dealt with that dilemma? Is there a political dimension to that dilemma?

Position: What do you believe about the issues of the dilemma? How was your belief in conflict in the dilemma? What do you hope for regarding the dilemma? What formed your beliefs about this matter?

Apply

Insights and Questions: What do you see in a new way? What have you learned about facing this dilemma? What questions remain for you in this kind of dilemma?

Implications: Identify learning or insight that occurred for you during this theological reflection.

What do you want or need to do?

- social implications,
- actions you could take,
- what you need to learn,
- support that would help in the midst of such a dilemma,
- where you could find that support.

Close your personal reflection with a prayer that offers your learning and hopes and requests to God.

Theological Reflection Beginning with a Dilemma (Action Source) (2)

Identify

Describe an incident for reflection—an experience in which you felt pulled in at least two directions over something, and for which there are no decisions pending, that is, the incident is over, though there still may be feelings. For example:

> I had looked forward to my best friend's wedding for months and had my plane ticket and my new outfit. We had plans to enjoy the sights and catch up and just have fun. And then my surviving parent got sick, but told me I could go ahead with my plans. I felt so torn. There was no one else there.

Name the turning point in the incident.

What's the central moment of the incident? Where is the tension greatest? What was happening? What were you thinking and feeling at that moment?

Record the central moment in a short sentence and your thoughts and feelings at that moment.

State the issue.

Try to state what's at stake or what the central dilemma is at the moment of greatest tension.

To help get to the dilemma, list declarative statements about what you wanted at that moment or what interests were at stake at that moment. You may have several.

Record tension statements as "I wanted _____ and I wanted _____." For example:

> I wanted to attend my best friend's wedding and I wanted to stay to take care of my ailing parent.

Select a pair of statements that best represent the central tension.

Record the central dilemma/what's at stake. For example:

> Personal fun conflicting with caring for another. Dilemma: Plans affected by unforeseen circumstances.

Identify another time.

Clarify the dilemma by recalling another time when you experienced a similar tension.

Record your additional experience with the identified tension by completing the sentence: "It was a time when. . . ."

Explore the dilemma.

What is it like to live in that tension? Contrast the cost/promise of the dilemma.

Record your responses to the questions using either cost/promise or theological perspectives:

COST OF EACH SIDE OF THE TENSION	PROMISE OF EACH SIDE OF THE TENSION
Ex., Plans: caught off guard, decisions made that are hard to change	Ex., Know what is coming

OR use one or two theological perspective questions adapted from the Cycle of Gospel Living, developed by Eric Law (and used in Interlude One, Week 15).[91] This cycle focuses around power, loss or yielding up of power, and empowerment, and moves through four phases.

- Give up power, choose the cross—This is a point of entry for the powerful.

- Cross, death, powerless—This is a point of entry for the powerless.

- Empowerment, endurance

- Empty tomb, resurrection, powerful

Here are examples of asking questions of the dilemma or image. Use only one or two when exploring your image or dilemma:

Give up power, choose the cross: What are the power dimensions of the dilemma or image? Who has power? What has to be yielded?

Cross, death, powerless: What sacrifice(s) might be called for? What are the temptations of the cross, of powerlessness? To whom or what is power yielded?

Empowerment, endurance: How is power transmitted to the powerless party? What is required in order to enter the cycle that leads to empowerment? What builds endurance?

Empty tomb, resurrection, powerful: What is left behind in the image or dilemma? How does resurrection occur in the image or dilemma? What is the hope of the power received?

---

91. Law, *The Wolf Shall Dwell with the Lamb*, 74.

Connect

TRADITION

Identify some stories from scripture or church history that relate to the dilemma or image. How or where does the Gospel Living cycle occur in our Christian story in scripture? In the lives of women and men of faith? Or perhaps some prayers or hymns come to mind that relate to this reflection.

DIALOGUE

Compare and contrast what your Christian tradition has to say about that dilemma or image. What choices would the tradition support? Not support? Why?

CULTURE AND POSITION

Where is that tension or dilemma experienced in our culture? Have there been news stories about it? Have you read a book or seen a movie that dealt with that dilemma? Is there a political dimension?

What do you believe about that dilemma? How was your belief in conflict within the dilemma? What do you hope for regarding the dilemma?

Apply

INSIGHTS AND QUESTIONS

What do you see in a new way now? What have you learned about facing this dilemma? What questions do you have about the dilemma in your life?

IMPLICATIONS

What do you want or need to do about this dilemma? Are there social implications? Are there actions you could take? Is there something more to learn? What support would help? Where will you find that support?

Theological Reflection Beginning with a Wide-Angle Lens (Action Source)

Why this title? Instead of the usual first step to **Identify** a focus from one of the four sources, the wide-angle lens begins with a variety of perspectives, then isolates a thread/theme/idea/image that connects them, that in turn becomes the focus for the reflection. A theological reflection beginning with a wide-angle lens can begin in any of the four sources. The key is that it requires initiation from something that could produce several themes or ideas. There are innumerable options. An individual can begin with movies, assigned readings, incidents from one's life, or several personal positions. In an EfM group, the beginning point can be themes from the spiritual autobiographies, themes from the week's reading, themes from any on-board time of the group, or some other starting point from which a variety of perspectives can be elicited. The initial step always is to list themes and find a thread that runs through several of them.

Identify

FIND A COMMON THEME OR THREAD

Begin by finding the threads or themes present in several personal incidents that indicate a gap between your belief and your behavior.

What are the common themes or elements that emerge? Is there a burning question, struggle, or issue? A theme may be expressed as a simple statement, an image, a metaphor, or an issue.

Select one thread that connects various themes. For instance, a review of several incidents (either ones identified by an individual or those identified in a group) could yield themes of frustration, tiredness, hurry, and feeling overwhelmed. Those themes would have shown up in two or more of the incidents. Asking, "What ties some of those themes together?" yields a thread that runs through some incidents. For example, "Having too much to do leads to impatience with others" could be named as a thread that ties two or more incidents.

Explore

REFLECT ON SOME THEOLOGICAL PERSPECTIVES

What image could paint a picture of the thread identified from your incidents?

Describe or draw that image. Examine the image for what's going on in it. Write about what's going on in that image.

Use theological perspective questions to explore the focus. Which theological perspective (creation, sin, judgment, repentance, redemption, celebration, the doctrine of God, grace, or others you think of) comes first to mind? Consider several. For example, what would repentance look like in that image? Or redemption?

Connect

Bring other sources into the conversation to help find meaning in matters of daily life and ministry.

CONSIDER CONTEMPORARY CULTURE AND SOCIETY

Focus on one or two areas of your culture or society so that the reflection will not be too broad. These connections might come from your local community or the larger world; our work environment, our education system, our health care system, our grandmothers, movies, TV, literature, art, songs, artifacts, architecture, government, the press, to name a few. Just pick one area of contemporary society with which to connect.

What does the world in which you live teach you about dealing with the identified focus? Where do you find evidence of people dealing with tiredness and anger in the world around you?

What have you learned from your culture that helps you or challenges you regarding the theme?

How do areas of Culture/Society speak to or about this thread? For instance, what does the world of employment teach us about tiredness and anger? What about our health care system? What about advertising? Again, just use one aspect of our society.

CONSIDER THE CHRISTIAN TRADITION

Identify biblical passages or other elements from Christian Tradition in which this common thread is evoked or brought to mind. Provide time to find and read passages. Select one text that seems to speak most clearly to the thread that was evoked.

Examine the passage with these questions: What do you know about the meaning of the text in its original setting? How have others interpreted this text? What does this text mean to you?

COMPARE AND CONTRAST CONTEMPORARY CULTURE AND CHRISTIAN TRADITION

From the perspectives of Culture and Tradition, what kind of a world emerges?

Where do these perspectives join or compete? Where do they clash or contrast?

Again use theological perspectives—creation, sin, judgment, repentance, redemption, celebration, the doctrine of God, grace, or others you think of—to shape your reflection. Likely, there is time to use only one or two of these themes during any one reflection. As an example, if the New Testament passage about Jesus cleansing the temple were used for the Christian Tradition and the work environment for the Contemporary Culture connection, how do those two perspectives compare and contrast? What messages do we hear from either or both?

CONNECT TO BELIEFS, POSITIONS, AND AFFIRMATIONS

What is your response to the messages from the Christian Tradition and Contemporary Culture?

What do you feel about where this reflection has led? What do you think about it?

Where are you in the reflection?

What positions or affirmations do you hold about this reflection?

Apply

IDENTIFY INSIGHTS AND PERSONAL IMPLICATIONS

What have you learned about coherence of belief and behavior? What moves or energizes you? What insights come to mind?

What are you personally called to do differently, to affirm, or to change? What prayer do you want to offer?

DECIDE ON SOCIAL AND CIVIC CONSEQUENCES

What actions will you take to carry out the implications you have discovered?

What will you investigate further in your community in order to make a difference?

Whom can you contact to join you or inform you? What action might you take?

The Tradition Source

Theological Reflections beginning with a text or artifact from the Christian tradition

Theological Reflection Beginning with the Christian Tradition (Scripture) (1)

This method of theological reflection focuses on a selection from scripture and uses it as the starting point for reflection. The passage may come from the readings for the week, or the group may select a passage that is of special interest.

Identify
SELECT A PIECE OF SCRIPTURE

A person in the group reads the selected passage of scripture.
Be silent for a couple of minutes.

FIRST RESPONSES

What word or phrase stands out for you? Share this in the group.

HEAR THE PASSAGE AGAIN

Another person reads the selected passage again. Perhaps a different translation may be used.
The group is silent for a couple of minutes.

Explore
EXAMINE THE PASSAGE

What do you know about the meaning of the text or its original setting?

What is happening in the text? What is going on?

How have others interpreted this text? What kind of a text is this? (sermon, parable, etc.)

What might it mean today?

EXAMINE THE TRADITION

What is the world like in this passage?

What human predicament in the world is revealed in this passage?

What indicates a change of mind, heart, or behavior?

What gives rise to celebration in this world?

Connect
MAKE CONNECTIONS WITH OUR OWN EXPERIENCE (ACTION)

With whom do you identify in this passage?

Can you recall a time in your life when you experienced an event or situation similar to the one in the passage? What were your thoughts and feelings?

What does that event or situation mean to you in light of this passage?

In what way does the tradition support, inform, and/or challenge your experience?

LOOK AT CULTURE

What does the Contemporary Culture say about the world described in the passage? Pick one aspect of Culture to discuss this connection, such as what books deal with the concerns of the scripture passage; what is happening in the world around us now that relates to the matter described in the scripture passage; what attitudes of our world of work connect to the concern of the scripture passage; how is God at work in our world in ways that relate to the scripture passage's concerns? Other ways that Culture can provide some help in reflection is to think of what movies are dealing with the scriptural issues under discussion; what family or social wisdom speak to the issue?

WHAT IS MY POSITION?

Where do you stand? What do you believe about the matters or issues raised in this reflection? What is your position on this matter?

Apply
IDENTIFY INSIGHTS

What new insights have emerged as a result of this reflection? What can you affirm or state that you have learned?

IMPLICATIONS FOR ACTION

Is there anything you intend to do differently as you live out your ministry?

What help might you need to carry out your intentions?

What are the consequences for others or for the future?

Example:

Moses was keeping the flock of his father-in-law Jethro, the priest of Midian; he led his flock beyond the wilderness, and came to Horeb, the mountain of God. There the angel of the Lord appeared to him in a flame of fire out of a bush; he looked, and the bush was blazing, yet it was not consumed. Then Moses said, "I must turn aside and look at this great sight, and see why the bush is not burned up." When the Lord saw that he had turned aside to see, God called to him out of the bush, "Moses, Moses!" And he said, "Here I am." Then he said, "Come no closer! Remove the sandals from your feet, for the place on which you are standing is holy ground." He said further, "I am the God of your father, the God of Abraham, the God of Isaac, and the God of Jacob." And Moses hid his face, for he was afraid to look at God. Then the Lord said, "I have observed the misery of my people who are in Egypt; I have heard their cry on account of their taskmasters. Indeed, I know their sufferings, and I have come down to deliver them from the Egyptians, and to bring them up out of that land to a good and broad land, a land flowing with milk and honey, to the country of the Canaanites, the Hittites, the Amorites, the Perizzites, the Hivites, and the Jebusites. The cry of the Israelites has now come to me; I have also seen how the Egyptians oppress them." –Exodus 3:1–9

A theological reflection starting from scripture begins in the Christian Tradition/Heritage source area.

Identify a focus point in the passage, i.e., where the key energy/heart of the passage seems to be, what the passage seems to be about. Perhaps the group can agree on an image or metaphor that pictures what the passage focus or energy is, such as the burning bush.

Explore the passage by considering what was going on at the time of this event; what commentaries say about this passage; what you have studied; what is described at the point of the burning bush.

What questions might occur in the face of such an event? What's the world like for Moses at this point (Creation)? What temptations are there for Moses at this moment (Sin)? What's surprising for Moses (Judgment)? What choices does Moses have (Judgment)? What makes things alright for him (Redemption)?

What questions would you have in such a moment?

Connect to other Sources/Life Areas as responses occur to anyone—not necessary to go in order or as steps. Just let these connections occur in whatever sequence they may come.

Personal Experience—when have you experienced something that you might call "a burning bush moment"?

Culture—what kinds of groups or events might be "burning bush" events in the world around us?

Personal Position/Belief—what do you believe about "burning bush" moments? What do you hope or doubt?

Apply

What new thoughts have occurred to you? What do you want to think about more? How might you engage in your life differently as a result of this conversation?

Theological Reflection Beginning with the Christian Tradition (Scripture) (2)

Identify

The following passages involve the people of Samaria, a group that fostered strong feelings among the Jews. Carefully read the passages and identify two or three topics common to both.

When the days drew near for him to be taken up, he set his face to go to Jerusalem. And he sent messengers ahead of him. On their way they entered a village of the Samaritans to make ready for him; but they did not receive him, because his face was set toward Jerusalem. When his disciples James and John saw it, they said, "Lord, do you want us to command fire to come down from heaven and consume them?" But he turned and rebuked them. Then they went on to another village.

Luke 9:51–56

But wanting to justify himself, he asked Jesus, "And who is my neighbor?" Jesus replied, "A man was going down from Jerusalem to Jericho, and fell into the hands of robbers, who stripped him, beat him, and went away, leaving him half dead. Now by chance a priest was going down that road; and when he saw him, he passed by on the other side. So likewise a Levite, when he came to the place and saw him, passed by on the other side. But a Samaritan while traveling came near him; and when he saw him, he was moved with pity. He went to him and bandaged his wounds, having poured oil and wine on them. Then he put him on his own animal, brought him to an inn, and took care of him. The next day he took out two denarii, gave them to the innkeeper, and said, 'Take care of him; and when I come back, I will repay you whatever more you spend.' Which of these three, do you think, was a neighbor to the man who fell into the hands of the robbers?" He said, "The one who showed him mercy." Jesus said to him, "Go and do likewise."

Luke 10:29–37

Note: Though the above scripture passages are quoted from the NRSV translation, reading the passages in a variety of translations may increase the sense of meaning.

Focus the passages by considering where the key energy/heart of the passage is, what the passages seem to be about.

Develop an image in words or a drawing that brings the point of the passages into focus.

Explore the image or central idea of the passages, using questions from the theological themes of Creation, Sin, Judgment, Repentance, or Redemption, such as:

- What kind of community does the image-world/theme suggest (Creation)?

- What might get in the way of relationships in that image-world/theme (Sin)?

- What could make those in that world realize there's something wrong; what choices are there (Judgment)?

- What would represent a change of direction (Repentance)?

- What might a new, life-giving creation look like (Redemption)?

Connect

Note: Connecting happens best if some freedom is allowed. Listen to each of the "voices" or "sources" below and let your responses emerge in any order. You may not make a connection in one area; that is okay. That may occur at a later time, or not at all. Mainly, allow your inner life to speak, connecting you to these areas of potential meaning and revelation.

Personal Experience—When has something happened in your life that is like the world of the image/metaphor? For instance, if the image created for the passages is "extending a party invitation," when have you given or sent such an invitation?

Compare your experience with the preceding theological exploration. How do your experience and the image relate to one another?

Contemporary Culture/Society—Who or what has taught you something that is helpful when life is like the image? In our world, how is there opposition to that image? How is there support for it? Where is God extending party invitations in the world in which you live?

Christian Tradition—What other scripture passages or church history events remind you of the image or central point of the passages from Luke?

Beliefs/Positions—What key issues do the metaphor and personal experience and contemporary culture raise? State your Beliefs and Positions relative to those issues.

Apply meaning and purpose to the reflection by identifying learning and clarifying questions.

How do the beliefs and insights of the exploration support you in ministry?

Notice where you might want to make some changes in action or viewpoint about the matter covered in the reflection.

Write a prayer in response to the discoveries in this reflection.

Theological Reflection Beginning with the Christian Tradition (3)

Identify the focus or a primary point of your EfM study this week.

Explore the primary point by identifying the theological perspectives of the world, sin, judgment, repentance, and/or redemption reflected in that focus. Apply any of these or similar theological questions to your consideration.

What view of the world is present in that focus?

What brokenness or sin does that focus address or reveal?

What questions or crises does that focus respond to or contribute to?

How does that concern or focus lead to repentance or reorientation?

How does that concern lead to restoration to a creative life?

What does the focus say about forgiveness?

What concern about God does the focus address?

Move to the other sources

Connect by stating how the focus is present in today's world *(Culture)*.

What book or movie has dealt with this focus?

Compare and contrast the connections to the world around you with the above exploration of the focus.

What issues or concerns do you become aware of?

What personal experiences (Action) have you had that relate to this focus?

State one or two personal beliefs (Position) you have about the focus that surfaced in this reflection.

How did those beliefs form?

When has it been difficult for you to act on those beliefs?

Apply

If you could do just one thing about the concerns that surfaced in this reflection, what would that be?

Theological Reflection Beginning with a Wide-Angle Lens (Tradition Source)

Why this title? The image of a wide-angle lens is used because this reflection begins with a variety of perspectives, then focuses on a thread/theme/idea/image that connects them. An individual starts by finding the threads or themes present—in this case in something he or she reads or watches. The key for use by an individual requires initiation from something that could produce several themes or ideas (in this case, two or more articles on a topic of interest). In an EfM group, the reflection's beginning point can be themes from the spiritual autobiographies, themes from the week's reading, themes from any on-board time of the group, or some other starting point from which a variety of perspectives can be elicited.

The key is first to list the themes in what is under consideration, then find a thread that runs through the themes.

Identify

FIND A COMMON THEME OR THREAD

Begin by listening carefully to the group as you share your reflections on the readings assigned for the week.

What are the common themes or elements that emerge?

Is there a central question, struggle, or issue that surfaces as those from each year level share?

State the central thread as a simple statement, image, metaphor, or issue.

For instance, a review of several articles could reveal themes of challenge of the *status quo,* support of a particular view, and/or revelation of something new. Asking "What ties some of those themes together" yields a thread that may have run through the articles.

Explore

THEOLOGICAL PERSPECTIVES

Write about what's going on in the image, issue, or statement you created in the Identify step above.

Sit quietly and let the image or statement and your writing rest in you.

What questions does your image or statement raise?

What questions does that image or statement answer?

Identify the perspectives contained in the questions, that is, wholeness, brokenness, recognition, reorientation, or restoration.

Connect

This is the point at which one looks at the various sources in life to help find meaning in matters of daily life and ministry. The object is to find connections between the image, statement, or issue and other aspects of our life that teach us something.

CONNECT TO CULTURE AND SOCIETY

Focus on one or two areas of your culture or society so that the reflection will not be too broad. These connections might come from your local community or the larger world: your work environment, the education system, the health care system, your grandmothers, movies, TV, literature, art, songs, artifacts, architecture, government, or the press, to name a few.

Pick just one area of our contemporary society with which to connect. For instance, what does the world of employment teach you about the theme you have identified? Or, what have you learned from the news media in your culture/society that helps you or challenges you regarding the theme?

How does the selected area of culture/society speak to or about this thread?

CONNECT TO CHRISTIAN TRADITION

- Identify biblical passages or other elements from Christian tradition (scripture, hymn, prayer, church history document) in which this common thread is evoked or brought to mind. Read the passages.

- Select one passage that seems to address the image, statement, or issue.

- Examine the passage:

  - Note how the passage offers insight into the image, statement, or issue you are considering.

  - Note how the passage challenges the image, statement, or issue.

  - What does the passage mean to you?

COMPARE AND CONTRAST CULTURE/SOCIETY AND CHRISTIAN TRADITION

From the perspectives of each, what kind of a world emerges?

Where do these perspectives join or compete? Where do they clash or contrast?

Note what seems to be "at stake" as you compare and contrast your Culture and Tradition connections.

CONNECT TO PERSONAL EXPERIENCE

When have you experienced something that relates to what seems to "be at stake" above?

CONNECT TO BELIEFS, POSITIONS, AND AFFIRMATIONS

What positions or affirmations do you hold in relation to what is at stake?

Identify how that belief formed for you. Was it from personal experience, from something you learned in your faith tradition, or from the cultural messages you have inherited or encountered?

What "gaps" are there for you between what you believe and how you act in relation to the theme considered in this reflection?

Apply

IDENTIFY INSIGHTS AND PERSONAL IMPLICATIONS

What have you learned about coherence of belief and behavior?

What are you personally called to do differently, to affirm, or to change?

What skills did this reflection help you learn in thinking theologically about something you read or watched?

DECIDE ON SOCIAL AND CIVIC CONSEQUENCES

What actions will you take to carry out the implications you have discovered?

Consider how this reflection supports you in living in a multicultural world.

Theological Reflection Beginning with a Mind Map (Tradition Source)

Identify a focus:

Construct a mind map with the centering theme "re-formation," placed in the center of a sheet of paper. As you make associations from your assigned reading over the past few weeks, write those associations around the theme and draw a line between the theme and each association. The figure below is an example. Your associations may be anything you choose.

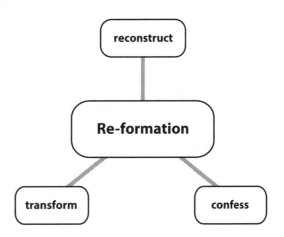

Additional levels of associations will radiate out. Straight lines are not required. Using different colors, drawing images, and forming metaphors in addition to the words will enhance the creative process of the mind map.

After making several levels of associations, study the entire map and select one metaphor or image to explore.

Explore the world of the metaphor/image:

Identify a specific point from which to explore the chosen image. For example, if the image is "Jumping into an Abyss," then be sure to explore the image from a specific standpoint such as the person jumping into the abyss. Do not shift to other possible standpoints such as observing someone jump into the abyss or leading someone to the edge of an abyss. It is important not to shift the focus if the reflection is to process smoothly.

Develop two or three theological perspective questions and explore the image through those perspectives. For example, what questions would explore the destructive dimensions of the image (Sin)? What questions would explore the nature of the world of the metaphor-image (Creation)? What questions help to bring in the Judgment dimensions of the metaphor? Or the Repentance and/or Redemption perspectives? *For example, what would cause someone to reconsider jumping into an abyss?*

Connect with other areas of life:

Begin connecting with your life by briefly stating when you experienced the world depicted in the image/metaphor. Remember to work from the standpoint previously identified. *For example, when have you metaphorically jumped into an abyss?*

Connect with contemporary culture and society. *For example, what recent stories in the news remind you of jumping into an abyss?*

Bring in your personal beliefs. What do you believe? What do you hold to be true? *For example, for what are you willing to risk metaphorically jumping into an abyss?*

Apply to your life going forward:

Notice how what you learn from the reflection applies to your life. *For example, what light does this reflection shed on how you engage opportunities for ministry?*

Theological Reflection Beginning with a Provocative Word (Tradition Source)[92]

Identify: Select a word that has impact.

For the purpose of this reflection and the practice, try the word "ATONEMENT."

What revelations on the meaning of the word do you have? Anything it denotes or connotes?

Explore: Ask the questions.

Next, ask the six "journalist's questions" about the feeling the word conveys:

WHO was involved when you were feeling a need to atone for something?
   (Action Source . . . tell the stories from your life)

WHAT image comes to mind about the feelings involved when you experienced a need to atone?
   (Image . . . explore the metaphor–its reflection of Wholeness, Brokenness, Recognition, Reorientation, and/or Restoration)

Connect: Go to the other sources we use to help explore meaning.

WHERE does this feeling come from and WHERE is it found in society?
   (Culture Source)

WHEN does this feeling come up in the Bible, lives of saints, hymns, and so forth?
   (Tradition Source. . . explore the world of tradition)

WHY is this feeling manifest in our lives?
   (Position Source)

HOW might God redeem any negatives in this?
   (Hope in Christ)

Consider insights and implications:

What have you learned for the next time you feel a need to atone?

Apply: Write a collect using the outline:

Dear God . . .   (naming of God's aspects)

You . . .   (connect situation of the image to that aspect)

We pray that . . . (petition of our hearts)

So that . . .   (result we desire)

Amen.

You might also want to try this using a different word, such as TRANSFOR-MATION, CONVERSION, or SALVATION.

---

92. Adapted from a design by Patricia Bleicher, EfM mentor.

The Culture Source

Theological Reflections beginning with a text or artifact from culture and/or society

Theological Reflection Beginning with a Social Concern (Culture Source) (1)

Focus

Find something that challenges you in a news article, an essay, a cartoon, a book, or the like.

Locate the central idea of the item you chose. Write a sentence stating that idea. This will be the focus to explore.

Explore the focus theologically.
Scan these perspective questions and bring two or more of them into a conversation with the focusing idea.

What does the focus idea say about the world?

What kind of world does the idea describe?

How does that idea-world describe brokenness?

What vision of wholeness is broken?

What crisis does the central idea recognize or present? What conversion is that idea calling for?

What would have to change?

How would the central idea promote a reorientation towards wholeness?

How would things look if they were made right?

What is the theology of the central idea?

Connect the focus with the sources of Christian Tradition, personal beliefs/Position, and personal experience/Action. This movement provides access to "voices" that can guide us in moments like the focus.

When you respond to the focus idea, do you think of an incident in your life or of something you have encountered in your EfM study or of some personal belief that relates to the focus?

List all connections you make to the focus idea.

How do those connections, those voices, guide you in relation to the focus idea?

Apply the reflection to your life.

What insights occur as you reflect on what you have found challenging about this culture or society?

Now that you have reflected on that challenge, what is God calling you to do, be, or change?

Theological Reflection Beginning with a Social Concern (Culture Source) (2)

Philosophical anthropology studies the nature of humankind. Questions of identity, both individual and communal, comprise the field of study. Theological anthropology addresses human nature in relation to God. Both philosophical and theological anthropology address related questions: What is the end (*telos*) of human beings? What does human flourishing involve? What is "the common good"—the actions, values, and policies that allow people to flourish? In theological terminology, what is God's vision for all people? Such questions involve thinking about the meaning of terms such as the Kingdom of God, heaven, and the *eschaton* (end-time).

The following theological reflection outline provides a way to consider philosophical and theological anthropological matters.

Identify a focus.

Develop a list of social concerns that are presently being deliberated in your Culture/society. The items on the list might come from politics, news media, documentaries, current cinema, or advertisements.

For example:

• Environmental concerns

• Universal health care

• National security

• Distribution of wealth

• Economic wellbeing

Select one topic from the list you create and reflect theologically on that voice from the Culture source. You will have a chance to make additional connections to the voice of Culture when you add the Connect movement to your reflection.

Explore some dimensions of your selected social concern. For example:

• Notice what is revealed about human nature in the identified concern, both individually and corporately. What human values seem to be operating around the social concern? Describe what the identified social concern seems to assert about "the common good"; that is, if the concern you are working with is "economic wellbeing," how does that concern relate to the common good?

• What characteristics of God are present or absent in that concern? Possibly, a social concern around national security could reflect God's characteristic of protector. What about God's self-emptying?

- Identify the deep hopes that are present or implied in the nature of the social concern.

Connect

Describe various ways the identified social concern gets manifested at the present time. For example, if universal health care is the identified concern under reflection, then identify the ways in which that concern has come to the foreground in the culture/society where you live, such as:

- U.S. news report on congressional action

- Canadian experience of universal health care

- English experience of universal health care

Where do you hear God's voice in your social structure, or your culture?

Learn something new. Find a way to hear the voice of Cultures/societies other than your own, such as how other countries handle the same or similar concern. How do varying cultural groups handle such a matter, perhaps even within the same country? Please resist the temptation to "talk off the cuff" about another place or people; rather, try to talk to someone from that culture or look up information that you could consider authoritative and reliable.

Personal Experience: Name concrete ways in which the issue has intersected your life. For example:

- Retirement brought change in how medical insurance was obtained

- Got ill and had to receive medical attention over an extended period of time

- Health of a friend's parent deteriorated and he/she required extended health care

- Visit to emergency room of hospital and noticing who was there and why

- Change in a person's life that required addressing the need for medical insurance

When have you had personal experience related to that concern or issue? What emotions have you experienced as that concern has intersected your life: fear, frustration, sorrow mixed with gratitude? Name your thoughts and feelings in relation to the focus you have selected.

Personal Belief/Position: What seems to be at stake in the reflection as you have explored and connected to the identified concern? What statements of conviction are you willing to make? What is alive for you in this matter?

- State what you value and hold important that is touched by the identified social concern.

- State your best vision or hope for the world. For creation.

Tradition: Listen to the voice of Christian tradition, especially the way Christian tradition speaks to the questions of God, common good (reign of God), or human nature.

What specific stories from the Christian tradition speak to the concern? Note what scripture stories, perhaps ones you remember from your childhood, give shape to the concern.

As you access the various voices in Personal Experience, Christian Tradition, Culture(s), Personal Beliefs, what rings true for you or seems new to you? Express, as best you can, any intuitive sense of what "should" be, "ought" to be, could be, or "must" be done relative to the social concern. In other words, what matters to you about this?

Describe actions that you could take that might contribute to the reign of God, the common good, in the matter of the social concern on which you reflected.

Apply

Apply the insight and new awareness from the reflection within the context of the social concern you named above.

How do the dimensions of the social concern point to the common good?

In what way does participation in the social concern/issue contribute to a vision of God's reign?

How does human flourishing revealed through the reflective theological conversation point toward action and behavior and practices?

In other words, what are you going to do (ministry) with what you have considered?

What would support you? Where/how will you reach out for that support?

Theological Reflection Beginning with the Culture Source

Identify

Explore another social culture in some way—by reading, watching a video or film, talking with someone from that culture, etc.—noticing differences in social custom or mores that challenge you. Create an image or metaphor for your (admittedly limited) understanding of the aspect that you find challenging.

Explore the focus from some theological perspectives, such as:

- What beliefs about creation are reflected in the image?

- What is considered sin in the world of your image?

- How does one find forgiveness in that image world?

- What constitutes ultimate fulfillment as that culture understands it?

- What do you regard as the meaning of life for that culture?

- What is the meaning of death?

Connect by listening to other voices. (Reminder: You can do the following in any order.)

Christian Tradition—What passages in scripture or church history come to mind as you explore the image above? Read the passages or material you recall.

Compare and contrast the world you found in the scripture or church history passage with the world you explored with the theological questions.

Personal Experience—What has occurred in your life that provides answers to some of those theological questions?

Compare and contrast your personal experience with the experiences of those in the culture you explored briefly. What differences and similarities are there? What begins to matter to you as you make the comparisons?

Contemporary Culture/Society—How does your culture/society view that of the one you explored? What are the challenges and possibilities?

Personal Beliefs—What beliefs of yours are challenged by those of the other culture? How could that challenge create road blocks? How could it create opportunity? What would you have to give up in order to change your beliefs? What might someone from the culture you explored have to give up?

Apply the reflection by noting your insights and how those insights might make a difference in ministry in your life.

Theological Reflection Beginning with a Wide-angle Lens (Culture Source)

Why this title? The image of a wide-angle lens is used because this reflection begins with a variety of perspectives, then focuses on a thread/theme/idea/image that connects them. An individual starts by finding the threads or themes present—in this case in something he or she reads or watches. The key for use by an individual requires initiation from something that could produce several themes or ideas (in this case, two or more articles on a topic of interest). In an EfM group, the reflection's beginning point can be themes from the spiritual autobiographies, themes from the week's reading, themes from any on-board time of the group, or some other starting point from which a variety of perspectives can be elicited.

The key is first to list the themes in what is under consideration, then find a thread that runs through the themes.

Identify

FIND A COMMON THEME OR THREAD

Begin with the articles chosen for the Respond section above.

What are the common themes or elements which emerge?

Is there a central question, struggle, or issue contained in the articles?

State the central thread as a simple statement, image, metaphor, or issue.

For instance, a review of several articles could reveal themes of challenge of the *status quo*, support of a particular view, and/or revelation of something new. Asking "What ties some of those themes together" yields a thread that may have run through the articles.

Explore

THEOLOGICAL PERSPECTIVES

Write about what's going on in the image, issue, or statement you created in the Identify step above.

Sit quietly and let the image or statement and your writing rest in you.

What questions does your image or statement raise?

What questions does that image or statement answer?

Identify the perspectives contained in the questions, that is, wholeness, brokenness, recognition, reorientation, or restoration.

Connect

This is the point at which one looks at the various sources in life to help find meaning in matters of daily life and ministry. The object is to find connections between the image, statement, or issue and other aspects of our life that teach us something.

CONNECT TO CULTURE AND SOCIETY

Focus on one or two areas of your culture or society so that the reflection will not be too broad. These connections might come from your local community or the larger world: your work environment, the education system, the health care system, your grandmothers, movies, TV, literature, art, songs, artifacts, architecture, government, or the press, to name a few.

Pick just one area of our contemporary society with which to connect. For instance, what does the world of employment teach you about the theme you have identified? Or, what have you learned from the news media in your culture/society that helps you or challenges you regarding the theme?

How does the selected area of culture/society speak to or about this thread?

CONNECT TO CHRISTIAN TRADITION

- Identify biblical passages or other elements from Christian tradition (scripture, hymn, prayer, church history document) in which this common thread is evoked or brought to mind. Read the passages.

- Select one passage that seems to address the image, statement, or issue.

- Examine the passage:

  - Note how the passage offers insight into the image, statement, or issue you are considering.

  - Note how the passage challenges the image, statement, or issue.

  - What does the passage mean to you?

COMPARE AND CONTRAST CULTURE/SOCIETY AND CHRISTIAN TRADITION

From the perspectives of each, what kind of a world emerges?

Where do these perspectives join or compete? Where do they clash or contrast?

Note what seems to be "at stake" as you compare and contrast your Culture and Tradition connections.

CONNECT TO PERSONAL EXPERIENCE

When have you experienced something that relates to what seems to "be at stake" above?

CONNECT TO BELIEFS, POSITIONS, AND AFFIRMATIONS

What positions or affirmations do you hold in relation to what is at stake?

Identify how that belief formed for you. Was it from personal experience, from something you learned in your faith tradition, or from the cultural messages you have inherited or encountered?

What "gaps" are there for you between what you believe and how you act in relation to the theme considered in this reflection?

Apply

IDENTIFY INSIGHTS AND PERSONAL IMPLICATIONS

What have you learned about coherence of belief and behavior?

What are you personally called to do differently, to affirm, or to change?

What skills did this reflection help you learn in thinking theologically about something you read or watched?

DECIDE ON SOCIAL AND CIVIC CONSEQUENCES

What actions will you take to carry out the implications you have discovered?

Theological Reflection Beginning with a Provocative Word (Culture Source)[93]

Identify

Select a word that has impact. For the purpose of this reflection and the practice, try the word "DESIRING."

What revelations on the meaning of the word do you have? Anything it denotes or connotes?

Explore

Next, ask the six "journalist's questions" about the feeling the word conveys:

WHO was involved when you were feeling _____?
(Action . . . tell the stories from your life)

WHAT image comes to mind about the feeling(s) _____?
(Image . . . explore the metaphor—its reflection of wholeness, brokenness, recognition, reorientation, and/or restoration)

Connect

Go to the other sources we use to help explore meaning.

WHERE does this feeling come from and WHERE is it found in society?
(Source/Culture)

WHEN does this feeling come up in the Bible, lives of saints, hymns, and so forth?
(Source/Tradition . . . explore the world of tradition)

WHY is this feeling manifest in our lives?
(Source/Position)

HOW might God redeem any negatives in this?
(Hope in Christ)

Consider insights and implications.

WHAT have you learned for the next time you feel _____?

Apply

Write a collect using the outline:

Dear God . . .	(naming of God's aspects)
You . . .	(connect situation of the image to that aspect)
We pray that . . .	(petition of our hearts)
So that . . .	(result we desire)
Amen.	

---

93. Adapted from a design by Patricia Bleicher, EfM mentor.

Theological Reflection Beginning with a Movie, Video, or Television Episode (Culture Source)

This theological reflection was designed by EfM Canada to meet the particular needs of groups who are wanting to engage in theological reflection beginning from a movie, video or television show (or episode). The design is intended to raise particular questions about the group's engagement with the movie/video/television episode and draw connections to the larger theological themes. Theological Reflection on a movie can be done as an individual reflection, however this exercise is framed for a group.

Identify

Begin by identifying a movie/video/television episode. The group agrees to view it either together or individually. The movie may be viewed during an EfM seminar meeting time or as "homework" in anticipation of the reflection. (If a full-length feature is to be viewed during the seminar, the group will need to decide beforehand whether to extend the meeting time in order to have adequate time for viewing plus the full reflection or if the movie will be viewed during one week's meeting and the reflection done during the subsequent meeting.)

After viewing:

- Classify the genre [comedy, drama, action, documentary, nature, adult, children, etc.] and the period in which the piece was made.

- What is the film about? Avoid a detailed plot summary, but describe the themes, overarching concerns, or prominent features.
  - Where was this evident in the film?
  - What scene captured the essence of what the movie was about?

Identify a focus for reflection (someone may list various suggestions from which to choose).

- A broad focus will look at a particular character or theme
- A narrow focus will look at a single scene

After the focus is chosen, invite the group to share briefly how each identifies with the focus.

Explore

Use theological perspective questions to explore the focus:

- For a scene
  - What happened? what is the world like?
  - What went wrong/right? what was broken/mended?

- What was surprising?
- What was cause for celebration?
- Where in this scene did you see joy, pain, surprise, coming together?

- For a character
  - What happened?
  - What went wrong/right?
  - What surprised him/her?
  - What was cause for celebration?

- For a theme
  - Where in the movie do we find the theme?
  - How is it depicted? what makes it bearable?
  - What enhances/destroys/builds up the theme? what obstacles are encountered?
  - Is there a resolution?
  - Is there change?

Connect

The question for connecting to the Christian Tradition depends on whether the group is exploring a character, theme, or scene. Where do we find resonances with characters in scripture or the tradition? OR Where do we find similar themes in scripture or the tradition? OR Where do we find similar scenes in scripture or the tradition? Identify/choose one similarity and explore it using the theological perspective questions used above.

Are there other voices from culture/society that address these themes, ideas, perspectives? Does the scene/theme/character confirm or challenge some aspect of culture/society? What does this scene/theme/character express in or for the culture/society that created it? At the time of its creation? Now? Are there underlying values, attitudes, etc.?

Apply

Consider your own position. What do I believe about what we have discussed? Has my position changed from my initial impression? Were I to view this film again, how might I view it differently?

What insights arise for me from this reflection? Can I make use of them in my life? What would help me? What resources would I need? How does this relate to my ministry? What is God calling me to be, do, or change?

What do we want to bring from this reflection into our current life together? What would our community look like if we could implement the values and perspectives we have discussed? What are we called on to do or change together? (The group may want to form a consensus statement.)

The Position Source

Theological Reflections beginning with closely held beliefs, values, and opinions

Theological Reflection Beginning with a Personal Position (1)

Identify a focus.

Begin with a focus on the value of music and poetry in worship and prayer.

Explore the focus.

Make a statement or image that reflects a connection between music and poetry and prayer or worship. For instance, someone might express that he only likes a certain type of music in worship because another kind destroys the sense of peace and beauty. Or another person might create an image that depicts people singing or playing instruments and the music notes floating outward towards God and the world.

Explore your statement or image theologically, using a few of the questions provided, or create your own questions for the image:

How does the overall statement or image reflect wholeness or goodness?

What view of the world is contained in your statement or image?

What view of the relationship between God and creation exists in your statement/image?

How would someone experience God in that statement/image?

What might disrupt someone's relationship with God and others in that focus?

What view of restoration to wholeness is contained in the focus?

Connect to other sources.

State your personal belief that undergirds your initial image or statement.

How do your personal belief and the exploration above coincide and how do they conflict?

What troubles you about the comparison? What comforts you about the comparison?

Find one or two scripture references to the place of music and poetry in liturgy and worship. Or, select one or two hymns to connect to. How do those hymns relate to your focusing image or statement and to your position? How do they relate to the exploration?

What view of the world around you is contained in your personal belief statement, in the image, in the hymns you chose?

Apply what is learned to daily life.

Once a person takes a stance or affirms a position, implications for ministry begin to emerge.

What do you see for your ministry as you live day to day?

Close by composing a prayer adapting the structure of Jewish prayers:

Blessed are you, O Lord God, _____
(description of God),

for you _____

and make us _____

through _____. *Amen.*

Theological Reflection Beginning with a Personal Position (2)

Identify a focus.

Begin with a focus on the value of music and poetry in worship and prayer.

Explore the focus.

Make a statement or image that reflects a connection between music and poetry and prayer or worship. For instance, someone might express that he only likes a certain type of music in worship because another kind destroys the sense of peace and beauty. Or another person might create an image that depicts people singing or playing instruments and the music notes floating outward towards God and the world.

Explore your statement or image theologically, using a few of the questions provided, or create your own questions for the image:

How does the overall statement or image reflect wholeness or goodness?

What view of the world is contained in your statement or image?

What view of the relationship between God and creation exists in your statement/image?

How would someone experience God in that statement/image?

What might disrupt someone's relationship with God and others in that focus?

What view of restoration to wholeness is contained in the focus?

Connect to other sources.

State your personal belief that undergirds your initial image or statement.

How do your personal belief and the exploration above coincide and how do they conflict?

What troubles you about the comparison? What comforts you about the comparison?

Find one or two scripture references to the place of music and poetry in liturgy and worship. Or, select one or two hymns to connect to. How do those hymns relate to your focusing image or statement and to your position? How do they relate to the exploration?

What view of the world around you is contained in your personal belief statement, in the image, in the hymns you chose?

Apply what is learned to daily life.

Once a person takes a stance or affirms a position, implications for ministry begin to emerge.

What do you see for your ministry as you live day to day?

Close by composing a prayer adapting the structure of Jewish prayers:

Blessed are you, O Lord God, _____
(description of God),

for you _____

and make us _____

through _____. *Amen.*

Theological Reflection Beginning with Multiple Personal Positions[94]

This method of theological reflection can be used when members of the seminar group hold a number of differing positions on a specific subject such as "confidentiality." This method of reflection requires maturity and tact since someone must be able to offer a belief with which others may disagree. We tend to defend and protect our beliefs. They are "precious" to us, and so it is essential that there be a high degree of trust in the group, a consensus to uphold each person with respect, and a clear understanding that this is not a debate or an attempt to change anyone's mind.

Identify

Begin by affirming the Respectful Communication Guidelines from the Kaleidoscope Institute, page 345 of this Guide.

Using mutual invitation (page 344 of this Guide), each member states a belief about a significant topic for which there are a variety of opinions. Allow some time for silence.

> For example, each participant answers the question, "How do you understand 'confidentiality' within the context of EfM?" by stating specifically what he or she means by "confidentiality." It may be helpful to have a mentor or other group member listen carefully and record each position.

Explore

Each person explores her or his position statement from the Action source, answering the following questions, again by mutual invitation:

- When have you felt tension in acting on the belief you have stated?

- In what situations have you been unsure how to apply your stated belief?

Connect

Brainstorm cultural messages that address the topic (not the individual position statements) presented to the group. The mentor facilitates "conversation" as members compare and contrast their own position statements and actions with messages from culture and society.

The group generates a list of selections from the tradition that speak to the heart of the matter explored so far. The group selects the one piece it

---

95. Adapted from *Common Lessons and Supporting Materials* (2006), 2-5-1–2-5-3.

wishes to explore. Read the selection aloud, if possible. Explore the selection of tradition, paying attention to how it affirms or challenges what has emerged in the course of the reflection thus far.

Apply

Identify insights and challenges. Share by mutual invitation.

Each member considers how the reflection has "spoken to" the position statement he or she shared in the beginning. Allow time for discerning implications for action and identifying what help is needed to follow through.

Resources for Community Life

Group Life: The Seminar

The Nature of Groups

We all live in groups. Whenever two or three gather together, we have a group. Because we take this so much for granted, we often fail to note that groups have lives. They begin, they grow, they encounter changes and mood swings, they calcify, they end. When we pay attention to the life of the group, we can keep patterns healthy and vibrant. We can make them into creative centers for learning and productivity. Other groups may degenerate into destructive patterns that feed on negativities, breed destructive behaviors, or just simply become ineffective, unproductive, stale, and dissatisfying. These groups usually collapse in conflict or abandonment.

The goal of the EfM seminar is to discover our theology with others on a common path. We know that certain considerations must be met in order for this to happen in a group that maintains a productive and creative life.

The key element of any seminar is **TRUST**. Without it every discussion becomes a defensive encounter and learning is limited by tactics of self-protection. An effective seminar develops because the leadership provides a venue in which leadership can be shared, responsibility for the common wellbeing can be assumed by everyone, and each person can enter the discussion with a sense of value, acceptance, and the ability to make distinctive contributions. Such a pattern does not just happen. It grows in an environment of caring and nurturing. Its growth validates that we learn more effectively by cooperation and enthusiastic participation than by competition and argumentation.

Essential Elements

We have determined that certain elements need to be present in the life of a seminar to make it effective and satisfying as **a learning environment**. Seating in a seminar should be arranged with no one dominating the group as if chairing a meeting. Members should be able to see each other, and the room should afford a sense of privacy. Different styles may dominate. Put aside barriers, such as a table in the center of the room, that may reduce personal communications. Seminars do not work well with interruptions such as might take place in a large hall open to the public. Restrooms and hospitality can be very helpful, including access to liquids, at the very least water. Nourishment that maintains a sense of comfort and wellbeing are suggested.

EfM offers participants an opportunity to share their "spiritual autobiographies." **Self-revelation** is a part of every encounter, when we state our names, shake hands, and offer information about ourselves. Typical information beyond our names includes our address, occupation, and family status. Of course we also reveal a great deal in non-verbal ways by appearance, body posture, and tones of voice. All these features highlight our encounters everyday. To develop a seminar group requires that we reveal a bit more. What we reveal depends upon our own comfort level in a group. Some personal information is obviously not appropriate in a seminar group, but members must make decisions about "how free" they can be. Usually this is an evolving process, like a marriage. As we grow in trust and support for one another, we reveal more and become more open. Secrets tend to restrict our freedom to express ourselves, resulting in a smaller and narrower world view. We cannot grow by ourselves, and we also cannot grow if we fail to participate. Self-revelation is our participation. Feedback from others is how others can contribute to our learning process.

While we begin with Spiritual Autobiographies in EfM, this is only one aspect of our continuing self-revelation and growth. Theological reflection only works well if it speaks to events in our lives. We can find it difficult to engage in theological reflection unless we can reveal enough of our lives to examine with the theological tools we acquire through the process of study.

A mentor has certain leadership functions assigned by the task, but **shared leadership** has more to do with style than with function. Shared leadership means that a group takes sufficient time to arrive at a consensus, that is to say a willingness of all to pursue a certain course. Consensus does not mean that all agree, but it does mean that everyone is willing to pursue a given option. Sharing the leadership requires that group members check with each other. Those who are most vocal need to give place and to encourage those who have less to say, but may indeed offer significant contributions. Shared leadership means looking out for one another, taking time for one another, and recognizing that unless we move together, our seminar will end.

No seminar works well unless there exists **a common enterprise**. This is the subject of our inquiry, in this case the theological enterprise in all its complexity. Our common enterprise includes the history of theology and the sources for our faith, the Bible, the experience of the people of God throughout history and through liturgy, and the interpretation of those experiences that have been handed to us in countless libraries as well as through a shared tradition of experience.

In academia the pattern or discipline used in seminars frequently follows that of the lecture hall. Instead of faculty, seminar members offer papers or "talks" which may be critiqued and discussed. For participants such seminars are often dry and uninteresting, unless either the subject is scintillating or the discussion takes on a polemic level that energizes at least some of the participants. We do not believe, however, that disputation as a technique to manage a seminar is very helpful.

The **general pattern** for conducting an EfM seminar is as follows:

- There is time to catch up with one another. This is kept short unless there is a crisis.

- There is time to worship together. The kind of worship will depend upon the needs of the participants.

- There is time to discuss the lessons, not in detail, but to note highlights, ask questions for clarification, and elicit themes and information that catch or surprise students.

- There is time to engage in reflective work such as a spiritual autobiography or a theological reflection; or time to examine spiritual needs, to plumb for theological meaning, or to examine the meaning of Christian ministry.

- This is a time to harvest the fruits of the seminar. Often we learn without knowing it and we fail to use what we have discovered. We have to name our discoveries in order to truly "own" them. It is important from time to time to ask: What have I learned? What are the implications of what I have learned? What must I do to put what I have learned into practice? What difference will what I have learned make in the way I am now? Tomorrow? In the future? What difference will it make for us, our families, our friends, our church, our communities?

- There is adequate time for breaks and refreshment.

We advise that the group produce a set of statements about the purpose, expectations, and norms by which it will work (e.g., the time to begin and to close each session). It also helps if everyone agrees to a schedule about various tasks associated with the seminar.

Social groups and work groups usually create opportunities to **celebrate** life. This is also true of an EfM seminar group. Remember special events in the life of the group with appropriate festivities. Just how and when this is done will vary from group to group. These celebrations may include a meal and alcohol may be served; however, whenever alcohol is served, the group must be sure to offer non-alcoholic beverages in an equally attractive manner.

Celebration may provide an occasion to bring in significant persons who are not part of the group. Spouses or special friends may be included so that they will have an opportunity to meet the group.

We often fail to say goodbye properly, to grieve for what will be no more, to celebrate what we have enjoyed and to give thanks for what we have received. Celebration may be part of **closure**, but closure is more than simply enjoying festivities. Only when we mourn are we ready to release and move on to the next opportunity. We do ourselves and others no service when we fail to mourn, for that failure means that we remain fixed to the past and our creativity diminishes. Certificates, diplomas, remembrances we exchange in token and in words, all serve as epitaphs and tombstones for the past. It is important that seminar groups find ways to express closure adequately.

Issues in the Life of a Seminar Group[95]

Whenever two or three gather together, a group exists. No individual can be born and exist alone. We live in family groups, church groups, educational groups, groups of friends, and in groups that are merely an association of individuals who happen to be in the same time and place.

Whether we know each other well or have hardly met, our life together in groups evolves through patterns that can be understood. When we do not understand these patterns, we are open to manipulation, someone moving us to do something against our will and without our knowledge.

EfM's learning style depends upon trust. Participants who strive for honesty and charity can support the kind of vulnerability and openness that allows everyone to interact as peers on a common quest.

Some groups do not work well together and may be called dysfunctional. It is possible to ensure that an EfM group is functional, works effectively, and engenders respect for all members. This does not mean that there will never be conflict. Conflict indicates that there are people who care and are willing to maintain something that is important to them. How we handle conflict is crucial.

There are issues that arise in the life of any group, and some will certainly arise in the context of your EfM group.

Three Basic Concerns

William Schutz developed the following theory from the premise that every member of a group experiences concerns in three areas of participation and membership within the life of the group: inclusion, control, and affection. At the beginning of a group's life, the concerns of members primarily involve the issue of inclusion. Soon, however, concerns evolve on how each is to participate in controlling the group's life. Finally come the affection concerns. At the end stage of the group's life, the order reverses. Participants who are aware of a group's life cycle may recognize the dynamics surrounding different issues and help the group take responsibility to address these.

The following questions arise at the beginning of a group's life:

INCLUSION

Who else is here?

What is the personal cost in joining?

How much am I willing to pay?

---

95. From *Common Lessons and Supporting Materials* (2006).

Can I entrust my real self to others?

Will they hold me up if I am falling?

CONTROL

Who is calling the shots here?

How much can I push for what I want?

What do others require of me?

Can I say what I really think?

Can I take it when others say what they really think?

AFFECTION

Am I willing to care?

Can I show my caring?

What will happen if I show care for one person before showing it for others?

What if no one cares for me?

What if they do?

What if I don't really ever care for some people in the group?

Will the group be able to bear it?

At the end of its life together the group reverses the questions to ease out of what has become a functioning body:

AFFECTION

We pull back from affectional ties that have no real future.

CONTROL

We again get embroiled in a game of "Who's boss here anyway?"

INCLUSION

We start wondering if we really want to put the time and effort into holding onto some or all members of the group.

The three areas of concern also overlap during the life cycle of a group. And, from time to time, a concern that is more usual at the beginning and ending phases of group life may emerge in the middle of things for one reason or another.

Three Areas of Need in Group Life

A helpful analysis of group life defines three main areas of need within a group: task needs, individual needs, and group maintenance needs. These different areas of group life require ongoing attention. No group will function very effectively if individual or personal needs go unmet or if the relationships of people in the group become totally dysfunctional. Finally, a group without a task is like children looking for mischief. A group without a task will invent one.

Some tasks usually draw a group together (e.g., Education for Ministry), though it will not by itself necessarily hold the group together.

TASK NEEDS

- need for a worthwhile goal
- need for a clear goal
- need for consensus about the goal
- need for a plan to meet the goal
- need to recognize when the goal has been met

Any group gathered for a purpose will push to learn and complete that task.

INDIVIDUAL NEEDS

Each individual brings his or her own needs to the group, including:

- need for acceptance
- need for contributing
- need for affirmation
- need for power
- need for freedom
- need for recognition

These needs affect the performance of each member and may hinder accomplishing the task.

GROUP MAINTENANCE NEEDS

Members must relate to one another so as to preserve the life of the group until it completes the task. These needs include:

- need for improving understanding
- need for facilitating cooperation between the members
- need for members to support each other
- need for fun and enjoyment together

Unseen tension may develop between accomplishing the task and fulfilling individuals' needs in the group. Good group maintenance involves recognizing both areas and keeps them in healthy balance.

At first sight only some of a group's task needs are visible and obvious. As the group develops, other areas begin to surface. The task of EfM groups mostly revolves around discussing the texts and reflecting theologically. But it is important to focus occasionally on group maintenance needs for preserving group cohesiveness, and to attend to individual needs so every member will feel integral to the life of the group.

The whole group is responsible for maintaining a balance between these different areas of need. The following design can help your group members recognize the different needs and begin to take responsibility for answering them.

Evaluating Group Life

Regular evaluation of progress is a healthy exercise for your seminar group. This can be done using written evaluations or open discussions during a seminar session.

Group satus reports twice a year provide natural opportunities for a group to evaluate itself.

Regular attention to the group's norms set at the beginning of the year is also wise.

When evaluating, members may consider these questions:

- How do you assess your understanding of and participation in this program?

- What is a stumbling block for you?

- What do you like about the leadership of the group?

- What would you like to change?

- How are we doing as a learning community? As a caring community?

- What needs attention?

Activities that Nurture Group Life

There are actions that group members can take that promote a productive life in the group. While we do many of these things naturally, without thinking, or simply because we have learned to be polite, it can be helpful to be aware of some of these actions. Thus we can encourage one another or take initiative without feeling that it should be left to a designated leader. Activities that nurture group life belong to everyone, so that the leadership and responsibility (ability to respond) may be shared, and that we may grow and learn together.

Some of these activities are:

INITIATING: proposing tasks or goals; defining group problems; suggesting procedures or ideas to solve problems.

INFORMATION/OPINION SEEKING: requesting facts; seeking relevant information about group concerns; stating beliefs; giving suggestions or ideas.

INFORMATION/OPINION GIVING: offering facts; providing relevant information about group concerns; stating beliefs; giving suggestions or ideas.

CLARIFYING/ELABORATING: interpreting or reflecting ideas and suggestions; clearing up confusion; indicating alternatives and issues for the group; giving examples.

SUMMARIZING: pulling together related ideas; restating suggestions after group discussion of them; offering decisions or conclusions for the group to accept or reject.

CONSENSUS TESTING: sending up "trial balloons" to see if the group is nearing a conclusion; checking degree of agreement in the group.

AWARENESS: what is my body telling me? Where is my tension?

OWNING: acknowledging to myself the sources of the tension.

DECIDING: how much do I want to share and how much can I shelve?

LEVELING: letting others know what's going on in me—stating what I think, feel, or want.

Tools from Kaleidoscope Institute

The following processes for gracious communication and leadership are from the Kaleidoscope Institute with whom EfM has been in a collaborative relationship since 2011. Learn more about KI at www.kscopeinstitute.org

The Cycle of Gospel Living

The difference in attitude toward the powerful and the powerless was very clear throughout the ministry of Jesus. Jesus never told the poor and powerless to sell all they own and give to the poor. That would obviously be an absurd thing to say. Jesus healed them, loved them, ate with them, touched them, comforted them, blessed them, served them, encouraged them, taught them, and liberated them by his own suffering, death, and resurrection. Finally, Jesus breathed on them to infuse them with the power of the Holy Spirit—the power to teach, heal, and forgive in the name of God. On the other hand, Jesus never told the rich and powerful that they are blessed. Instead, Jesus warned them and challenged them to serve and to humble themselves. He reminded them of what the law and the prophets had said.

The Gospel invites the powerful to take up their cross and follow Jesus. Salvation for the powerful comes from the decision to give up power and take up the cross. The Gospel, however, never asks the powerless to choose the cross because the powerless, by the condition of their powerlessness, are already on the cross. There is no need for them to choose it, just as there is no need for the poor to give up what they have and give to the poor because they are already poor. Because the powerless are already on the cross, salvation comes from endurance and faithfulness in the hope of God's deliverance through the resurrection.

Choosing the cross and the resurrection of Jesus are part of the same Gospel story. But we interact with the different parts of the story differently depending on our place of power in a particular situation. As a Chinese American working in the Episcopal Church, I often find myself in situations where I am set up to be powerless. For example I am sometimes invited to be the token Asian in a meeting. When I am in this kind of situation, I actually spend some time before I enter the meeting to get in touch with the empty tomb, the resurrection side of the Gospel. I tell myself that I am blessed and a child of God no matter what happens. I ask God to breathe the Holy Spirit through me to give me strength to endure and power to speak and challenge the system I am about to enter.

On the other hand, as a trainer and consultant I also find myself in situations where I am given power and authority to influence others.

In my preparation for each training session, I spend time reflecting on what it means to choose the cross. I tell myself that I am a servant to the participants. I tell myself that even though I may be treated as an expert, I must be humble. I tell myself that my job is to work myself out of my job by giving my knowledge, skills, and power away freely, so that at the end of the session the participants will know what I know and my services are no longer needed.

It is crucial to determine in a given situation which side of the cross we are on if we are to experience the wholeness of the Gospel. No one can stay on one side of the cross all the time. That would be neglecting the wholeness of the Gospel. Living the Gospel involves moving through the cycle of death and resurrection, the cross and the empty tomb, again and again. The moment I am resurrected into new life of empowerment, I must begin to think about serving and giving away my power and take up the cross again, or I stand the chance of abusing my power. The moment I take up the cross and become powerless, I must begin to think about faithfulness and endurance and look toward empowerment through the empty tomb. It is in this dynamic of death and resurrection, cross and empty tomb, Lent and Easter, that the Gospel comes to life in each one of us.[96]

Law uses this diagram to illustrate his Cycle of Gospel Living.

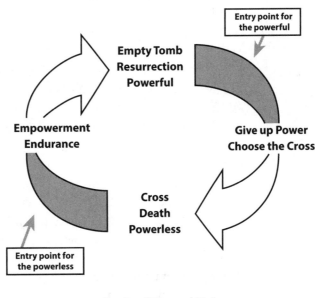

Cycle of Gospel Living

---

96. Eric H. F. Law, *The Wolf Shall Dwell with the Lamb: A Spirituality for Leadership in a Multicultural Community* (St. Louis: Chalice Press, 1993), 41–43. Used with permission. Reprinted under license #2018OZEFM. For personal use only.

Mutual Invitation

In order to ensure that everyone who wants to share has the opportunity to speak, we will proceed in the following way:

The leader or a designated person shares first. After that person has spoken, he or she then invites another to share. (Whom you invite does not need to be the person next to you.) After the next person has spoken, that person is given the privilege to invite another to share.

If you are not ready to share, say "I pass for now" and we will invite you to share later on. If you don't want to say anything at all, simply say "pass" and proceed to invite another to share. We will do this until everyone has been invited.

We invite you to listen and not to respond to someone's sharing immediately. There will be time to respond and to ask clarifying questions after everyone has had an opportunity to share.

(adapted from *The Wolf Shall Dwell with the Lamb* by Eric H. F. Law[97])

© 2010 Kaleidoscope Institute. Used with permission. Reprinted under License #2018OZEFM. For personal use only.

As you practice Mutual Invitation you are enacting the Gospel Cycle of Living. The person speaking is powerful. The persons refraining from speaking have given up power, but will take it up again when invited. A person who passes has the power to offer power to another through invitation. Notice and reflect on this cycle as you become more adept and comfortable with the process.

---

97. Atlanta: Chalice Press, 1993.

Respectful Communication Guidelines

R = take RESPONSIBILITY for what you say and feel without blaming others

E = use EMPATHETIC listening

S = be SENSITIVE to differences in communication styles

P = PONDER what you hear and feel before you speak

E = EXAMINE your own assumptions and perceptions

C = keep CONFIDENTIALITY

T = TRUST ambiguity, because we are not here to debate who is right or wrong

(from *The Bush Was Blazing but Not Consumed* by Eric H. F. Law)

I agree to uphold these guidelines for the time we have together.

Signature _____ Date _____